Praise for Terry Frei's Previous Books

Olympic Affair

"Give a talented journalist an engrossing storyline—especially a sports writer accustomed to the drama of games—and he will keep you mesmerized by the who, what, where, when and why of the unfolding adventure. And so it is with Terry Frei's *Olympic Affair*. Set against the 1936 Berlin Olympics—remembered primarily for Jesse Owens' four gold-medal performance and Adolf Hitler's disdain for him—Frei focuses on the decathlon champion, America's Glenn Morris, and his affair with the renowned German actress and Olympic film director, Leni Reifenstahl. It is, then, a compelling look at an historic sporting event and a love/sex scandal cloaked in intrigue and danger. Frei's style is reporter/novelist, cleanly balanced between event and character, offering a panorama of human triumph saddened by failure. Of the books I've read in the past four or five years, this one is near the top of the list." —Terry Kay, author of *To Dance with the White Dog* and *The Book of Marie*

"Historical fiction is a dangerous game: where does history leave off and fiction begin? How to draw the line between what happened and what might/should have happened? Frei takes these challenges head-on and succeeds brilliantly. . . . This is history as historians seldom write it and should be required reading for everyone." —David Milofsky, professor of English, Colorado State University, novelist and author of *Playing From Memory* and *A Friend of Kissinger*

"[T]he most intriguing sports book I've read in the last 12 months. . . . What makes the book special is that it's actually a novel, with Frei's exhaustive research filling in the blanks of the love story and what has been largely an untold tale. The book is written with care and sensitivity and works on several levels—not only as straight entertainment but as a history refresher on what the world was like during that explosive time. And hey, any book featuring sex, sports and Nazis is bound to be pretty good, right? Obviously, this is an adult book but one I recommend highly. Frei's Glenn Morris is a fascinatingly tragic hero that you will not soon forget." —Dwight Jaynes, Comcast Sports Northwest

Horns, Hogs, and Nixon Coming

"We had a few friends over who thought we had lost our minds as we whooped and hollered through a football game so exciting it was billed as the Game of the Century. For a few hours, we were innocent again, totally caught up in the contest. The game and its cultural contexts have been beautifully chronicled by Terry Frei in his book *Horns, Hogs, and Nixon Coming.*" —Bill Clinton in *My Life*

"[O]ne of the better—and most readable—books of social history published in recent years." —Paul Greenberg, Pulitzer Prize–winning editorial writer, Arkansas *Democrat Gazette*

"A superb blending of sports, history, and politics." —Si Dunn, *Dallas Morning News*

Third Down and a War to Go

"Many times you hear athletes called heroes, and their deeds and accomplishments on the field are characterized as courageous. After reading *Third Down and a War to Go,* I am embarrassed to have ever been thought of as brave or courageous. . . . Enjoy this adventure in history, life, and courage and take it from a so-called 'tough guy'—keep the hanky close by." —Dan Fouts, Hall of Fame quarterback and CBS sportscaster

"Brings to life, in shades of black and blue and blood red, the idea that certain things are worth fighting for." —Rick Morrissey, *Chicago Tribune*

"Mythology is nice. Truth is better. What a powerful piece of work . . . a telling detail in the great portrait of America at war, young men and women who saw their duty and did it no matter how much it scared them." —Dave Kindred, *The Sporting News*, and author of *Sound and Fury*

'77: Denver, the Broncos, and a Coming of Age

"Ahh, the memories. And they all happened right here in the forgotten time zone. Those magical moments came back with a rush last week reading *'77: Denver, The Broncos, and a Coming of Age*. What a fantastic read. . . . '77 is more than just a Bronco football memoir. It was a time when our Centennial State exploded on the national scene. . . . [T]hanks to Terry Frei's wonderful work, we get to live that magical moment all over again." —Dick Maynard, *Grand Junction Sentinel*

"No one knows more about Denver and its sports than Terry Frei does, and here in '77, he describes nothing less than the transformation of a city with a special focus on Denver's most magical team. To know why and how the Mile High City exists as it does today, this is essential history." —Sandy Clough, sports talk host, Denver's FM Sports Radio 104.3, The Fan

"You didn't have to live through it in Denver to appreciate this account of the flowering of a franchise and its love affair with a town, but this book takes those of us who did straight back to those thrilling days of yesteryear in unforgettable fashion." —Michael Knisley, senior deputy editor, ESPN.com

The Witch's Season

"Events carry the story forward swiftly, and that alone would make it a good read. But Frei has a larger point to make. It's during times of upheaval, when the very foundations of normalcy are being shaken, that personal courage, honor and the willingness to stand fast on principle matter most. All of the central characters in Frei's story will have to decide whether to make that stand, and if so, how to make it. Frei has written three nonfiction books, most notably *Horns, Hogs, and Nixon Coming*. This book proves he can write fiction too." —Ken Goe, Portland *Oregonian*

Playing Piano in a Brothel

"For every story, there's a story behind the story, and Frei's book captures hundreds of them. Frei provides never-before-read tales of legendary athletes, monumental events and games behind the games, as well as his own opinion of newspaper sports journalism as a whole—and its future. . . . A must-read for every sports fan."
—Doug Ottewill, *Mile High Sports Magazine*

March 1939

Also by Terry Frei

Nonfiction
Horns, Hogs, and Nixon Coming
Third Down and a War to Go
'77: Denver, the Broncos, and a Coming of Age
Playing Piano in a Brothel

Fiction
The Witch's Season
Olympic Affair: A Novel of Hitler's Siren and America's Hero

March 1939

Before the Madness

The Story of the First NCAA Basketball Tournament Champions

Terry Frei

TAYLOR TRADE PUBLISHING

Lanham • Boulder • New York • Toronto • Plymouth, UK

Published by Taylor Trade Publishing
An imprint of Rowman & Littlefield
4501 Forbes Boulevard, Suite 200, Lanham, Maryland 20706
www.rowman.com

10 Thornbury Road, Plymouth PL6 7PP, United Kingdom

Distributed by NATIONAL BOOK NETWORK

British Library Cataloguing in Publication Information Available

Library of Congress Cataloging-in-Publication Data

Frei, Terry, 1955–
  March 1939 : before the madness : the story of the first NCAA Basketball
Tournament champions / Terry Frei.
      pages cm
  Includes bibliographical references and index.
  ISBN 978-1-58979-924-0 (cloth : alk. paper) -- ISBN 978-1-58979-925-7 (electronic)
  1. NCAA Basketball Tournament (1939)—History. I. Title.
  GV885.49.N37F74 2014
  796.323'6309043—dc23

                                                                        2013033163

♾️™ The paper used in this publication meets the minimum requirements of
American National Standard for Information Sciences—Permanence of Paper for
Printed Library Materials, ANSI/NISO Z39.48-1992.

Printed in the United States of America

To Helen

To Jim Beseda, a real pro, true friend, and great help

*To the memories of Howard Hobson
and the 1938–39 Oregon Webfoots*

Contents

PROGRAM! GET YOUR PROGRAM!

Oregon Webfoots
1938–39 Roster

COACH: Howard Hobson, Oregon '26

STARTERS					
20 Bobby Anet	Guard	5-8	175	Senior	Astoria, Oregon
32 Wally Johansen	Guard	5-11	155	Senior	Astoria
22 Slim Wintermute	Center	6-8	195	Senior	Longview, Washington
18 John Dick	Forward	6-4	200	Junior	The Dalles, Oregon
28 Laddie Gale	Forward	6-4	195	Senior	Oakridge, Oregon
RESERVES/TRAVELING SQUAD					
15 Red McNeeley	Guard	6-2	180	Soph.	Portland, Oregon
13 Ford Mullen	Guard	5-8	165	Junior	Olympia, Washington
11 Matt Pavalunas	Guard	6-0	170	Junior	Raymond, Washington
40 Bob Hardy	Forward	6-3	180	Senior	Ashland, Oregon
25 Ted Sarpola	Forward	6-2	160	Junior	Astoria
36 Earl Sandness	Center	6-4	190	Soph.	Astoria
ADDITIONAL RESERVES					
14 George Andrews	Guard	5-11	180	Soph.	Victoria, B.C.
34 Archie Marshik	Center	6-6	195	Soph.	Eugene
16 Toivo Piippo	Guard	6-0	160	Soph.	Astoria
12 Wimpy Quinn	Forward	6-2	180	Junior	Portland

OTHER TEAM MEMBERS: Robert Blenkinsop, Don Mabee, Warren Smith, Stanley Short, Gilbert Wylie.

Introduction

How could the selection committee leave out Kansas State?
Anybody know which Loyola that is? Chicago? Baltimore?
New Orleans? Does it matter?
How could I be dead in the water already . . . in all 27 of my
pools?
Could you believe that shot?
Think the boss noticed the three-hour lunch to the sports bar?
Oh, he was there, too?
Where're we watching the championship game?

Before the NCAA Basketball Tournament became a mega-dollar, mammoth affair captivating the nation, there had to be an inaugural event that started the tournament's evolution . . . and the sport's revolution.

It came in 1939.

The first championship team—the University of Oregon Webfoots, coached by Howard Hobson and ultimately called the "Tall Firs" because of their towering height along the front line—was part of my early sports fascination. I was raised in Eugene, and my father, Jerry Frei, was on Oregon football coaching staff from 1955 through 1971, serving as an assistant under the legendary Len Casanova for 12 seasons and then as head coach for 5 before moving on to a long coaching, scouting, and administrative career in the National Football League. Early in his stay at Oregon, he helped coach the freshman basketball team, too . . . because that's what young coaches did then. The football coaching offices were in a wing attached to McArthur Court, the Ducks' home arena. I visited my father on the job often enough to be able to now conjure memories of smoke wafting through the darkened back room and the 16-millimeter projector loudly whirring as "Cas," my father, and the other assistants, including John McKay; and then my father and his staff, including John Robinson, George Seifert, and Bruce Snyder, watched the black-and-white game films. After the switch from the on-campus Hayward Field to the new off-campus Autzen Stadium for football games in 1967, the Ducks still practiced on fields near what we all called "Mac Court." The dank football practice locker rooms, with rickety plumbing that made the players wonder if the pipes were going to explode any minute as they showered, were in the arena basement.

My older brother, David,[1] and I spent many hours in the ivy-draped arena, attending Oregon basketball games and the on-campus Casanova sports summer camps for boys aged 9 to 14, hanging around, or even playing in recreational games with coaches and their families. (We knew where the light closet was . . . and how to get in it.) For the Oregon basketball games, our tickets were for the first row of the overhanging balcony's section 2-R, where I felt as if I could have spit down on John Wooden's dynastic UCLA Bruins if I had chosen to do so. I admit I was tempted.

The display cases on Mac Court's floor level were history courses, touching on all Oregon sports programs, including football and legendary coach Bill Bowerman's track and field teams. Hobson and the Tall Firs had honored spots, and we were indoctrinated in the lore. To some, the men on that 1938–39 Webfoots team were an answer to a trivia question; to many of us, they were heroic, bordering on the mythic. I could name Hobson's five starters: guards Bobby Anet and Wally Johansen, forwards Laddie Gale and John Dick, and center Slim Wintermute. I also knew that one of the Webfoots, a former flyer in World War II, was a high-profile career Navy officer who periodically visited his alma mater, was a booster in the good sense of the world, met my father, and probably was one of the few who knew the part of the Oregon football coach's life that never was mentioned in his press guide biography, that Jerry Frei had been a decorated P-38 fighter pilot in the Pacific Theater.

When I attended the 1965 NCAA championship game in Portland with my father, many of the 1939 Webfoots, then in their late 40s, were introduced and drew applause, and a two-page feature

---

1. David, who also has worked in college and pro sports, now is familiar to many as a fellow author and the longtime television analyst on the Westminster Kennel Club and National Dog Shows.

on the first champions in the official program included a Tall Firs team picture. Princeton's Bill Bradley scored 58 points in the third-place game against Wichita State before left-handed senior guard Gail Goodrich had 42 points to lead UCLA past Cazzie Russell and Michigan for the Bruins' second straight national title. I realized only later that the Bruins' guard was Gail Goodrich *Junior*, and that Gail Goodrich *Senior* in 1938–39 was the University of Southern California's star guard, competing with the Webfoots in the Pacific Coast Conference.

As I immersed myself in sports and school, I also was a voluminous reader. In elementary school, one of my favorites was the Chip Hilton Sports Series, from the same publisher—Grosset and Dunlap—as the famous Hardy Boys detective stories. My brother started the family collection, and I added to it as new books came out. On the back of the Chip Hilton dust jackets, I was told that the author, Clair Bee, coached "many winning basketball teams at Long Island University" and that he "knows what makes boys tick!" When the books began being published with picture covers rather than dust jackets, the Clair Bee mini-bio on the back eliminated any mention of LIU. Many years later, I had a better understanding of why that was.

The Oregon Ducks, in all sports, were my "real" teams.

Chip Hilton's teams—the Valley Falls High School Big Reds and the State University Statesmen—were my fantasy teams . . . before the term meant something else. Chip was an All-American in three sports, a gentleman and scholar working his way through college while refusing to accept a scholarship tied to his sports prowess. For 23 books and re-readings, I was Chip's teammate.

At some point, I became aware that Bee had coached LIU to the championship of the 1939 national invitation tournament in New York, and that some Eastern partisans considered that accomplishment to be as significant, and perhaps even more so, than the Webfoots' NCAA championship. Heck, although they were coached by Chip Hilton's creator, which for that reason alone made them worthy of salute, I considered ridiculous the thought that any team could be better than the Tall Firs. (And in my cynical adulthood, my conclusion is . . . well, you'll see.)

I left Oregon when I was a junior at South Eugene High School. But in the mid-1980s, after living in Colorado for 13 years and beginning my professional career with an 8-year stint at *The Denver Post*, I became a sports columnist for the *Oregonian* in Portland. I was reintroduced to Tall Firs Coach Howard Hobson, beloved and almost always called "Hobby," and was fortunate to get to know him better in his final years.

I wrote a whimsical column about Chip Hilton and Bee's series in *The Denver Post* in the early 1980s, and a similar one later in the *Oregonian*. Both drew considerable "me, too!" reaction. I became known as one of the most enthusiastic Chip Hilton nuts out there, and many of my media brethren shook their heads when during a Portland Trail Blazers' playoff series in 1992, I spent what seemed to be hours talking about Chip with Jack McCallum, who had written a landmark tribute to the books and Bee in *Sports Illustrated* in January 1980. I became friends through correspondence with Bee's daughter, Cynthia Farley, and her husband, Randy, when they were teaching in Indonesia. When they teamed to update the Hilton stories as paperbacks for Broadman & Holman in the late 1990s and early 2000s, I wrote an afterword for them. The full afterword ran in the 13th book of the series, *Fourth Down Showdown*, and a snippet was included on the back-cover copy on many of the other new versions. In fact, if you search for my name and my book listings on Amazon.com, *Fourth Down Showdown* is among the books that show up.

I covered several NCAA Final Fours, including at Kansas City in 1988. The NCAA considers the number of tournaments and not year anniversaries, so in 1988, the Tall Firs were among those honored at events commemorating the 50th tournament, which culminated in the Larry Brown–coached Kansas Jayhawks knocking off league rival Oklahoma for the championship.[2] At the gala, master of ceremonies Curt Gowdy said: "The first college championship was won by Oregon. There was no network radio, no TV, not much press. But these were the men and coaches who laid the foundation for what has become the Final Four."

When the Webfoots won the first championship, the sport wasn't yet a half-century old and still was evolving from James

---

2. It can be confusing. As documented in *Horns, Hogs, and Nixon Coming*, the NCAA celebrated 1969 as the centennial season of college football, saluting the 1869 Rutgers-Princeton game as the first played. In basketball, the 75th anniversary of the first tournament is 2014. If you were married in 1962, the 50th anniversary came in 2012, right?

Naismith's original peach-basket game of nine players per side, unveiled at the International YMCA Training School in Springfield, Massachusetts, in 1891.[3] In 1939, Dr. Naismith attended both the national invitation tournament and the NCAA tournament, being a good sport and proud parent, but also expressing skepticism about what his "basket ball" had become after a half-century of "progress." That "progress," of course, has continued, in part because of integration but also advancement in training methods, equipment (e.g., basketball shoes), and facilities. Judged with today's standards, both the game and the players of that era were slower and far less athletic. But that type of judgment can be made for virtually every other sport, too—yes, including baseball—and as clichéd as it is, evaluations of teams and individuals have to be framed within the context of their eras. Plus, it wasn't *easy* to shoot a basketball then. The ball still had laces, adding to the awkward feel and making it more difficult to dribble than in future years. The first ball without laces was manufactured in 1948.

Officiating wasn't "good" or "bad" as much as it was a mystery, with different interpretations from game to game and, especially, region to region. Consider that this was the definition of a foul in Naismith's original rules, published in 1892: "No shouldering, holding, pushing, tripping, or striking in any way the person of an opponent shall be allowed."

Even on outside shots, usually launched with two hands, players often aimed for the backboard. Part of it was conventional wisdom and geometry, but on rare occasions, shooters were trying to keep the ball out of reach of a "goaltender." The few men tall enough and athletic enough to jump and get a hand above the rim could swat away shots on their way down. Yes, goaltending was legal. Shooting percentages were barely mentioned and not considered much of an issue, but 30 percent could be a good night. Tossing up a shot and, if it didn't go in, hoping to get it back off the carom for a closer-in shot was a legitimate strategy. The center jump after every basket had been eliminated before the 1937–38 season, changing the game's tempo and giving an advantage to coaches, including Howard Hobson, who emphasized pushing the pace in a patterned fast break, trying to get down the floor quicker than

---

3. Now Springfield College.

the defenders, even after opposition baskets. And if the Webfoots didn't get a fast-break bucket, their set plays also were run at a breakneck pace. Players who could do such things as palm the ball, maneuver, run rather than lope, and accurately shoot one-handed on the move were revolutionizing basketball. The Webfoots, with All-American and virtually ambidextrous one-handed-shot wizard Laddie Gale, were at the forefront.

That Oregon team was and still is in the NCAA tournament programs and historical listings, first among past champions. In 2013, when the Dana Altman–coached Ducks won two games in the NCAA tournament before falling to Louisville in the Sweet 16, broadcast crews several times pointed out that Oregon was the first NCAA champion, offering grainy, black-and-white photographic evidence. They even amusedly noted that Oregon's official nickname then was Webfoots, not Ducks.

The tournament the Webfoots won in 1939 was new and considered a risky financial undertaking by the sponsoring National Association of Basketball Coaches. The NCAA, while lending its name to the proceedings, regarded it with wariness. The nation's major press outlets—newspapers, magazines, wire services, and radio networks—weren't sure how seriously to take it. About all they knew was that the event began as a response to, and a rival for, the six-team national invitation tournament in New York's Madison Square Garden. Later, retroactive comparisons of the two tournaments often created the mistaken impression that the NIT was deeply entrenched when the "upstart" NCAA tournament was founded. Actually, the New York tournament, sponsored for its first two years by the Metropolitan Basketball Writers Association (by *sportswriters!*), began in 1938 . . . only one year earlier than the NCAA tournament. Yet primarily because of the successful regular-season doubleheaders staged in the Garden beginning in 1934, New York unquestionably had become the showcase venue for the college game. Many prominent national college coaches took advantage of that in the regular season, bringing their teams into Manhattan. They didn't want New York to have an uncontested claim to primacy in the postseason, too. So they put together their own national tournament.

The undisputed powerhouse New York team of that period, and a powerful draw in the Garden in both the regular and post-season, was Clair Bee's Long Island University Blackbirds.

In that 1938–39 season, the Webfoots and Blackbirds each won a national tournament.

They remain linked by history.

In 1939, both March tournaments—the NCAA's first, the national invitation tournament's second—were played as drumbeats in Europe became louder and war fears heightened. The players of that season were born either during or shortly after the Great War. They knew the toll, including about 117,000 American dead, was horrifying. They also knew that many Americans had come to believe that France and Great Britain, or profit-driven American bankers and industrialists, or all of the above, maneuvered the U.S. into unwise and costly intervention in what became known as World War I. That view especially came into vogue thanks to the advocacy of isolationists in the U.S. Senate, including Republicans Gerald Nye of North Dakota and William Borah of Idaho. The North Dakotan chaired the infamous Nye Committee, which in 1934 held hearings and, with self-fulfilling prophecy methodology, concluded that America indeed had been, essentially, suckered into the war. By early 1939, as on-campus forums and fraternity living room discussions of the ominous events in Europe and the issue of U.S. involvement continued to be part of the ongoing debates, many young Americans and their elders *tried* to ignore the events on the other side of the Atlantic and, secondarily, in the Second Sino-Japanese war, which had broken out in 1937. Many optimistically assumed we'd manage to stay out of the rest of the world's squabbles this time. Some wanted to make sure of that, arguing for nonintervention as official, or even legislated, national policy, except in the case of an attack on the U.S. That sentiment, in formative stages as Hitler's aims and evils became more obvious, would lead to the founding of such groups as the America First Committee and the League of American Writers' Keep America Out of War Committee after Great Britain and France declared war on Germany following the invasion of Poland. The young men on these 1938–39 basketball rosters, and the young people in the bleachers and on their campuses, at least subconsciously wondered as the season progressed: *Could we be drawn into war again? And could we have to fight it?*

Basketball and sports could be diversions, but this was a month when world events became harder to ignore, even on campuses where goldfish swallowing was an escapist craze.

On more than one level, then, theirs was an eventful and even tumultuous March.

A March before the Madness.

I

SETTING THE STAGE

1.

Hobby

Howard Hobson was young enough—35 at the time of the 1938 National Association of Basketball Coaches (NABC) convention where the idea for a national tournament was hatched—for him to feel deferential, allowing the veterans of the business to take the lead in setting up what became his career-defining accomplishment. Also, he had been the Webfoots' head coach only since 1935, after advancing through the ranks to land the job at his alma mater in his home state.

Hobson was raised in Portland, Oregon's largest city, at the confluence of the Columbia and Willamette Rivers along the Washington-Oregon border, and at the north end of the fertile Willamette Valley. "I grew up with a basketball in one hand and a baseball in the other," he wrote in his 1984 book, *Shooting Ducks: A History of University of Oregon Basketball.*

Characteristically for the humble Hobson, that book was an omnibus work about the Oregon program from its inception to the early '80s and only scratched the surface of his own background and involvement, even with the championship team. Fortunately, he passed along more details about his upbringing and life to his sons, including David Hobson, and in a taped June 1982 interview conducted by Linda Brody for the oral history archives at the Oregon Historical Society in Portland.

His father, George Edwin Hobson, was a bookkeeper, the sort of human adding machine who could have a long column of figures dropped in front of him and, without taking pencil to paper, come up with a sum almost instantly. Howard's mother was a much-feared figure, even under her own roof, as a Portland Public Schools truant officer. Money was tight, but Hobson later said that one of the most important dates in his life was December 12, 1915, when at age 12, he played in his first basketball game at an athletic club. His coach challenged him to stop the opposing team's top scorer, and he did it clumsily. The collision left Hobson minus two teeth, which got him in trouble at home. On the spot, he told himself that if he were going to play the game, he would learn to play it with skill and the proper technique, rather than simply rely on his precocious athletic talent.

At Franklin High School in southeast Portland, Hobson played football, basketball, and baseball and was on the track team. When he fell asleep in class one day, the teacher joked, "Don't bother him; he has a game tonight." And he probably did. His reputation, justifiably, was as a serious, intelligent, and intense young man, but his mischievous sense of humor showed when he called the star of an opposing high school team on the telephone, identified himself as a sportswriter doing a story on an upcoming game, and told the opponent, "You better watch out for this Hobson guy; he's a star." The opponent didn't catch on that it was Hobson.

As a Franklin senior in 1921, he was captain of Oregon's state championship basketball team and president of both the student body and senior class. He headed to Eugene, 110 miles south at the head of the valley, thinking he would study law at the U of O and become an attorney. The exact timetable is unclear, but either right after high school or after his freshman year, Hobson took a year off from school to make and save money to go toward his college expenses. Regardless, the system at the time called for students to move to begin studying for a bachelor degree in law (LLB) after their sophomore years. For Hobson, that was after he earned the first of his three letters with the Webfoots' basketball team in the 1923–24 season. The dean of the law school, mindful of the time demands involved, told Hobson he could play only one sport from then on if he was studying law. Hobson said he considered that ultimatum to be the same as asking him which arm he should cut off. He switched his major to economics and stayed with both basketball and baseball. Playing for Coach Bill Reinhart, young Hobson was captain of the Webfoots' basketball squad his final two seasons, 1924–25 and 1925–26, and also a baseball star, majoring in economics while also taking enough education courses to qualify for teaching and coaching accreditation.

Reinhart also was an assistant football coach, and Hobson said he and his teammates essentially practiced on their own in the fall until football season was over and the coach joined them.

With Hobson as the pseudo-coach, the boys tinkered with a new offensive approach and Reinhart embraced and refined it. "We spent many, many hours together figuring out a new system, and a new strategy for the games," Hobson said. "Reinhart was a great teacher and a great fundamentalist and the system we finally decided on was more of Piggy Lambert's than anybody else. We settled on the short-pass, fast-break offense."

Ward "Piggy" Lambert was the head coach at Purdue at the time, and he would end up serving in that role from 1916–46, with one season off to serve in World War I. From 1929–33, one of his players was John Wooden.

By Hobson's later college years, in the mid-1920s, he earned his spending money running and working in the commissary at his fraternity, Phi Delta Theta. "We sold candy and cigarettes," he said. "We had punchboards [lottery-type cards] and various inducements for the brothers to help me along. I did very well in that venture. . . . I think I averaged about $80 a month on it, which was adequate."

Eligibility and amateur rules were loose, so Hobson didn't cause any problems when he played what amounted to semi-pro baseball for company-sponsored teams in the summer. The money, relatively speaking, was very good, and the players usually were considered nominal company employees as they played for the teams.

He was a big man on a small campus. When he arrived in Eugene, the U of O still was relatively young for a U.S. university, having opened in 1876, starting with one building, Deady Hall, and expanding. Oregon didn't have an on-campus gym suited for games in Hobson's playing days, after the program outgrew the Men's Gym. Hobson and his Webfoot teammates played in the City Armory, increasingly inadequate each season. The students lobbied for a new arena and agreed to an additional student fee designated to pay for it. "McArthur Court was built by the efforts of the students—not the administration, not the alumni, not the townspeople," Hobson declared proudly.

Construction on the new arena began on the southern edge of campus during the 1925–26 season, when Hobson was the senior team captain. Under Reinhart, the Webfoots went 10-0 in the Pacific Coast Conference's Northern Division, but then lost to California 32-17 and 29-23 in the best-of-three league championship series.

There was an asterisk, though: during the week after the Webfoots finished the regular season with a 25-15 victory over Oregon State, Reinhart jovially ordered Hobson, his captain, to take his fellow starters to dinner. With the coach apparently taking care of the bill, the boys had a good time, topping it all off with mountains of ice cream. But the Webfoots' top scorer, junior Swede Westergren, ordered his favorite dish, Crab Louie, and by the next morning was terribly ill with ptomaine poisoning. He wasn't able to make the trip to Berkeley. The Webfoots might have lost anyway, but without Westergren they were in over their heads. Regardless, the excitement that team generated on campus was important for the program, setting the stage for the move into a new arena the next season.

Later, the lore was that during construction, its detractors claimed it "looked like an overgrown Eskimo ice house," giving rise to its nickname of "The Igloo." Whether that was true or otherwise, "The Igloo" became an affectionate term, not a scornful one, in use until "Mac Court" supplanted it as the nickname. The building was officially named after Clifton "Pat" McArthur, the U of O's first student body president and first athletic manager (when the term essentially meant athletic director), who also was a four-term Republican U.S. Congressman from 1915 to 1923. He died in late 1923, and he was honored in part because he had helped raise money to keep the university afloat during tough financial times in the early years of the 20th century.

"At that time it was probably the greatest basketball pavilion in the Pacific Coast Conference, if not the entire nation," Hobson said of McArthur Court. Its seating capacity was 6,000, with 1,700 in bleachers and 4,300 in permanent sections. (Second- and third-level balconies wouldn't be added for many years.) The university's enrollment was 3,600, and Eugene's population was about 18,000, so it was quite an accomplishment to fill The Igloo.

When the new arena opened, Hobson was in his first of two years of coaching and teaching at Kelso High School in southwest Washington. His young wife, Jennie, also taught there and the couple was happy. But then Hobson decided to seek his master's degree in physical education at Columbia University in New York, and he and Jennie moved to Manhattan. They loved the life there, attending—at Hobson's count—57 Broadway shows and keeping the *Playbill* magazines, enabling them to refer to them over the years.

On the side Hobson played for the Brooklyn Bushwicks semi-pro baseball team. Ex-major leaguers sometimes appeared in the Bushwicks lineups as drawing cards, and the team also played off-season exhibition games against teams of big leaguers. Hobson drew interest from major-league organizations, but Jennie Hobson made it clear to her husband that she wouldn't be happy with him stepping away from the coaching and teaching career path to embark on the minor-league baseball life with only a long-shot chance of making the major leagues, where the financial rewards were minimal for all but the greatest players, anyway. Hobson also played basketball for the Montclair Athletic Club in the Eastern Athletic club league. The post-graduate life was enjoyable but expensive, and the Hobsons ran through their savings as Howard obtained his P.E. master's degree. He and Jennie both accepted teaching positions at Cortland State Teachers College, 215 miles from New York City. But Wall Street's October 1929 disasters came early in the school year and the picture changed dramatically. The next spring, they headed back to Oregon. "I thought with a master's degree from Columbia University I could choose my spot, but the stock market crash had come on and things were very tight," Hobson said.

With artful strategy in the interviewing, he caught on to teach and coach at Portland's Benson Tech High School.

"What do you teach?" the principal inquired.

"What do you need?" Hobson asked.

"General science."

"That's my specialty," said Hobson, the economics major.

He joked that he stayed a chapter ahead of his students in his two years at Benson, where the Hobson-coached basketball team dominated the Portland league. With that on his résumé, he stepped up to the college games, moving to Southern Oregon Normal School (SONS) in Ashland, near the California border. There, he was adaptive, too, coaching multiple sports. He accepted that his teams had to use a junior-high gym in basketball and a hilly gravel field for football. He said that there was only enough hot water for the first player into the shower at the "shack" they called a dressing room. Conferring with the editor of the *Ashland Daily Tidings*, Coach Hobson pleaded for coverage of his basketball team, but was told the newspaper didn't have the staff or budget to do much. The editor told Hobson if he wrote the stories, the paper would run them, and Hobson jumped at the offer. He later labeled it "the best press I ever had" and didn't once claim to have been misquoted. At first he taught only physical education but soon added economics. As if he didn't have enough to do, he played semi-pro baseball in the summers. He was busy but called his time at Southern Oregon "a wonderful three years," and he drew a lot of attention because his small-school basketball teams went 6-2 against the Reinhart-coached squads from Oregon. Reinhart had backed off the fast-break approach, running more of a pattern offense again, and Hobson couldn't understand why.

Reinhart left in March 1935 to become the coach at George Washington University, and that turned out to be significant not only because it opened up the Oregon job for Hobson. At GW, Reinhart went back to the fast-break approach and one of his players, Arnold "Red" Auerbach, ended up coaching virtually the same system to his Boston Celtics.

Hobson got the news of Reinhart's departure and the multiple-sport opening at Oregon for a basketball and baseball head coach when he was in Denver with his Southern Oregon team, competing in the national AAU tournament. A friend told Hobson he was recommending him and urged him to send a wire assuring Oregon decision makers he was interested. He did that immediately. Technically, the Associated Students of the University of Oregon (ASUO), the student body organization, did the hiring. Hobson dealt with Hugh Rosson, the graduate manager of the university, discussing salary and other issues, and his selection was approved and confirmed at the April 1, 1935, meeting of the ASUO's executive and athletics councils. In making the announcement, Rosson said: "We feel that in Hobson, we have selected a young man who is thoroughly grounded in coaching work, is an inspirational leader, and one who will most capably handle both basketball and baseball assignments."

Hobson said he was "tickled to death," but noted that not only was he the head coach in two sports, he also had agreed to be an assistant coach in football and teach up to a half-load of classes. His salary was $3,000.[1]

---

1. That's roughly equivalent to $50,000 today.

He was the new coach of the Webfoots.

Oregon's athletic nickname had nothing to do with a bird. A group of fishermen in Massachusetts who served the American cause during the Revolutionary War were called "Webfoots," referring to their footwear, and some Oregonians claimed to be their descendants. So the original Webfoots nickname in U of O sports was intended to honor *fishermen*.[2] Connecting it to Ducks in Eugene, though, was inevitable, and students gathered up various live ducks, all nicknamed "Puddles," from the industrial, man-made Millrace waterway near campus and brought them to games. Headline writers also jumped on the shorter "Ducks," and it came to be used as an alternative in stories and in informal conversations. In line with a 1932 student referendum, though, Webfoots remained the official nickname.

Hobson quickly disowned Reinhart's tendency to court and accept out-of-state players, from as far away as New York, as the foundation of the Oregon roster. Perhaps because he was from Portland, and he was embarrassed that the Oregon State Beavers had more Oregonians on their roster and often seemed more popular within the state, Hobson sought to land more players from the state's high schools. When he went beyond the borders, it usually was to southwest Washington. Eventually, after he had made over his roster, all five starters on the 1938–39 team were born in Oregon. Also, both starting guards plus two reserves from the usual 11-man traveling squad all were from the same historic fishing town.

2. It's also why the football team modeled after the Woodstock-era Oregon Ducks in *The Witch's Season* is the Cascade Fishermen.

2.

Fishermen

Bobby Anet and Wally Johansen lived across the street from each other in Astoria, on the south shore of the Columbia River and only six miles from where it flows into the Pacific Ocean at the extreme northwest tip of Oregon. Both born in August 1917 and only 15 days apart in age, the boys were inseparable ever since . . . well, since at least as far back as they could remember.

Despite its well-deserved image as a haven for Finnish immigrants, many of them gill-net fishermen, Astoria's populace was diverse. Heck, there weren't *only* Finns; there also were many Swedes and Norwegians. And, as years went on, Chinese and Japanese immigrants also joined the labor force.

Anet and Johansen were raised in Astoria's Uniontown, or what also was called "Finntown" or "Little Helsinki." Although their Lincoln Street was too hilly for a hoop, they knew the other hotspots in town, and if local drivers came across a street basketball game in progress, they stopped for a suitable break in the action and a wave-through before they proceeded.

Everybody knew the local protocols in Astoria—and, for the most part, followed them.

Founded in 1811 as Fort Astor by John Jacob Astor's American Fur Company, the town's character and economic lifeblood were reflected in Astoria High's athletic team nickname: Fishermen. In the late 19th century, the area was the world's largest source of salmon, but the aggressive harvesting took its toll and by the 1920s, the fishing industry, while still viable, had slowed. A devastating 1922 fire destroyed 32 blocks, roughly one-quarter of the downtown, and about 200 businesses, including a logging mill. Wooden plank streets fueled the fire, and the rebuilding efforts and strategies recognized that it was imperative to replace all streets with pavement, an expensive proposition. For a brief time, the Ku Klux Klan gained a foothold in Astoria, but its influence waned and a Klan burning of a 35-foot cross on the area's Coxcomb Hill in 1925 was considered a last hurrah.[1]

Bobby Anet's grandfather and grandmother came to the United States in the late 1870s, shortening the family name from its original Anetjärve ("people by the lake") and settling in Astoria after a brief residency in Michigan. After a failed 1896 fishermen's strike against the canneries and their fish trapping methods, about 200 of the Finns formed their own Union Fishermen's Cooperative Packing Company, and it flourished, becoming the biggest in Astoria. Bobby's father, Charles Anet, became the secretary-treasurer of the cooperative and also was involved in other businesses, including the area lumber mills. He married Hilda Urell, a Swedish-Finnish woman seven years his junior, and they had four children, two boys and two girls. The family's four-bedroom home reflected an upper-middle class status, even in the Depression years. One of the family pastimes was to look out from the house on the hill, down to the Columbia River, and watch the ferry run between the Oregon and Washington sides. At one point, Bobby and his younger brother, Cliff, and their friends constructed homemade sailboats out of salmon boxes and tried to race the ferry across the river. If Bobby's ramshackle boat had capsized, someone else might have been the Oregon Webfoots' captain in 1938–39. Some folks on the ferry grinned at the boys' nerve, but the crew was not amused.

Hilda Anet got a phone call from the captain. "Get those kids off the river right now!" he roared.

From then on, Hilda was even more encouraging of Bobby's passion for sports.

Across the street, Wally Johansen's father, Arthur, was a fireman and his mother, Anna, was a housewife.

In the wake of the huge fire, Anet and Johansen and all the Astoria boys of their generation were excited when the new Liberty Theater opened in 1925 as part of the rebuilding of downtown. In the tradition of the times, silent movies were shown around Vaudeville-type acts. The next year, schoolchildren reveled in a three-day Astoria celebration to commemorate the opening of the Astoria Column, a 125-foot high monument decorated with 14 paintings of Astoria historical significance. The Column became

---

1. Karen L. Leedom's *Astoria: An Oregon History* is an omnibus look at the city.

a mandatory stop for visitors and tourists and a source of pride for local residents.

Anet and Johansen went though the town's youth basketball program together, winning a state age-group title playing for young YMCA physical director and coach Dick Strite, who took great pride in the progress of his young charges. Born in Maryland and raised in New York, Strite was a star athlete at the YMCA-run McBurney Prep School in New York and a lifeguard on Long Beach in the summers. He then attended the YMCA-run school in Springfield where James Naismith, then a YMCA physical director himself, invented the game. (At the time, it was called the International YMCA College.) After returning to New York, he got his YMCA career started in Brooklyn. Soon, though, he succumbed to the urge to head west to join his brother, Dan, and they worked together in the lumber trade in the forests near Garibaldi, in Oregon's Tillamook Bay area. Calling on his YMCA experience and connections, Strite soon landed the physical director job at the Astoria Y and got out of the forests.

Astoria's population dipped from around 14,000 in 1920, to about 10,000 in 1930, and basketball could be a distraction. As Anet and Johansen reached Astoria High, their coach was the beloved "Honest John" Warren, a native of eastern Oregon who got into coaching at Astoria following his football career at the U of O and his 1928 graduation. Realizing he knew far more about football than basketball, he attended summer basketball coaching camps in the early years of his Astoria tenure. A quick learner, he guided the Fishermen to four state high school basketball championships in six seasons—in 1930, '32, '34, and '35. In writing about Warren's early teams, the *Oregonian*'s L. H. Gregory, who became sports editor at the state's largest newspaper in 1921 and never felt as if writing about high school sports and athletes was beneath him, labeled them the "Flying Finns," but was corrected and told there was only one Finn on the team. By the time the 1934 and '35 teams also won state titles, though, the nickname fit. The boys from Lincoln Street, plus several other Finnish boys, were instrumental in winning those final two titles. The Fishermen were 39-4 and beat Klamath Union in the 1934 championship game, then repeated in '35, going 40-4 and knocking off Portland's Jefferson High to win the title.

By the time they were leaving high school, Anet and Johansen had been working in the fishing industry for several years. That was typical in Astoria for the teenaged boys, even in a time when the U.S. economic malaise considerably weakened the industry. While working for the cooperative in his teenage years, Bobby Anet was captain of several gill-net boats and cannery tenders, the boats that transported the fish to the cannery so the fishermen could stay out on the water. He was out both on the Columbia River and on the Pacific Ocean. Johansen's experience likely was similar, in part because the two boys seemed to do everything together.

Between Anet and Johansen's high school championship seasons, Chancellor Adolf Hitler assumed complete and undisputed power in Germany following the death of President Paul von Hindenburg in August 1934. With so many immigrants from Europe in Astoria, the situation was the topic of discussion in the bars and on the docks. That is, they talked about it when they weren't talking about those boys who were making the town the high school basketball capital of Oregon—including those two guards who played so well together.

Using the designations that appeared in lineups, programs, and box scores, Anet was the "lg" (left guard), Johansen the "rg" (right guard). At Astoria and almost everywhere else, offensive diagrams and plays were drawn up with both guards roughly parallel on each side, and either could handle the ball and start the play. As the energizer and leader, Anet ran the show for the Fishermen, and he didn't need to score to be effective: his highest-scoring game in high school was only eight points. Johansen was the quiet, steady, and reliable complement in the backcourt, both in Astoria and later in Eugene. He could keep up with Anet, and he was a steady, two-handed outside shooter with a perfect follow-through that coaches used as an ideal for others.

Bobby and Wally didn't have to look for each other on the floor. They knew where the other was. They headed off to the U of O together. The catch, though, was that Anet went to Eugene on a football scholarship as a quarterback, and while he intended to play two sports, the "second" sport was baseball.

That plan would change.

Other Fishermen followed Anet and Johansen to Eugene. The first, Ted Sarpola, was a year behind Anet and Johansen and led the Fishermen in scoring for three consecutive seasons. In an era of haphazardly kept records, he generally was considered the first Oregon high school player to score 1,000 points in a career. Another year behind him, the lanky Earl Sandness took advantage of his deft inside moves and broke Sarpola's record for most points in the four-game 1937 state tournament, scoring 68. A fifth ex-Astoria player, Toivo Piippo, also was on what Coach Hobson later listed as his full 20-man Oregon basketball roster for the 1938–39 season.

The Astoria pipeline didn't involve only players, but also a coach and a sports writer.

As Hobson was about to be hired at Oregon in the spring of 1935, after Anet and Johansen's senior high school seasons, he got fully behind "Honest John" Warren as the choice for the coach of the Oregon freshman teams, including in the basketball program. Warren's hiring, in fact, was announced at the same time as Hobson's. Any Fishermen who chose the U of O would be playing for their former high school coach in their first year in Eugene.

All of that was stunningly similar to a plotline of Clair Bee's Chip Hilton books. When Chip and a handful of his Valley Falls High School teammates left their small town and all went to State University, so did their high school coach, the beloved and sage Hank Rockwell. Bee's book about Chip's senior high school baseball season, *Pitchers' Duel*, ends with the guest speaker at the Valley Falls baseball banquet, State's athletic director, announcing the hiring of Rockwell as the university's new freshman coach in football, basketball, and baseball. Chip and his pals, of course, are ecstatic that "The Rock" will be joining them at college.

Bee knew and coached against Hobson many times in the years leading up to the period when he began writing the Hilton books in the late 1940s. He undoubtedly noticed how the Webfoots' coach assembled a significant portion of his glory-years roster from one small town. In fact, New York scribes jumped on the Astoria angle when writing about the Oregon team, and Bee couldn't have missed that, either. Bee knew that Oregon also had brought in the town's beloved coach to head up the freshmen programs. Bee acknowledged he drew on his background and experiences in writing the Hilton books, including when he used Seton Hall star Bob Davies as the model for Chip. He made Valley Falls High School's teams the Big Reds; he could have called them the Fishermen.

And what of Anet and Johansen's YMCA coach? Dick Strite left Astoria before his youth team stars reached high school, transferring to become physical director at the YMCA in Spokane, Washington. Next, he moved to the Eugene Y, and apparently after dabbling in sports writing on the side, he ended up the sports editor of the *Eugene Morning News* in 1933, and then took over the same job with the afternoon *Eugene Register-Guard* in 1937. The YMCA man became a newspaperman. In his travels, he played basketball on various town and amateur teams. He also served as a referee for a while, until he groused that anyone who paid a fee and passed a lightweight rules test could officiate and that the standards were too low, so he didn't want to be part of it any longer. By the 1938–39 season, he was in his mid-30s, married with two children, and with the two-finger typing eccentricities and habits common to the business.

A Eugene native who briefly worked for Strite after graduating from high school right after the end of World War II was Paul Simon, the son of the pastor at Eugene's Grace Lutheran Church. Much later, Simon recalled: "Dick Strite wrote good stories, and expected the same of me. He also had the affliction of most journalists in that day, a love of whiskey and smoking. His top right-hand drawer had a fifth of whiskey in it, which he made clear I should not touch." That was a decade after the Tall Firs passed through Eugene, but it's reasonable to assume Strite hadn't just taken up smoking and drinking at the time. Yet it's also perilous to apply modern standards to that, considering a bottle in a desk drawer wasn't much of a rebel act in those times, and it could involve a toast of relief when another edition was put to bed. In addition to newspaper traditions, in which alcohol seemed as much a part of the business as typewriters and carbon paper, think of Ed Asner, as news director Lou Grant, occasionally pulling a bottle out of the drawer on the *Mary Tyler Moore Show* in the 1970s. It didn't seem irresponsible at all, did it? It was the way it was in newsrooms.

During the late 1930s, Strite occasionally mentioned his connection to Anet and Johansen in print, but didn't overdo it.

So Warren, Anet, and Johansen—and, in a way, Strite—turned out to be a package deal, with other ex-Fishermen following them in subsequent years.

3.

Laddie and Slim

In the 1930s, the NCAA rules governing recruiting were virtually nonexistent.[1]

It's also a misconception that coaches didn't pursue the top prospects and instead just coached whoever showed up. They recruited, recruited hard, and recruited with virtually no restraints. There were scholarships, but they were loosely defined, and the aid often directly drew on the support of athletic department boosters. So that was the system—and a chaotic one at that—as Coach Hobson went after the two boys who would be his senior star big men by 1938–39.

Because his father was an engineer with the Southern Pacific Railroad, Lauren "Laddie" Gale moved around in his youth. Laddie was born in Grants Pass, in southern Oregon, but in his early years, he lived with his father, also Lauren, and mother, Charlotte, in the rural country nearby. His early swimming hole was the Rogue River, near Hellgate Canyon.

Soon, though, his parents were divorced, and Laddie's father eventually was married five times. Charlotte married another railroad man, Bill Smith, who worked in the Southern Pacific's Bridge and Building (B&B) department. In the custody of his mother and stepfather, Laddie lived for a while in Portland. His next move, as he was about to enter high school, was to Oakridge, another small town along the McKenzie River about 40 miles east of Eugene. There, he rejoined his engineer father. With a roundhouse for maintenance of locomotives, Oakridge was a Southern Pacific "helper" station at the base of the Cascade Range, on the Cascade Line that went over Willamette Pass. Laddie enjoyed the small-town life much more than he had Portland, though he occasionally

---

1. Most acronym references to the governing body in that era included periods, but for simplicity's sake, it will be NCAA throughout here.

returned to the city to visit his mother. There was no estrangement there. He simply decided he was more suited for Oakridge.

Young Laddie was popular, mischievous, and adventurous, with a terrific barbed sense of humor. That stayed with him for life, and he enjoyed pulling the legs of those who asked about his upbringing in Oakridge, leaving the impression that Laddie had lived in the woods alone or even in a boxcar. There's no doubt that he was poor during his Oakridge period, as so many were in those Depression years of the early 1930s. His father often was gone with trains, leaving Laddie on his own. It helped that he enjoyed hunting and fishing, and it was for more than sport. But he wasn't Tarzan in the jungle, either. His son, Hank Gale, chuckles and affectionately says he heard his father tell many tales to others, with variations each time, and that when Hank winced or tried to speak up, Laddie would say good-naturedly, "Shut up, kid." They were stories spun from the fabric of truth, not falsehoods.

The even smaller town of Westfir was four miles away, and the Number 22 railroad tunnel was between the two. Laddie landed a job cleaning up at the Westfir hall where each week movies were shown on one weeknight and a dinner was held the next. Once, he was cutting through the railroad tunnel when a train came along. He first tried to outrun it, and then jumped to the side and suffered a broken kneecap. (He had scars and visible remnants of wire, used for repairs in those times, to back up his story.) That slowed his high school basketball career, but once he recovered, it kicked into high gear. For a summer, he also worked atop nearby Larison Rock, a forest fire lookout station with a tiny cupola-type house, and he later told Hank—and this one seemed to add up, too—that he sometimes would run into town, three miles away, for a date, and run back to be on the job at the lookout the next morning. A Civilian Conservation Corps camp was in the area, also, and one of the rituals became the CCC men lined up along one wall and the local men lined up along another at the local dances, glaring at each other and competing for the attention of the local girls and women.

In the 1935 Oregon state high school tournament, the Gale-led Oakridge Warriors met the loaded Astoria Fishermen.[2] John

---

2. Some newspaper accounts later said that Gale came to Warren's attention because Oakridge won Oregon's Class B state tournament, received a Class A tournament berth as a

Warren and several of his players were impressed with Gale in a losing cause, in part because his one-handed shooting was so accurate and audacious, especially for a kid who, at 6-4, usually was the tallest player on the floor. After joining the Oregon staff, Warren urged his new boss to go after Gale—and Hobson did it with great enthusiasm. Gale originally intended to attend Oregon State, but the coaching changes in Eugene altered the picture and Gale changed his plans and told Hobson, all right, he would become one of the Webfoots. That left veteran Beavers coach Slats Gill, a former OSC player himself, steaming because it came not long after Hobson also poached the even taller Urgel "Slim" Wintermute, the 6-foot-8 giant.

Wintermute was born in Portland, but his family had moved to Longview in southwest Washington, and that's where he played his high school ball. Hobson gave Wintermute's high school coach, Scott Milligan, considerable credit for being patient with the gangly Wintermute at Longview and nurturing him. At the time, having a big man (or boy) in the middle wasn't universally valued, especially if a coach favored the sedate game featuring outside set shots. In fact, a big man's major attraction for some coaches was that he could win so many of the jump balls held after every basket. Many agreed that procedure was stultifying and cheered the rules change before the 1937–38 season. Also, many of the coaches who *did* appreciate the big men for more than that wanted them to attempt to play the role of goaltender, swatting shots away as they were about to drop into the net.

Slim's father, a mill worker, was killed in an accident in 1933, and Slim and his mother returned to Portland to live as he was about to head to college. Pencil-thin at 165 pounds, Slim deserved his nickname.

After Slim indicated he planned to attend Oregon State, Hobson, the new Oregon coach, didn't back off. Actually, a coach couldn't even be sure he had landed a player until the young man showed up on campus, enrolled, and attended classes, so Hobson's persistence wasn't surprising or dirty pool. He became more hopeful when

result of the championship, and then lost to Astoria. But the Oregon High School Athletic Association's records indicate that there was only one classification through 1935, and the Class B tournament wasn't instituted until 1936.

Wintermute agreed to visit the Oregon campus in the summer of 1935. Hobson made plans to pick him up and drive him to Eugene, but when the coach arrived at the Wintermutes' home, he was told that Slim was at a dental appointment. Rather than wait, Hobson went to the dentist's office—and the first person he saw was Oregon State star football player Frank Ramsey, there to keep watch over Slim. Soon, Slats Gill showed up, too. Gill lectured Hobson that he needed to accept that the young center wanted to go to Oregon State. Hobson said they were friends and both had been Phi Delta Theta men on their respective campuses, but that wasn't going to save the relationship if Gill prevented Wintermute from visiting the Oregon campus, as planned. Gill said no, insisting he was taking Wintermute to the Oregon State campus for the weekend.

When Wintermute emerged from the dentist's examination room, he was embarrassed. He rode home with Gill, but Hobson followed and waited outside. Finally, Wintermute emerged and told Hobson he had decided to go to Corvallis for the weekend. But he got in the car and began a deeper conversation with Hobson, and eventually Wintermute consented to give Oregon a chance and visit Eugene instead.

He soon said he was going to Oregon.

Hobson estimated that he visited Wintermute seven times more before the center actually enrolled at the U of O, and much of it involved the details of lining up Wintermute's mother with a place to live and a job at Washburne's department store in Eugene, plus a part-time job for Slim himself, and then getting them moved to the college town.

*   *   *

As that summer wound down, Congress passed, and first-term President Franklin Roosevelt signed, the Neutrality Act of 1935, banning the U.S. from trading arms and other military materials with belligerents in a war. Roosevelt protested that he should have the power to judge which nation was the aggressor and adjust policy accordingly, but when it was clear a bill wouldn't pass with that kind of provision, he went along. To many, the Neutrality Act was another means to lessen the chances of America being drawn into another European war, and of the men heading off to college—and so many others—someday having to fight in it.

In Corvallis, Slats Gill was determined to make one more run at Wintermute and Gale before the fall term opened. But the Beavers coach couldn't find the two prospects in Eugene. The savvy Hobson, expecting Gill's final moves, sent them to a cabin along the McKenzie River and told them to stay there, lay low, and have a good time. Laddie and Slim fished, hiked, boated through the white-water rapids on the river, and talked. By the time they enrolled at Oregon in September, they had forged the foundation of a lifelong friendship. It wouldn't be, and couldn't be, as tight as the relationship between Bobby Anet and Wally Johansen, the Astoria Fishermen, but it was significant in the Webfoots' success. The two big men knew their games and even their personalities were complementary. An entrenched starter, forward Dave Silver, was a year ahead of them, so as they looked around them, they thought about which teammate might be the third member of the starting front line by the time they were seniors.

4.

From the Gorge

John Henry Dick's story was quintessential Oregon, and he passed along details of his family history to his three sons.

His father, Franklin, was a young, successful chicken farmer in Iowa who became ill and visited a country doctor. He was told: *Mr. Dick, sorry to break the news, but you have consumption. You have perhaps six months to live.* Facing that diagnosis of tuberculosis with bravery but determination, Franklin decided to see more of the world in his time left, sold his chicken farm, visited the East Coast, and, running low on money, returned home. He visited another doctor for a second opinion, or at least for an update on his timetable and prognosis. The second doctor was incredulous. *Consumption? No, what you have, Mr. Dick, is an ulcer. We can fight, and maybe even control, that!*

Bolstered by the new diagnosis but determined to get a fresh start, Franklin took the money he had left, jumped on a train, and headed west. Deciding his cash wouldn't last all the way to the coast, or long in Portland or any other major city, he disembarked in The Dalles, the small farming community at the eastern end of the Columbia River Gorge. Franklin landed a job as a clerk in a local lawyer's office. Showing an aptitude for the work, he studied and passed the bar examination, becoming a small-town lawyer himself. He married a J.C. Penney seamstress, Louise, and started a family, and John was the second oldest of the four Dick sons, behind big brother Bill. The twist was that because both Astoria and The Dalles were on the south bank of the Columbia, in theory, if young John Dick had dropped a bottle with a message into the river, young Bobby Anet or Wally Johansen eventually might have been able to fish it out as it was about to reach the Pacific.

Dick discussed his upbringing and more in a lengthy interview with Oregon athletic department official Jeff Eberhart for the *Order of the O* newsletter, distributed to former lettermen. Only part of the interview ran in the newsletter. Eberhart graciously passed along an entire transcript.

"Sports and the local trials were the biggest things in town," Dick told Eberhart. "The entire business district would close an hour before a high school football game and wouldn't reopen until about an hour after the game had ended. We had 5,500 people in The Dalles at that time and we'd seat about 4,000 to 4,500 people at those high school games."

When John was a sophomore and big brother Bill was a junior and star of the team, The Dalles High lost a playoff game and the townsfolk were distraught. Bill Dick told his father that his "little" brother, John—already a shade over 6-foot-4 but still a string bean—showed promise but wasn't yet tough or strong enough. Franklin owned farmland he intended to turn into a wheat ranch. Part of it was still heavily wooded. Every day over the next summer, Franklin drove John to the farmland, handed him a lunch, and left him behind to work on clearing the acreage. When The Dalles High School opened again the next fall, John was beginning to look a lot more like the powerful forward who played for the Webfoots. In the next two years, both with Bill as a teammate and after Bill graduated, John became known as a football star playing end and linebacker.

Howard Hobson and John Warren recruited Dick for basketball, and they insisted he could be a college star in the sport if he put his mind to it. They knew they had a leg up in the recruiting because Bill was at Oregon, playing both football and baseball. (He eventually transferred to Willamette University.) John Dick went to the Oregon campus several times to visit his brother and attend games.

"I wanted to be a student at the university long before I came here," John said. "I was also recruited to play baseball and football at Oregon, but you couldn't play any other sport if football was giving you the scholarship. I chose basketball because I knew we were going to have a pretty good team, and it also gave me the chance to play baseball, which was great because 'Hobby' was the baseball coach as well."

Dick was charismatic and a natural leader, and he was elected the freshman class president. He remained involved in student-body politics and spread thin and reluctantly gave up baseball after his freshman year. But his baseball connection allowed him to become friends with former Webfoot infielder Joe Gordon, then in the Yankees' minor-league system and about to reach the major leagues. The friendship lasted decades.

"Managing my time became an issue, so I chose to concentrate on one sport," Dick said. "You have to remember that these were the Depression years, so we had to work for our scholarships. Our room, board and tuition were paid for, but we had to buy our own books."

Dick joined the Sigma Nu fraternity, which had several members from The Dalles and also many athletes, including his eventual basketball teammates Wally Johansen, Bobby Anet, and Ted Sarpola—three of the Astoria boys. Dick made pocket money stocking campus cigarette machines. Despite the lingering effects of the Depression, the good-times mood was prevalent on campus, and Dick unabashedly joined in the partying. The students didn't have to hide it, either, in the wake of the December 1933 end of Prohibition. As Dick became one of the most-liked men on campus and a student government leader, his attitude was reflected in what he later told his own sons: "You can't have too few enemies and too many friends."

5.

Basketeers

Howard Hobson caught a break in the late fall of 1935. Bobby Anet, on a scholarship as a quarterback, showed up in Hobson's office after playing for John Warren in his freshman football season. He told Hobson that varsity football coach Prink Callison was going to refuse to allow him to keep his scholarship if he insisted on going out for baseball in the spring.[1] Anet asked Hobson if he could receive a basketball scholarship instead and play basketball and baseball. The Webfoots' basketball and baseball coach said that would be okay with him. As it turned out, Anet gave up baseball, too, after his freshman year, but the moves were fortuitous for the Webfoots' basketball program.

As Anet, Wally Johansen, Slim Wintermute, and Laddie Gale were on the verge of becoming eligible for varsity play as sophomores, the Spanish Civil War between those loyal to the Republican government and the Nationalist rebels of Generalissimo Francisco Franco broke out in July 1936. One fear was that with Germany and Italy supporting Franco, and with the Soviet Union backing the loyalists, it could be kindling for additional conflicts in an unstable Europe.

Meanwhile in the U.S., Franklin Roosevelt easily won reelection for a second term on November 3, with Republican Alf Landon, the Kansas governor, carrying only Vermont and Maine and winning only 8 of the 531 electoral votes. It was an endorsement for Roosevelt's leadership in combating the Great Depression, even if many believed he had gone too far with radical New Deal programs and government intervention. Yet also entering into it was the perception that he was better equipped and qualified to deal with the deepening crises in Europe and around the world. Roos-

---

1. As John Dick related, he considered that same policy in deciding not to play football.

evelt repeatedly declared that his goal was to keep America from being entangled, and that he wouldn't allow it to happen.

John Dick played for the freshman basketball team and watched as several sophomores helped the 1936–37 Webfoots finish in a three-way tie for first in the Northern Division at 11-5. Laddie Gale showed flashes of stardom early, but he suffered a broken hand and missed most of the season. He scored only 45 points as a sophomore, eventually preventing him from dominating the career scoring lists at the U of O for a long time. Noting the Webfoots' scrappy play, mostly without Gale, *Oregonian* sports editor L. H. Gregory—who had called the Astoria boys the "Flying Finns"— nicknamed the sophomore-laden team "alley-cats." The Webfoots fell to eventual winner Washington State at the outset of a three-team playoff for the Northern Division title. That probably was just as well. In 1937, the Webfoots would have been overmatched in the ensuing PCC championship series against the Stanford Indians and their charismatic, trail-blazing superstar.

* * *

Because league-wide train travel up and down the coast would have been expensive and excessively time-consuming, the PCC had a two-division structure. In that 1936–37 season, when the core players on Oregon's eventual championship team were sophomores, the dominant team in the Southern Division and the league was Stanford, led by junior forward Angelo "Hank" Luisetti, from San Francisco's Russian Hill neighborhood. Defying convention and confounding coaches stubbornly wed to the "fundamentals" of careful ball control and the two-handed set shot, most often taken with feet planted together and from a stationary position, Luisetti rang up points with running one-handers. He would end up an All-American in all three of his collegiate seasons, and it was more than gimmickry. Other stars of the mid- to late 1930s, including Gale, utilized the one-hander, too, and the evolution was inevitable, but Luisetti was its most visible pioneer. Still, many coaches groused that it would diminish the game if it were allowed to catch on.

Before the Indians turned their attention to their Southern Division rivals that season, Luisetti took New York by storm with a Madison Square Garden appearance on a national barnstorming tour. On December 30, 1936, a crowd of 17,623 watched as the Indians snapped Long Island University's—and Coach Clair Bee's—win streak at 43 games. Luisetti had 15 points in Stanford's 45-31 victory, and in addition to his flashy shooting, what impressed the New York folks was his extraordinary passing ability, especially for a forward who sometimes also played center. LIU had gone 26-0 the previous season, and the loss to Stanford was the Blackbirds' first since they'd fallen to Duquesne 30-25 on February 15, 1935, in the Garden.

The Indians were the first team from west of the Mississippi to play in one of promoter Ned Irish's doubleheaders at the nation's best-known arena. The "new" Garden, the building's third incarnation, and the first to not be located at Madison Square itself, opened in 1925 on Manhattan's Eighth Avenue, between 49th and 50th Streets. Two National Hockey League teams, the Rangers and Americans, played there, and big-time boxing matches and the Ringling Bros. and Barnum & Bailey Circus were the other major attractions. Basketball at first was an afterthought. The professional New York Knickerbockers, founded by Irish as a charter member of the Basketball Association of America, wouldn't begin play in the Garden until 1946. Until then, the college game was the focus, largely because of Irish's doubleheaders in Madison Square Garden.

Before he hooked on with Madison Square Garden, Irish wrote for the *New York World-Telegram*. He also became a part-time public relations man for the New York Giants and the National Football League. The degree of his innovation in putting basketball in the Garden often has been overstated, but he certainly was its most influential promoter.

At the request of New York Mayor Jimmy Walker in January 1931, the early days of the Depression, Irish was among the New York sportswriters who helped put on a benefit tripleheader involving New York teams in the Garden. It drew over 15,000, and the proceeds when to unemployment relief funds. If someone didn't start thinking of the potential to mine the New York college game for profit after that, it would have been a shock. Another benefit card the next year did well, too. Until then, the New York college game mainly was a private act, played in tiny and often overflowing gymnasiums. Irish went along with the oft-told story of how he came up with the inspired idea of putting college games in the Garden when he had to sneak into an overflowing gym through a window to cover a City College of New York–Manhattan game, ripping his trousers in the process. That tale rarely includes mentions of the previous relief fund benefits in the Garden.

In 1934, while still working for the *World-Telegram*, Irish made his move, consulting with Garden president John Kilpatrick to book six nights during the 1934–35 season in the famous building. Irish knew the matchups of city teams had outgrown the small local college venues, but that they likely wouldn't steadily pack the much larger Garden, either. So his goal—and this is probably where he was most visionary, influential, and even daring—was to bring in opponents from outside the area to face the New York teams.

In recruiting teams for his doubleheaders, Irish also could emphasize that the playing conditions would be much better than for those at the previous basketball dates in the Garden. Because the earlier games were benefits, the complaints were muted, but those conditions were horrible and produced games considered low-scoring even in the chess match that often was the Eastern game of the time. In the original 1931 benefit tripleheader, for example, the *highest* point total among the three losing teams was 18. (Yes . . . 18.) The *New York Times'* advance story for Irish's first doubleheader noted that those earlier basketball events in the Garden were played on a makeshift, sagging canvas surface stretched over the stone floor, and that in time for Irish's doubleheaders, the Garden had acquired a real board floor and innovative glass backboards, designed not to block the view of the fans watching from higher levels behind the baskets.

In that inaugural doubleheader on December 29, 1934, New York University beat Notre Dame 25-18 and Westminster College of Pennsylvania beat St. John's 37-34. The attendance was 16,138, a college record crowd. So Irish, previously hopeful but knowing nothing during the Depression was a sure thing, exhaled. Called on the carpet by *World-Telegram* sports editor Joe Williams for spending so much time promoting his upcoming venture, Irish had rolled the dice, quitting his newspaper job altogether, and he also was on the hook for $4,000 rent each night at the Garden. That turned out to be a bargain.

A week later, on January 5, 1935, NYU knocked off the Adolph Rupp–coached Kentucky Wildcats 23-22 in the second double-header, and the drama included a controversial foul call on Kentucky at the end. The announced crowd was even better, at 16,500. On the day of the game, too, Rupp mused about an outlandish idea: why not hold a national championship tournament? "At the end of each season, four or five teams throughout the country lay claim to the mythical national title," Rupp said. "If the leading teams of each section would agree to play a round robin tournament in some centrally located city, like Chicago, a sort of Rose Bowl champion in basketball would be crowned each year." He went on to say such a tournament would lead to heightened interest in college basketball and perhaps even encourage more uniform rules interpretation across the country. The round-robin aspect of the tournament was unrealistic, unless the field was limited to no more than four teams. Yet it was one of the first times a credible college coach publicly supported the concept of a tournament to determine a national champion.

Four years later, his comments would be rendered ironic.

Irish plowed on with a series of doubleheaders each season. Emboldened, he sought to top himself, and bringing in Stanford to play LIU in late 1936, in Irish's third season as a Garden promoter, was part of his high ambition. Because a coast-to-coast train trip for one game was impractical, the Indians—with Irish's help—turned it into one long road trip with multiple games, and that model soon would come into play for the Oregon Webfoots, too.

After beating LIU, the Indians went 10-2 in the PCC's Southern Division in that 1936–37 season and easily handled Washington State in the championship series. The Webfoots, with Anet, Johansen, Gale, and Wintermute gaining experience as sophomores, took solace that they were making progress, and that Hank Luisetti had only one more season of eligibility.

*   *   *

The "peace" between Japan and China following their 1894–95 war was tenuous, with "incidents" over the years and periodic fighting since 1931. All pretense of peace was abandoned in July 1937, and the Second Sino-Japanese War started. American newspapers ran news, giving hints of the war's ferocity and the Japanese invaders' barbaric conduct, but for the most part it was considered worthy of only minor concern. It was *their* war.

* * *

Looking ahead to 1937–38, his fourth season in the Garden, Irish was determined to take advantage of Luisetti's senior year, too. He sold Stanford officials on making another trip to New York and scheduled the Indians for not one, but two, games in the Garden. In the span of three nights in December 1937, the Indians beat CCNY and LIU (again) and looked to be the undisputed best team in America. They even had more balance: Luisetti wasn't the Indians' leading scorer in the 49-35 romp over LIU. That honor went to center Art Stoefen, who hit for 20. The much-hyped Indians-Blackbirds rematch drew a Garden basketball record crowd of 18,148, and scribes were offended that "speculators" reselling tickets outside were getting up to 250 percent of the real price of the ticket.

As part of the barnstorming arrangements, the Indians' next stop was in Philadelphia, and there the Indians lost 35-31 to Temple, which slowed the game to a crawl. The mild upset proved that Stanford and Luisetti weren't invincible. On the way home, though, Luisetti drew major headlines across the country when he scored an astounding 50 points in a win over Duquesne.

Back in Palo Alto, the Indians stormed through the PCC's Southern Division, going 10-2 to reach the league championship series again.

This time, their opponent was Oregon.

The Webfoots went 14-6 in the North, beating out Washington by one game. Laddie Gale, also gaining renown for his flashiness, led the division in scoring as a junior. He averaged 12.4 points in all games, 12.5 in conference games only. His ability to palm balls in both hands at once was featured one day in a 1937 "Ripley's Believe it or Not," perhaps a day after the world's largest rutabaga. He also could do something quite rare—not only shoot effectively with one hand, but with either hand.

Slim Wintermute was making eye-popping progress, going from skinny and raw and easily pushed around in his first varsity season and part of his second, to talented big man, still full of potential, by the time his junior season was winding down. "I liked Wintermute from the start," Hobson said in a 1939 *Oregon Journal* story that seemed to have indulged in a style of the era and "punched up" his words a bit. "In his way," Hobson added, "he was willing, and for a big follow he wasn't awkward. But he was about as aggressive as a fire hydrant and his self-confidence was as low as a bank balance after the 10th of the month. But he was only 17 and he had grown up in a year. He wasn't even accustomed to his size. He began to acquire the winning spirit in his second varsity year. When I finally managed to convince him that he was unbeatable, he became unbeatable. He had everything else. For all his size, there's a boy who made a champion of himself the hard way." Hobson brought up the elimination of the jump ball after every basket for that season and said, "A lot of coaches began to neglect the big fellows. The smaller fellows who mature earlier are easier to coach. But the good big man is still better than the good little man in this game and the coach who has the patience to work with him until he 'arrives' will profit."

Averaging eight points in conference games, a surprisingly mobile Wintermute finished third in Northern Division scoring in 1937–38, behind Laddie Gale and Washington State's Al Hooper, and just ahead of Montana's Bill Lazetich and Idaho's Steve Belko. At the defensive end, Wintermute had become a major force without relying only on his height and legal goaltending to make his mark. "He was in his day the best center in the country," Hobson said years later. "I've always said that he was the best defensive center I've ever coached. In fact, he's the best college defensive center I've ever seen."

As that 1937–38 season wound down, L. H. Gregory, in almost throwaway, off-handed references in the *Oregonian*, coined what would become the team's famous nickname. He decided he had a better idea than the "alley-cats" he had made popular the season before. In his "Gregory's Sports Gossip" column on March 3, 1938, he noted that Oregon still was at the top of the division standings and added: " . . . and there the tall-fir Webfoots should certainly stay." On March 5, in a story advancing that night's game against the Oregon State Beavers, he wrote: "The only way Oregon's tall-fir basketeers can fumble that basketball title now . . . is to become falling pines at Corvallis tonight, and they're so far and away the league's best team that this just isn't a reasonable thought." Over the next year, there were a handful of similar references in news stories, almost always without capital letters and usually with the hyphen, and ultimately some "TALL FIRS" mentions in headlines. The truth is, though, they became the "Tall Firs" more in retrospect than they were during their Oregon careers.

As a junior that season, scrappy guard and team captain Bobby Anet cemented his image as the undisputed leader. Coaches couldn't communicate with the players on the floor and the captain had to call the time-outs. But even more striking was his energy and his pushing of the offensive pace, especially in the first season minus the jump ball after every hoop.

"Anet was an indifferent shot and his floor game wasn't always the last word in perfection, but his faith in himself and his team was unshakable," Hobson said. "With him there was never any question whether Oregon could outplay its opponent; it was simply a question of how much. He inflamed every other player. He was our high priest of Oregon invincibility."

John Dick called Anet "the greatest dribbler I have ever seen. Bobby was a real smart kid, but also a real tough kid. He had short legs, but long arms, and he didn't have to bend over to dribble, and he could dribble as fast as he could run. And he dribbled so low that I never saw anybody steal the ball from him. He was not a big scorer himself, but when you needed it, he was what you called a money player. He'd find a way to get the ball in the hole."

With Anet as the leader, the Webfoots were at least competitive against Stanford and Luisetti in the 1938 PCC championship series in the Bay area. In Game 1, Luisetti poured through 20 points in a 52-39 victory in the San Francisco Civic Auditorium.

About when the game ended, on the morning of March 12 in Europe, German Army troops marched into Austria, sealing the *Anschluss*—the annexation of Adolf Hitler's native land into the Third Reich.

Luisetti had 26 points the next night in Stanford's 59-51 series-clinching victory in the much smaller Stanford Gymnasium, but the overflow crowd of around 1,800 gave him a standing ovation when he was replaced late in the game. He was destined to be an All-American for the third season in a row, and the league title also was the Indians' third in succession.

After that season-ending game for both teams, Anet saw to it that the visitors' dressing room door remained closed and conducted a team meeting. Hobson, recognizing it was a frank talk among the boys, waited outside. Trainer Bob "Two Gun" Officer, who was allowed to remain, later filled him in on what was said. Anet emphasized to his teammates that the next season, in effect, had started that minute. While the national tournament still was an idea to come, Anet announced to his teammates: "Next year, we're going to win everything."

The Webfoots grudgingly admitted to themselves that they had lost to a better team. "After getting past us, had there been a national championship contested in 1938, I have no doubt that Stanford would have won going away," Dick said.

Dick might have been right. He probably *was* right. But Stanford's December loss to Temple always would come into play for those trying to determine a mythical national champion.

Gale and Johansen soon were named to the PCC's first-team all-star team after the season, and Wintermute was on the second-team, joined by, among others, Idaho's Steve Belko.

*   *   *

Meanwhile in New York, the first national invitation tournament was played on March 9, 14, and 16, 1938, so it sandwiched the PCC title series. It definitely was an outgrowth of the regular-season doubleheaders and involved the type of conflict of interest for writers that wouldn't have been tolerated later. Although Ned Irish's fingerprints were on the tournament, too, the Metropolitan Basketball Writers Association, made up of New York scribes, founded, sponsored, and promoted it—and promoted it to the point where they sometimes came off as carnival barkers imploring passersby to enter the tent. The writers' group was founded in 1934, and Irving T. Marsh and Everett B. Morris, both from the *Herald Tribune*, were its ringleaders. Morris also was the paper's boating writer.

The plan was to follow Irish's doubleheader formula in putting together tournament fields, mixing New York–area teams with intriguing squads from other parts of the country. One of the goals was to confirm New York's primacy in the college basketball world, and the tournament did that, but there was some confusion because nobody seemed to know what to call it. Most often, it was "the national invitation tournament," with the informality of lowercase letters, but it also was labeled the Metropolitan Basketball

Writers' tournament, the New York writers' invitation tournament, and several other combinations. Capital letters and/or the NIT acronym didn't come into play right away.

The participants in that six-team 1938 inaugural invitation tournament were Colorado, Oklahoma A&M,[2] and Bradley Tech,[3] joining eastern entrants Temple, New York University, and LIU. As those with the farthest to travel, Colorado and Oklahoma A&M had byes, and the writers probably were second-guessing the bracketing that matched two New York teams, NYU and LIU, in the March 9 quarterfinals, which guaranteed the early elimination of one local draw. In a shocker, NYU knocked off Clair Bee's Blackbirds 39-37. The Blackbirds finished the season with a 23-5 record, disappointing given the expectations and a soft schedule, with the other losses coming to Marshall, Minnesota, Stanford, and La Salle. In the other quarterfinal, Temple beat Bradley Tech 43-40.

Colorado had won the Rocky Mountain region's Big 7 league, but the Buffaloes were sought because they had the biggest star in the tournament—an event its home-state *Denver Post*, by the way, called "the first national Invitation Intercollegiate tournament." That star was a scholarly fellow from Wellington, Colorado. Byron "Whizzer" White was an All-American halfback for the Buffaloes and a solid starter for Colorado in basketball. The New York scribes couldn't get enough of him, just as they had enjoyed building up Luisetti when he came through with Stanford during the regular season. The Colorado hero was the toast of Manhattan from the time he arrived with the Buffaloes' traveling party. He had eight points in the March 14 semifinals as the Buffaloes edged NYU 48-47 on Don Hendricks's late basket. In the other semifinal, the Oklahoma Aggies, coached by 33-year-old Henry "Hank" Iba, lost a 56-55 heartbreaker to Temple. The New York scribes puffed out their chests as they typed, knowing the nip-and-tuck semifinals had been exciting, and hoped for a reprise in the March 16 championship game.

Instead, they and the fans got a stinker. Temple routed Colorado 60-36 to win the tournament title, and Whizzer White bowed out of his college basketball career with a 10-point night. Minutes after the championship game, he again was being asked which he

---

2. Now Oklahoma State.
3. Now Bradley.

would choose—the outlandish $15,000 contract from franchise owner Art Rooney to play for the Pittsburgh Steelers or a Rhodes scholarship to study in Oxford. "There are about 500 people trying to make up my mind," he said in the Madison Square Garden dressing room. One way to tell that White already was an extraordinary celebrity was that at least one scribe actually talked to him after the game instead of following the usual procedure of typing eyewitness accounts of the game and not seeking comment from anyone involved.

Temple, the tournament champions, finished the 1937–38 season with a 23-2 record. Many in the east advanced the Philadelphia squad as the nation's best, and it wasn't unreasonable. Their head-to-head victory over Stanford, the west's top team, bolstered the claim. There were scattered references to the Owls as "national champions," but for the most part, the national attitude—at least among those who noticed in other areas of the country—seemed to be that the Owls had won a new tournament for New York teams and invited guests, no more suited to select the best team in the land than, say, a holiday tournament. It was a tournament for select (and selected) teams, but not a national championship, and Stanford wasn't there. After beating the Webfoots for the 1937–38 PCC title, the Indians didn't go anywhere, except perhaps to their homes during spring break. They already had made two cross-country trips to New York and beyond in the previous sixteen months. That was enough.

Considered an experimental venture that first year, the invitation tournament was pronounced a success. The catch, though, was that organizers couldn't count on having a Whizzer White–type drawing card every year from among the teams brought in from outside the New York area or the East Coast.

Stanford coach John Bunn was one of many in his profession who began to wonder if there might be a way to both combat the national invitation tournament *and* determine a national champion, perhaps as soon as the upcoming 1938–39 season.

* * *

The week after the 1938 PCC championship series, Webfoots reserve guard Matt Pavalunas, then a sophomore, returned home to tiny Raymond, Washington, during spring break and spoke at a local function attended by a reporter from his hometown newspaper, the *Willapa Harbor Herald*. "In the last game, I got to check Luisetti for about the last minute of the game, and had to hold onto his pants to keep him from scoring," he said. "Luisetti is a very modest man off the floor, but he is quite a showman while playing. At one time, during a hushed period, a little boy yelled, 'Hi, Hank,' and Luisetti turned and waved to him." Pavalunas promised his hometown listeners that in 1938–39, the Webfoots would be "even better than this year. Oregon loses but one regular and one reserve and we have two freshman players who will go a long way toward replacing them."

To his listeners, or those who read the newspaper account, "even better" meant winning the PCC. Soon, though, there was another goal to shoot for—a national title.

6.

Floating Ideas

Two weeks after the first national invitation tournament, the nation's coaches gathered for their convention at Chicago's Morrison Hotel. Stanford's John Bunn brought up the idea of a tournament involving teams from all areas of the country, with the selections made by men who knew what they were doing. Other coaches joined in the chorus.

In a sense, the tournament idea can be tied to the coaching tree of longtime Kansas coach Phog Allen. Allen was a proponent, too, and so were three of his former players-turned-coaches—Bunn, Adolph Rupp (at least judging from his 1935 comments proposing a national tournament), and Northwestern's Dutch Lonborg. Also outspoken in support of the idea was Ohio State's Harold Olsen. These weren't coaches from obscure programs, in outpost parts of the country, whining about the potential to be overlooked by the New York tournament. These were coaches from prominent programs, wanting to prevent the post-season spotlight from shining *only* in Manhattan.

Bunn was certain his 1938 Stanford team would have won a genuinely open national tournament, whipping Temple in any rematch, plus any other teams the Indians found themselves matched up against. He was about to give up coaching to become Stanford's dean of men before the next season, but he remained involved with and passionate about the game.

Because the tournament would stretch from coast to coast, the initial skepticism among many members was understandable. Howard Hobson later said of the membership reaction: "Interest was not great." The majority of the 205 NCAA programs probably wouldn't contend for either the national invitation or the NCAA tournament, so they weren't going to be whipped into frenzies during the debate. The enthusiastic supporters of an NCAA tournament might not have had huge numbers; they had major influence, and others came around.

The NABC membership endorsed passing along the proposal for a tournament to the NCAA. The catch was that the national body then was barely 30 years old after its founding as the Intercollegiate Athletic Association of the United States (IAAUS) in early 1906, and it still had limited resources and power. It was formed as part of the response to President Theodore Roosevelt's call for rules changes in football to protect players—the "Flying Wedge" repulsed him—and his summons of college presidents to the White House for discussion of possible reforms. Sixty-two schools signed up as charter members of the IAAUS in late 1905, and it officially opened for business in March 1906. The name change to NCAA came in 1910, and the organization began sponsoring a national track and field championship as soon as 1921. But that was conducting individual competition among athletes who made it to a single-site meet and then tallying team points, and it was relatively uncomplicated compared to team tournaments involving a series of games. While the coaches could argue to the NCAA that a national tournament wasn't an unprecedented project for the organization, its scope and ambition certainly were.

The NCAA was wary and officials essentially told the coaches: *Let us think about it.* Back in Eugene, Coach Hobson at least mentioned the possibility of a new national tournament to the Webfoots. They didn't get too excited, but they filed it away.

*   *   *

As the next season approached, the Munich Conference in late September 1938 essentially endorsed the beginning of Czechoslovakia's dismemberment through the German annexation of the Sudetenland. After returning to London, British Prime Minister Neville Chamberlain stood outside 10 Downing Street and declared of the agreement, signed by Germany, Italy, France, and Great Britain: "I believe it is peace for our time."

*   *   *

It wasn't until October 3 that the NCAA went along with the inception of a national tournament, and with a significant caveat. The NCAA agreed to sanction the event, to be held at the end of the 1938–39 season, but declared that the NABC assumed all the financial risk. In addition to not being convinced of the tournament's financial viability, the NCAA had minimal staff and didn't want to get in over its head, administering a far-flung national championship on short notice.

Ohio State's Olsen was named chairman of both the tournament and selection committees. The Wisconsin native and former Badgers star player started his coaching career at Ripon College in his home state, but took over the Buckeyes' program in 1922, when he was only 27. He was one of the major voices behind picking up the pace of the game through the early 1930s implementation of the rule calling for teams to have no more than 10 seconds to advance the ball past a center-court line. Also, the first tournament was going to be held as part of only the second season without the jump ball after every basket, and already some coaches were complaining that the innovation made the game far too strenuous and even potentially risky for the young athletes.

After the NCAA gave the go-ahead for the tournament, it wasn't put together overnight. The coaches involved had their own teams to worry about, their own seasons to play, and the first tournament always had a bit of an impromptu, by-the-seat-of-the-pants feel to it. Once that approval came, Hobson and many other coaches made their players aware that while they didn't know all the details, there would be a new tournament played at the end of the 1938–39 season.

"From that moment on, winning the national title became our primary focus," John Dick said.

Hobson was all-in on the national tournament concept. That was consistent with his image as an original thinker and a statistics devotee, reflecting his father's human adding-machine aptitude. He advocated awarding three points for a successful longer shot, two points for anything from medium range, and one point for lay-ins. Hoping to get the game away from the hoop, he also advocated doubling the width of the lane from 6 to 12 feet. Hobson became more public with his recommendations in the late 1940s, but the ideas were percolating long before that. He was all for eliminating the center jump after every basket. In a game of desultory paces and considerable standing around, Hobson, like Ohio State's Olsen, argued for the wisdom of pushing the ball up the floor with energy and having movement in the offenses. After helping devise a fast-break system as a player at Oregon, he still was in the first wave of coaches teaching the strategy with precision. The outlet pass would go to a forward or, ideally, a guard on the side, then the ball would go to a guard cutting diagonally to the middle to lead the break. The center would trail as the safety net. "It was not a helter-skelter fast-break," Hobson said. "We had a single and a secondary trailer. It had definite organization to it, so that if we were intercepted, the center, who happened to be the intermediate trailer, could go back to the hole to fend off any fast-break attempts by the other team."

The key was that the forwards and center could get up and down the floor, too. "I used to kid Anet all the time," Laddie Gale said. "He was pretty quick, but I'd tell him that if he was so damn fast how come it was that I'd pass the ball out to him and then I'd be down at the other end of the court waiting for him to pass it to me?"

Coach Hobson insisted on keeping track of statistics that went far beyond the sparse summaries, listing for at least in-house consideration assists, steals, rebounds, and turnovers, and he was one of the first coaches to also keep shot charts. The players learned to expect and live with his experiments, including tinkering with the height of the basket and seeing if there might be a more optimum level than the standard ten feet. His original thought about raising the basket was that it might make the misses carom farther, thus leading to more rebounds for the smaller men on the floor. After conducting trial runs, he admitted he was wrong about that. Yet just when the boys thought he was settling down, he'd start talking about those three-pointers and another of his innovative proposals, establishing a time limit on a possession before a team had to shoot—a shot clock, in other words. He wasn't alone on that: Clair Bee also mentioned the concept and Syracuse Nats owner Danny Biasone later was instrumental in the shot clock's introduction in the NBA, and many others favored some sort of time limit on a possession before its adoption. But Hobson was among the concept's first credible advocates.

Later, in a letter nominating Hobson for the Basketball Hall of Fame, Bobby Anet said: "He was the first coach to plot a player's moves on the court and while at Oregon, and before, had other members of his teams in the stands charting an individual who was playing—where he best reacted, his 'spot' to shoot from, and the best style for him to play. This not only involved the player watched, but also taught the 'student' various maneuvers and forced his concentration on the game." So even when Hobson had 20 players on his roster, he found ways to put them all to work, on the floor in practices and scrimmages, and the extras as observers at home games.

By the beginning of Hobson's fourth season, the Webfoots had gone 63-28 under the young coach, and he had earned respect and tolerance for innovative approaches while settling in as head of both the basketball and baseball programs in Eugene. "He was relatively soft-spoken," John Dick said. "He was never a shouter, a ranter, or a raver. He was analytical. At halftime, he would analyze the game. He was a great user of charts. He was not the fiery, inspirational, pep-talk type of person. He was very businesslike, and I think that part of his personality carried over to his coaching. I always thought we were better prepared than most teams that we played against, because Hobby was such a student of the game."

Hopes were high for Hobson's 1938–39 Webfoots.

He decided they were ready for Broadway.

The Oregon coach had become a part-time area scout for the New York Yankees, and they were grateful for how he gracefully accepted and aided the storied franchise's signing of his star infielder, Joe Gordon, in early 1936. Gordon had played only two varsity seasons for the Webfoots—and only one under Hobson, the new baseball coach. Gordon, from Portland's Jefferson High School, also played freshman football before concentrating on baseball. A gifted violinist who had played in the Portland Symphony at age 14, he also was in the U of O orchestra. The Yankees signed him after Southern California–area Yankees scout Bill Essick took a look at him in Los Angeles–area summer league competition, and Hobson had lost the man who was certain to be his best player in 1936.

Gordon spent only two seasons in the minor leagues before joining the Yankees in the spring of 1938 and having a tremendous rookie season, which culminated with a New York sweep of the Cubs in the World Series.[1] Game 2 in Chicago was especially notable because Cubs starter Dizzy Dean gave up two-run homers to Frank Crosetti and Joe DiMaggio in a 6-3 New York victory. In

---

1. No, that *wasn't* the Cubs' most recent Series appearance. They made it again in 1945.

the clinching Game 4 in New York, Tommy Heinrich homered and Yankee starter Red Ruffing went the distance, winning 8-3. Gordon, the kid second baseman, hit .400 in the Series, and his former college coach was at Yankee Stadium for the finish. The Yankees paid for Hobson's trip to New York for the final two games, and then he stuck around after the Series for Yankees organizational meetings. On October 15, he attended the Purdue-Fordham football game to scout Fordham, since the Rams were scheduled to play host to the Oregon Webfoots the next Saturday in New York, in a rare intersectional regular-season football game involving that much travel. As it turned out, his scouting report didn't do much good: coached by former Notre Dame Four Horseman halfback Jim Crowley, Fordham easily beat the Webfoots 26-0. This was two years after Vince Lombardi's senior season as one of the "Seven Blocks of Granite."

During his New York stay, Hobson completed the arrangements for his basketball team to play in New York early in the 1938–39 season.

Although Hank Luisetti had just graduated, Ned Irish at first hoped to bring Stanford in to New York for a third consecutive year. Stanford officials turned down the invitation and recommended their fellow Pacific Coast Conference team, the Webfoots. Hobson said that Irish at first "wasn't sure that Oregon existed." It helped that Hobson was able to meet Irish face-to-face in New York, and the promoter came around and invited the Webfoots to play in the season's first doubleheader, scheduled for Saturday, December 17. It turned out to be Oregon vs. CCNY and Northwestern vs. St. John's. Another Irish doubleheader was set for New Year's Eve. The first game would match St. John's vs. Colorado. The 1938 national invitation tournament runner-up Buffaloes would be making their second trip to New York in nine months, but this time minus Byron "Whizzer" White. LIU would be in the second game, playing Southern California.

As part of the deal to bring in Oregon, Irish made it clear to Hobson that the Garden would want an undefeated team to promote, so while scheduling pre-trip "breathers" at home would be acceptable, the Webfoots would be expected to travel straight to New York from Oregon and only play additional games on the way back. Hobson consented, and the trip ended up resembling a baseball team's barnstorming excursion. The Webfoots were scheduled to play nine games in 15 days—or ten games in 22 days if you counted a stop in Portland to face the Signal Oil AAU team before the Oregon traveling party continued east.

The commitment alarmed U of O athletic board officials. *There goes Hobby again.* They made it clear to the young coach that it wouldn't accept or make up financial losses, so if the trip turned out to be a money-loser, it was Coach Hobson's Folly and his responsibility. Even local sportswriters, normally aboard Hobson's bandwagon, wondered if it was wise to have the players on the road that long, for all those games and with limited opportunities to practice, before the conference schedule opened on January 6.

Hobson had faith that the trip would be at least a push financially, but there was more to it. "He felt that the benefits of the trip, educational as well as athletic, would far outweigh any negative impact, and he was right," John Dick said.

Back home, Howard and Jennie by now had two young sons, Howard Jr. and David. They were too young to hang around practices or sit on the team bench—that would come later—but they hung a play hoop on a door in the family home and did what a lot of kids were doing as the Tall Firs prepared for that season. They pretended to be the Webfoots, playing on that hoop as they, doubling as sportscasters, called out the passes from Anet to Johansen to . . .

Their father's Webfoots were about to become well known outside Oregon.

7.

Bee and the Blackbirds

In late 1938, the Long Island Blackbirds were coming off the disappointing five-loss season and the upsetting loss to NYU in the quarterfinals of the first national invitational tournament. Forward Irv Torgoff, a 6-4 senior and a local boy from the Brownsville section of Brooklyn and Tilden High School, was the leading scorer among New York–area collegians that previous season, and he had a strong supporting cast returning with him. The New York scribes again built up Torgoff and the Blackbirds as one of the nation's top teams, realizing that LIU would be a major draw for their tournament if Clair Bee's boys, often called the "Busy Bees," had another successful season and warranted a second consecutive invitation.

LIU was an unlikely basketball power. A private school, its campus was in the heart of Brooklyn and had started out in an abandoned warehouse in 1926. With no suitable gym on what passed for their "campus," the Blackbirds played their home games at the 800-seat Brooklyn College of Pharmacy Gymnasium in Bedford-Stuyvesant.[1] The gym was on the top floor of the BCP building, completed in 1929, on Lafayette Avenue. For several years, LIU's schedule had featured low-profile opponents at home, decent or better programs with marquee names on the Garden doubleheaders, and few true road games. Still, the Blackbirds put together a string of impressive seasons and came to be regarded as one of the top programs in the country, and Bee gained renown.

A native of West Virginia, Bee was born in Parkersburg and raised in Grafton, 25 miles south of Morgantown and 100 miles from Pittsburgh. He and his friends sneaked into the local church gym for pickup games. "After a while," Bee said, "the priests caught on, but they turned their heads the other way and let us

---

1. The College of Pharmacy opened in 1886, became affiliated with LIU in 1929, and officially became part of LIU in 1976. It is now the Arnold and Marie Schwartz College of Pharmacy.

keep playing. They were happy to see us in church even though it was only for basketball." For a *Sport* magazine profile in 1951, Bee told writer Milton Gross that in his early teen years, he worked in a coal mine, on a farm, and at the railway, in part to help support his stepmother and family following his father's death. He served in the Army's 16th Regiment of railway engineers in Europe during the Great War, even before he finished high school, and he joked that he had been the craps champion of the Allied Expeditionary Forces. Returning to finish high school after the war, he was older than most of his classmates and was the captain of the football, basketball, and baseball teams.

He attended four colleges—Waynesburg, Ohio State, Rider, and Rutgers—and earned three bachelor's and two master's degrees. At Rider, he was both the football coach and headed the business administration program, then moved to LIU as football coach in 1931. Despite a 7-1 record, the program was discontinued after that season. He took over the Blackbirds' basketball program, and the rise was meteoric. As a basketball coach, he was an authoritarian who, as so many coaches did, expected his players to listen and follow instructions without questioning them. He won with strategies and philosophies that he eventually passed along in a series of detail- and diagram-filled coaching books and then the Chip Hilton books for young readers. He plotted strategy using thread spools to represent players on a table replica of a court, and his practices were laboratories. One of his trademarks was coaching both man-to-man and 1-3-1 zone defenses, and switching back and forth during games. There, he and Hobson utilized very similar strategies. Offensively, Bee would prove to be adaptive. Especially after the elimination of the center jump after every basket, a move he at first opposed, he emphasized getting down the floor with some speed, but also preached the value of the set shot, taken if unguarded and able to come to a complete stop.

This is a fast forward to later years, but in 1950's *Hoop Crazy*, the fifth book in the Chip Hilton series, a new resident of town, T. A. K. Baxter, tries to sell Chip and his Valley Falls High School teammates on the merits of the one-handed shot. When some of them get carried away, it causes problems within the team. Chip, a master at the two-handed set shot, is very reluctant and muses that he agrees with the sage coach Hank Rockwell that most things can be done better with two hands than one. Eventually, though, Chip is a much more active and athletic player when he leads the State University Statesmen to glory in his sophomore and junior years, in five books written in the late 1950s and early '60s. (Alas, Grosset and Dunlap pulled the plug on the original series before three-sport star Chip got to his senior year at State.) Also worth noting about *Hoop Crazy* is Bee's dedication: "To William 'Dolly' King. Student, athlete, gentleman and friend." King was a star multi-sport athlete at LIU and joined the Blackbirds' basketball team when a new term began late in the 1938–39 season. Bee apparently didn't hold it against King that he left the Blackbirds late in the 1940–41 season to join the all-black professional New York Renaissance, better known as the Rens, in time for the Max Rosenblum Invitational Pro Basketball Tournament in Cleveland. Signing with the National Basketball League's Rochester Royals in 1946, King eventually was one of the trailblazers in the integration of what morphed into the NBA. *Hoop Crazy* also dealt with the integration of the Valley Falls Big Reds, with new junior-varsity player Clem Barnes, generally labeled the "colored boy" by the Big Reds' supporters, overcoming the resentment of his teammates—with Chip's help, of course.

As did Hobson, Bee emphasized honor, sportsmanship, and teamwork. The prominence of the basketball team helped the school gain a name and a foothold in the New York market, so in that sense, his program was a spectacularly successful investment for the young university. The soft schedules weren't all Bee's fault, either. Coach Nat Holman of CCNY was among the many New York–area coaches who refused to regularly schedule LIU. He said it was because of his problems with the program's academic and other standards, but jealousy likely entered into it, too.

As aloof and gruff as Bee could seem when coaching, he was quite different away from it. Milton Gross's *Sport* piece declared: "He is salty, profane, a two-fisted fighter, and a two-fisted drinker—until he bowed to his ulcers. He loves to sit up all night playing stud poker." He didn't develop those traits suddenly when older, so the man coaching the Blackbirds in the 1930s was both cerebral and sassy.

His program gained considerable attention when the Blackbirds went undefeated in the 1935–36 season, beating Duquesne, St.

John's, and Rice in Garden doubleheaders, and then turned down an invitation to participate in the multiple-team trials to select a roster for the notorious 1936 Summer Olympics at Berlin. The decision was principled, but it soon was distorted into something it wasn't—and it *still* is inaccurately portrayed at times.

The U.S. basketball trials culminated with an eight-team tournament in April 1936 at the Garden that was designed to be a tryout showcase and, perhaps even more important in an Olympic year when officials were scrambling to raise money to finance the sending of full U.S. teams to Berlin, a money-maker. The plan *never* was to automatically designate the championship team of the Garden tournament as the U.S. squad for Berlin. Five college teams would play in the eight-team field, selected through qualifying in ten districts. Those ten teams would be matched up for one additional qualifying game, with the five winners advancing to New York. The other three teams in the Garden field were the AAU national tournament champions and runners-up, plus the national YMCA champions.

For a while, actually, there had been considerable doubt about whether the U.S. would send *any* teams to Berlin. Reacting to the Hitler regime's anti-Jewish measures, the U.S. came close to boycotting the Games altogether, and it wasn't until the Amateur Athletic Union's December 1935 national convention voted by a slim margin to proceed with sending teams to Berlin that U.S. participation was assured.

In March 1936, Bee took a vote among the Blackbirds—the majority of the players, but not all, were Jewish—and the decision was to turn down the invitation to the trials. "Our conviction that the United States should not participate in the Olympics has not been altered by the fact that our basketball team is recognized generally as a possible Olympic representative," LIU dean[2] Tristram Walker Metcalfe said in a statement issued by the university. "Such participation would be indirect, if not direct, contribution to the raising of funds to finance such participation."

Subsequent references to the Blackbirds "boycotting" the Berlin Games, then, were well meaning but misleading. The invitation was to participate in a trials process to select *individual* players on

2. Walker served as the school's CEO from 1932 to 1952, with the title changed to president in 1943.

a U.S. team. At least five other U.S. college teams—NYU, Notre Dame, Purdue, Illinois, and Ohio Wesleyan—for various reasons, including principle, turned down chances to play in the trials, also. After regional qualifying, the five college teams in the New York trials tournament turned out to be Arkansas, Utah State, De Paul, Washington, and Temple. The AAU teams made up of older former college players were the McPherson Globe Oilers of Kansas and Universal Pictures of Hollywood, mainly a team of former UCLA and USC players, and they both won their way to the trials championship game, besting the college boys. The 14-man U.S. Olympic team roster was a pooling of the two AAU squads' top players, plus Washington Huskies center Ralph Bishop.

Two years later, the Blackbirds' publicized schedule for the 1938-39 season was familiar: a parade of soft touches coming into Brooklyn; five games against solid opponents (Southern California, Kentucky, Marquette, Toledo, and Duquesne) in the Garden; only one game against another major New York team (St. Francis); and just two games outside the New York area. The five Garden opponents were legitimate tests, but the famous Manhattan arena in no way was a neutral site for the Blackbirds. Their two scheduled road trips were for a game against New Mexico A&M on a neutral floor in Chicago on February 1 (and, as it turned out, that game was canceled), and then a matchup with La Salle in the Philadelphia Convention Center in the regular season's final game. Their only game against a major New York program was against St. Francis, meaning they did *not* play St. John's, Columbia, Manhattan, CCNY, Fordham, Brooklyn, or NYU. Columbia, also with only one game against a major metropolitan-area opponent, and LIU were the only teams scheduled to play fewer than five games against the other teams in the mythical metropolitan league, chronicled with unofficial standings in the newspapers.

That all sounds as if it's intended to be belittling of Bee and his program. It isn't. Despite the scheduling that seems to have been largely ignored by the New York scribes, this much was indisputable: when matched up against good teams, the Blackbirds almost always managed to win. And Bee was a brilliant coach.

8.

Taking the Show on the Road

With Oregon starters Bobby Anet, Wally Johansen, Laddie Gale, and Slim Wintermute returning for the 1938–39 season, the major decisions Howard Hobson faced involved filling out his roster and selecting a fifth starter. As practice began, the top contenders to replace the departed Dave Silver at forward were junior John Dick and senior Bob Hardy, from Ashland. The left-handed Hardy starred as a sophomore, averaging around 15 points a game, at his hometown Southern Oregon Normal School, Hobson's previous stop, before transferring to Eugene. He missed most of the Webfoots' 1937–38 season after suffering a broken ankle, but had proven himself capable on the court. Most of the boys indeed considered Hardy a future pro, but in baseball, where he was a flame-throwing "southpaw" pitcher for Hobson's Webfoots in the spring. The consensus was that Hardy might get a serious look for the starting forward position by Hobson, who generally used seniority as a tiebreaker in lineup decisions, but that Dick, especially dangerous with whirling moves and pivot and hook shots from the low post, would end up in the starting lineup either by the start of the season or before long. The only demerit against Dick was that he was such a serious student with such broad interests, he didn't consider basketball his first priority, and didn't even seem upset about not being moved into the starting lineup.

Behind Anet and Johansen, the reserve guards included two more of Coach Hobson's Webfoot baseball players, both infielders from Washington state and both juniors—Ford Mullen from Olympia and Matt Pavalunas from Raymond.

Mullen, raised at a small resort his family owned on Washington's Lake Lacey, was a fine infielder, also with pro potential. He was self-effacing about his basketball skill, leading him in later years to good-naturedly claim to have guarded the water bucket.

But he was much better than that, and his teammates knew it. They had faith that if Anet ever suffered a significant injury, Mullen, the fine all-around athlete, could step in and run the team. At 5-8, he was a physical duplicate of Anet and could play the same way, meaning the rest of the Webfoots wouldn't have to change their games. They had similar confidence in the 6-foot Pavalunas, who couldn't match Johansen's chemistry with Anet but was considered roughly on a par with Johansen in talent.

Pavalunas's parents—Charlie, a worker in the shingle mill near Raymond, and Ruth—were immigrants from the Baltic region, and Lithuanian was the first language in their home, including for young Matt. He struggled with English and repeated a grade in elementary school as he adjusted. In high school, he was a four-sport star, in football, basketball, baseball, and in the 440- and 220-yard races in track. His son, Bob, notes that his father's nickname became "Once in a Blue Moon Boy" when the local paper opined that "an athlete like this comes along once in a blue moon."

The other three reserves on the usual 11-man traveling squad seemed fairly set, too. Two of them, junior Ted Sarpola and sophomore Earl Sandness, were the additional Astoria Fishermen.

Sophomore Evert "Red" McNeeley was born in Pacific Beach, Washington, but when he was six, his family moved to Portland and his father landed a job with the sanitary department. Red graduated from Portland's Jefferson High School, where he was a year behind Joe Gordon, but didn't head straight to college. Instead, with his parents divorcing and no money available, McNeeley worked for two years, including in a gas station, and was playing AAU basketball when Hobson, impressed with his outside shooting, offered him a scholarship to Oregon. He was thrilled to have the opportunity, so he didn't gripe about not being in the starting lineup as a sophomore. His bright red hair, usually meticulously parted in the middle, inspired the nickname that would stay with him for life. Although only a sophomore, he was 22 when the season started—and the oldest player on the team.

The other nine players, including ex-Fisherman Toivo Piippo, provided practice fodder, kept statistics, and took notes during home games. They hoped to catch Hobson's attention and perhaps be promoted to the regular traveling roster and/or get in some games.

References to the squad as the Ducks were becoming more frequent, but it was all unofficial. By 1938–39, a Duck cartoon-type caricature was on the Oregon warm-up jackets and in such things as game programs. The makeshift press guide for that season, featuring Anet on the cover, was a combination of nicely printed sheets around mimeographed supplemental information on newsprint, and was called "Duck Dope." In the guide, sports publicist Bruce Hamby promised "no change this season from the spectacular fast-break style made famous on the coast by Coach Hobson. Oregon's offensive tactics, in a nutshell, are to beat the defense back down court for a quick shot at the basket. When this is not possible, the Webfoots establish fast-moving set plays."

Hamby's guide dutifully listed the Webfoots' official heights. As often happens on team rosters, the heights weren't correct. Yet this was a rare case of understatement. The Tall Firs actually were *taller* than the official roster figures. Dick and Gale both were listed at 6-foot-4, but Dick was just a shade under 6-5 and Gale was about an inch taller than that. Dick later told his sons that Wintermute was at least 6-10.

Why the gamesmanship?

In Wintermute's case, it was self-consciousness and a desire to avoid being labeled a "freak," and he was steadfast in his refusal to be re-measured. Slim said he was 6-8 and as far as he was concerned, that settled it.

In general, too, the thinking was that if opponents were "shocked" at how tall players were when they came across them for the first time, that could be a small advantage.

Before heading east, the Taller-Than-Advertised Firs beat the University of Portland 51-24, Portland's Multnomah Athletic Club 83-25, and Signal Oil 46-34, all in The Igloo. They worked on disguising their defensive strategies, alternating between zone and man-to-man and, with their hands in the air, often causing opponents to only belatedly recognize when they'd switched to a man-to-man.

At Portland's Benson Tech High School on December 10, 1938, the Webfoots easily handled another AAU team, the Pacific Packards, 54-39, and then filed onto the train the next night and headed for New York. Because of the trip's length, Hobson expanded his traveling roster. Sophomore forward Don Mabee, who had just finished a standout season as an end for Oregon's football team, was the 12th man.[1]

The train berths were made for conventionally sized passengers, and the Webfoots did some re-engineering. In the upper berths, they took the headboards out, turning two berths into one long one.

The boys could stretch out.

* * *

The long trip was going to take the Webfoots out of only one week of classes, and for most of the players, that wasn't a major problem. Wally Johansen, though, was among about 30 U of O seniors finishing up study for undergraduate LLB degrees in law and was determined to keep up. If he let his work slide, he might hear from, among others, Wayne Morse, who had been the dean of the law school for nine years, but still was only 38 years old. The joke on campus was that the boys studying law kept the tobacco salesmen flush, since chain smoking seemed to be one of the prerequisites for the law curriculum. Not all law students smoked; it just seemed as if they did. The pressure heaped on them as undergraduates was enormous. The law library all along was closed on Sundays, but Morse was among the administrators who noticed how jammed it was on Saturdays and decided to close it that day as well to encourage students to take weekend-long breaks from studying—or at least studying in the library. Morse wanted his charges to have outside interests but wouldn't excuse away sliding marks for athletes.

* * *

While the Webfoots were on their way to New York, Ohio State coach Harold Olsen in Columbus announced that his National Association of Basketball Coaches committees had roughed together an outline for the first national tournament. Notably, the December 14 Associated Press story about Olsen's announcement began: "The National Collegiate Athletic Association's plan to select America's undisputed college basketball champion advanced a step today . . . "

---

1. At one stop on the barnstorming swing, the wire service scribe assigned to the game listed Webfoots reserve Toivo Piippo in the box score, but he wasn't on the trip. Piippo was No. 16 on the preseason roster in the *Duck Dope*, but that jersey was assigned to Mabee for the eastern swing.

Declaring it to be the case, whether from the Ohio State campus or from an Associated Press bureau, didn't make it so, of course, but it nonetheless seemed significant that the "undisputed college basketball champion" phrase made it onto the national wire without significant qualification or paying homage to New York as the true center of the basketball universe.

Olsen announced plans for two four-team "sectionals," one for teams east of the Mississippi River and one for teams west of it. In the ensuing months, those events also were called "regionals," the variations were numerous, and the most common was "Eastern (or Western) championships." One thing the new tournament and the year-old New York national invitation tournament had in common was a lack of uniformity in what they were called, whether in print or anywhere else.

The Ohio State coach said those NCAA sectionals would be played on March 10–11 or March 17–18, in New York or Philadelphia in the East, and in Kansas City, Denver, or Los Angeles in the West. Then the two surviving teams would meet for the national championship at an as-yet undetermined site. Also, Olsen said one team from each of eight districts would be in the tournament. His statement gave geographic specifics for each of the eight districts, listed the teams in each one, plus named district chairmen and committees. That much seemed to be straightforward and sensible. It truly would be a national tournament.

Olsen said it was up to each district to select its entrant, and there were no set rules. He indicated it was preferable if each committee could simply select a team as its representative in the eight-team national field, but said they also could hold qualifying playoffs, if they felt it necessary.

So this was the Ohio State coach issuing a statement in Columbus that drew national attention, with the wire stories running in many newspapers.

This was the Ohio State coach bringing up a plan that almost certainly would involve the Big Ten champion—if not the Buckeyes, then someone else from the league.

It's inconceivable that the Buckeyes players didn't get wind of this.

Yet . . .

More on that later.

Eventually, Olsen named John Bunn, in his first months as Stanford's dean of men, as chairman of the tournament's Pacific Coast district.

Because there *were* some "play-in"-type games when the tournament was played the next March, it's at least misleading to call the inaugural tournament an eight-team event. Later, that most often was brought up by those trying to say the NCAA tournament was no more inclusive than the national invitation tournament. That's not true. The committee's mistake arguably was not formalizing the "play-in" process and making it the same in all eight districts, essentially making the NCAA tournament a 16- or 32-team event from the start. That would have flaunted how much more national and democratic it was than the New York writers' tournament.

Again, it's amazing that so many of the NCAA tournament details, including the sites, still were up in the air three months before the tournament began. Even those vague plans changed considerably before the first tournament began. At the time, Olsen's Buckeyes had played only one game, beating George Washington in Columbus, and were preparing to make a cross-country jaunt of their own.

* * *

After arriving at Manhattan's Penn Station on the morning of Thursday, December 15, 1938, the Webfoots checked in at the Hotel Lincoln on Eighth Avenue between 44th and 45th Streets. It had an athletic pedigree: the 1936 U.S. Olympic teams had convened and stayed there before heading over to Berlin.[2]

The Webfoots went through what nominally was a practice at the West Side YMCA, at 63rd Street and Central Park West. With the Garden still trying to sell tickets and get attention, the session was little more than a glorified press conference, with Irish making sure the Webfoots wore their white game uniforms and spent most of the allotted time in the gym posing for the newspaper photographers and parading for the scribes, who mostly watched and didn't dream of actually trying to *interview* any of the Webfoots.

The next morning, or still on the day before the game, the Webfoots got prominent play in the New York papers. Across the top of its lead sports page, the *Times* ran a large picture of the Oregon

---

2. It's now the Milford Plaza.

starters, each dribbling a ball. Significantly, the five Webfoots shown were Wintermute, Gale, Hardy, Johansen, and Anet. At that point, Hardy still was starting. The headline on the story below the picture noted:

COAST GIANTS HERE
FOR C.C.N.Y. GAME
Oregon Five's Workout Augurs
Busy Night for Beavers
On Garden Court

On the front of *its* sports section, above Everett B. Morris's story, the *New York Herald Tribune* ran a huge picture of Coach Hobson speaking to the 12 Webfoots at the YMCA practice. An indication of how little the Webfoots got done at the YMCA was that Hobson also lined up the Manhattan College gym for an afternoon full practice, complete with a long intra-squad scrimmage. He hoped to allow the Webfoots to shake off the cobwebs and heavy legs caused by the long train trip. Bringing up the Astoria angle, Morris wrote that in the Columbia River town, "basketball rivals salmon fishing as the leading industry." He also had a reaction that was surprisingly typical of scribes watching the Webfoots in practice for the first time: He was most impressed with the ball handling of flashy junior reserve Ted Sarpola, another of the Astoria boys. Morris raved that the flashy Sarpola "could do more tricks with a basketball than Thurston could do with a rabbit." (Howard Thurston, a renowned magician of the era, had died in 1936.) He added: "If Sarpola could only shoot as well as he can do interesting but less important maneuvers, he would be phenomenal." Morris went to the full practice at Manhattan College, too, or at least pretended to have done so. He provided a scouting report of the Webfoots' style, remarking on their "terrifically fast break" and their tendency to alternate between zone and man-to-man defenses.

At some point during the New York stay, too, Wintermute and Gale met *New York Daily News* columnist Ed Sullivan, who tried to arrange a picture of one sitting on the shoulders of the other and dunking a basketball.

Several of the players went to Radio City Music Hall, which had opened in 1932 and still looked and felt new, to watch the leggy Rockettes perform in conjunction with the showing of the new movie *The Duke of West Point*, starring Louis Hayward and Joan Fontaine. Hayward played the title character, a chap from an American family who was raised in England and attended the U.S. Military Academy because it ran in his family. The Cadets' football and hockey teams were part of the story, but not the basketball squad. The Webfoots probably didn't mind basketball's exclusion; they were thinking about the Rockettes' precision and Fontaine's magnetism on screen. New York University law professor John MacGregor was a former Oregon student-body president, and he acted as the Webfoots' guide, also lining up Broadway show tickets. Among the choices were Raymond Massey in *Abe Lincoln in Illinois*, Helen Hayes in *Victoria Regina*, plus musicals *Hellzapoppin* and *The Boys from Syracuse*.

At least two Webfoots—Hardy and Mullen, Hobson's baseball standouts—were thrilled when Hobson arranged a visit to Yankee Stadium and they were able to stand on the mound and gawk at their surroundings. The stadium, which opened in 1923, was the House That Ruth Built, where Lou Gehrig and Joe DiMaggio, among others, played for the world champions. As the Webfoots played sightseers and imagined playing on the diamond someday with the Yankees' stars, they couldn't have known that Gehrig would play only eight more games with New York because of his as-yet undiagnosed illness.

As always, the "new" Garden was busy during the week of the Webfoots' visit. On December 15, their first night in town, Welshman Tommy Farr, the British Empire heavyweight champion, was the marquee name on a boxing card. He came in with consecutive decision losses to Joe Louis, Jim Braddock, and Max Baer, but he was popular because he was game and put on good shows. He lost again this time, on a 15-round decision to young Californian Lou Nova, but it was a spectacular and much-cheered fight, with both boxers barely able to stand at the finish. That's what "regular," or non-championship, Garden boxing cards were supposed to be about. On December 16, the arena's two National Hockey League teams, the Rangers and Americans, played to a 1-1 tie in front of 13,955.

On the morning of the Oregon-CCNY game, the *Times* jumped aboard the Astoria angle bandwagon. Respected sports writer

Arthur Daley, then 34, substituted for regular columnist John Kieran to pen the "Sports of the Times" piece, and he noted that the Fishermen had won the Oregon state high school championship in seven of the ten previous seasons. He obviously took someone's word for it, and whoever it was either deliberately exaggerated or got it wrong. The actual count at that point for Astoria High was four championships in nine seasons.[3] Like Everett B. Morris, Daley also made it sound as if every street in the little Oregon fishing town was turned into a court with hoops, which also was a bit overdone. Nonetheless, it was a nice tribute. His column in "relief" of Kieran came three years after Daley became the first *Times* sportswriter sent to Europe to cover an event—the 1936 Summer Games in Berlin.

Herald Tribune columnist Richards Vidmer reprised the tale of Ned Irish tearing his pants sneaking in to cover a game (he didn't specify that it was CCNY vs. Manhattan) in a "small hall that bulged at the seams after a few hundred people had entered through the door. The mishap preyed on Mr. Irish's mind and he carried around the idea that if people didn't have to tear their trousers climbing through windows, more of them would come to see basketball games. So, four years ago, he took his proposition to Madison Square Garden, sold them the idea and since then he has been bringing the better teams of the country to the Palace of Play."

Vidmer pointed out that the Webfoots' appearance would come as Irish began his fifth season of doubleheaders, adding: "From the very beginning the crowds came pouring in and the average over four seasons has been something more than 12,000 a night. This is much higher than the average attendance at hockey games and there aren't many fights that bring that many customers to the Garden. Jai Alai, indoor polo, squash and other indoor sports don't come even close to such figures."

Ned Irish still had a hit on his hands.

---

3. Under John Warren's replacement as the Fishermen's head coach, former Oregon State star Wally Palmberg, Astoria also won state titles in 1941 and '42. The ultimate haul, then, was 6 state titles in 13 seasons.

9.

Garden and Beyond

The game against CCNY was a fiasco for the Webfoots. Howard Hobson later said that the first hint of trouble was when one of the referees, Pat Kennedy, approached him and said off-handedly: "Now we aren't going to call every little brush a foul. That's okay with you, isn't it?" Because four fouls disqualified a player for the rest of the game and nobody wanted to see the game adversely affected by ridiculously scrupulous officiating, it was okay with Hobson, within reason.

John Dick later noted that while tugs or slashes on the arms weren't called, the CCNY players were adept at tumbling at any contact to draw offensive fouls, a concept that was completely foreign to the Webfoots.

Said Hobson: "They did a lot of things we didn't use or coach— they stepped on your feet, grabbed your pants, and the officials allowed more contact on the screens."

Arthur Daley noted in his *Times* game story that the Webfoots were "hampered in the beginning by the strangeness in the officiating. The Ducks could not understand many of the penalties called against them." The other major problem was that Gale was ill, leading Daley to note that the Webfoots' star was "slowed down to a walk by a heavy cold." Hobson limited his playing time.

Here's how bad the Webfoots were early in front of a crowd of 16,386: They trailed 8-1 after five minutes and were down 16-6 after not getting a field goal in the first 15 minutes. They finally got going and were within 19-14 at the half. CCNY's strategy was to keep smaller defenders Al Soupios and Babe Adler between the ball and Wintermute and Gale, when he was in. It worked—at least long enough.

"We were beaten badly in the first half, but it may have been the most important game for us that season," Hobson said. "At the half, the boys were complaining about the officiating. I told them,

'I can sympathize with your feelings, but if I were you big fellows and they did those things to me, I'd at least protect myself.' Well, they went out there and played a great second half."

The Webfoots managed to pull into a 30-30 tie on Wally Johansen's long set shot. In the final minutes, they trailed 37-36 when Anet missed the free throw that would have tied it. Adler made the second of a two-shot opportunity to make the CCNY lead two points, and the Beavers held on for the 38-36 victory. Anet led the Webfoots with 13 points, and Wintermute and the weakened Gale each had 6 in the wrenching loss. Dave Siperstein fired away from the outside for CCNY and led the Beavers with 14 points.

Daley's story called the game "a drab sort of battle in its early stages but it perked up brilliantly in the second half and finally wound up with the fans standing on their seats in wild delight."[1]

The *New York Daily News*' Jack Mahon characterized the winners as a "small, but mighty classy City College of New York quint" and the contest as a "thrill-a-minute first game" of the doubleheader. He noted that the Webfoots "couldn't quite solve the rushing, bullying attack of its smaller adversaries."

For the game, CCNY was called for 19 fouls, with two starters getting four personals and leaving the game early. The Webfoots had three fewer personals. So if Oregon had cause to complain about the officiating, it likely was more an issue of style than unfairness. Yet Hobson said that Irish and his assistant, John Gardner, were so embarrassed, they were waiting in the dressing room for the Webfoots and immediately asked Hobson to return with the team the next season.

On the spot, the Webfoots became determined to erase the ignominy of the showing against a mediocre-at-best CCNY team in the Garden. It wasn't their style to score only 36 points or to be a part of a game that—even if the scribes can be believed and it had the fans standing at the end—rang up only 74 points for both teams.

In the second game of the doubleheader, St. John's knocked off Northwestern 49-41, so it was a successful night for the New York

---

1. Slightly different accounts of this game were attributed to Daley, including by L. H. Gregory in a column soon after the game. They almost certainly were authentic and perhaps were from a different edition, but those passages don't show up in microfilm or digital archives. Also, this was one of several instances during the Webfoots' season when box scores and scoring figures weren't uniform in all publications. Writers, whether for papers or wire services, generally compiled their own statistics, so variation wasn't unusual. Also, the process of dictation over the phone led to frequent misspellings, especially when a team wasn't "local" and familiar to the fellows working in the office.

schools. The St. John's Redmen were in their second season under one of the most recognizable names in the game. Joe Lapchick still was feeling his way as a coach after a long pro career as a star center, mostly for the Original Celtics, the famous barnstorming team that also had a stint in the American Basketball League. At 6-foot-5, he was considered a "big" man in his time, and watching the Webfoots in at least part of the first game was an eye-opener for him. Officially, Slim Wintermute was three inches taller than one of the greatest centers of all time, and the difference in height probably was greater than that.

*   *   *

With the LIU Blackbirds not scheduled for their first Garden appearance of the season for two more weeks, they continued what was little more than a warm-up act against soft opposition in the first month. In Brooklyn two days before Oregon's appearance in the Garden, they walloped Princeton Seminary 82-37 and then, two days after the Webfoots' loss, whipped East Stroudsburg 69-33.

*   *   *

Keeping in mind that the trip was supposed to be part educational, Coach Hobson allowed the Webfoots to stay an extra night in New York. They headed down to Philadelphia on the morning of December 19, and that night the Webfoots faced St. Joseph's in front of about 6,000 fans in Philadelphia's Convention Hall. Oregon won 54-44, using a 13-0 run at the end of the first half to take a 24-15 lead and ensure no trouble the rest of the way. Wintermute and Gale each had 13 points.

Hobson noted that Ned Irish and John Gardner were in attendance, sitting behind the Oregon bench and gently suggesting that the Webfoots take it easy on St. Joseph's because the Philadelphia squad was playing in New York soon. The Oregon coach removed all his starters with five minutes remaining.

The next night in the Cleveland Public Hall, the Webfoots ran up an astounding point total against Miami of Ohio, winning 74-38. Considering that a team scoring more than 60 was evidence of revolutionary racehorse basketball or a ridiculous mismatch, or both, the rout was slight atonement for the lackluster showing against CCNY, especially since the Webfoots had traveled over 400 miles by train after playing the night before. Illustrating how early and how far the game got out of hand, Astoria's Ted Sarpola came off the bench to lead the Webfoots with 20 points.

The big news of the night, though, was that Wintermute suffered an ankle injury, serious enough that he left the arena to head to a local hospital for X-rays. Hobson immediately told John Dick that Wintermute could be out for the season and challenged the junior forward to step up, both in that game and beyond. Although Wintermute missed three of the next four games, Hobson almost certainly knew, both immediately and especially after the X-rays were negative, that he had exaggerated the severity of Wintermute's injury. But after Hobson's speech, Dick scored 12 points in the second half in the rout. Gale, playing sparingly, had 11. Also, the young Miami coach, an alumnus of the school and a former football and basketball star, congratulated Hobson after the game.

The Oregon coach said thanks to the young coach, Wilber C. "Weeb" Ewbank.

Ewbank was coaching at the school's affiliated high school and was pressed into service as the Miami basketball coach for only 1938–39 when John Mauer quit right before the start of the season.

* * *

Harold Olsen's Ohio State Buckeyes arrived on the West Coast for six games against Pacific Coast Conference opponents. The tour opened with a two-game set at Seattle against the Washington Huskies on December 22–23, and the Buckeyes were about to discover that the boys out west could play pretty good basketball. Although the Buckeyes' two stars, Dick Baker and Jimmy Hull, were on the trip, three other players had been ruled academically ineligible for the time being and weren't with the team.

* * *

With Wintermute out, the Webfoots managed an easy 53-41 win over Canisius in Buffalo's Broadway Auditorium on December 22. Gale had 15 points and Hardy 11. Dick started at center in Wintermute's place, but had only three points.

The next night in Detroit's Naval Armory, with Wintermute again watching from the bench and Dick playing center, the Webfoots beat previously undefeated Wayne University[2] 52-41. Wally

---

2. Now Wayne State.

Johansen had 14 and Gale 10 points for the Webfoots, and Anet and Dick pitched in with 9 apiece. The Associated Press writer, perhaps still unfamiliar with the barnstorming team from the west, called Gale by his real first name, Lauren, in his story, and that could lead to teasing from his teammates when they saw the stories and box scores in their travels. Of course, if Wintermute had played in that game, too, it would have been double-barreled, with Lauren and Urgel leading the Webfoots.

The Webfoots spent Christmas in at the Hotel La Salle in Chicago. Each player received a tinhorn stuffed with about $2. *Payola!* That was the Webfoots' Christmas bonus. They then moved on to Peoria for a game the next night against Bradley Tech, which had played in the national invitation tournament the previous March and lost to eventual champion Temple in the quarterfinals. The 4-1 Braves were coming off a pre-Christmas road trip of their own, when they beat Nebraska and New Mexico, but were clobbered 48-36 by the PCC's California Golden Bears at Berkeley.

Bradley Tech got a measure of revenge against the PCC and the Webfoots were awful that night in a 52-39 loss in Peoria's City Armory. Wintermute returned to the lineup and had eight points but still was hobbled, and the opposing center, Dar Hutchins, took advantage, racking up 17 points. Even on nights when Wintermute didn't score big, the Webfoots were accustomed to him being a defensive force, so this was a rarity and Hobson immediately decided he had made a mistake rushing his center back into the lineup. Forward Carl Schunk pitched in with 15 for the Braves, and Gale was the only Oregon player in double figures, with 14.

Bradley Tech beat the Webfoots at their own game, outrunning them to take an early lead and never letting Oregon back in it. The Braves led 31-14 at halftime. More so than the loss to CCNY, the loss to Bradley Tech was a black mark for Oregon, fair to bring up in any attempt to evaluate their accomplishments that season. The 5,000 fans in the stands that night in Peoria must have wondered what the fuss was about, then and later. But the Webfoots had been on the road for nearly three weeks, and the toll was beginning to show. The strange thing was that two nights later, Southern Methodist came into Peoria and knocked off the Braves 45-33, and that would be Bradley Tech's final loss until March.

Hobson held Wintermute out of the 60-45 rout of Western Illinois State Teachers College[3] at the Chicago Coliseum the next night. Sarpola again had a big game, with 18 points, and Gale and Anet were next, with 8.

The Webfoots had only one more stop to make before heading back to the West Coast, and they beat Drake 42-31 in Des Moines on December 29. Even then, though, they weren't going home.

*　*　*

Southern California arrived in New York to give the LIU Blackbirds their first legitimate test of the season, and the Trojans were coming off their eighth consecutive victory, a win over reigning national invitation tournament champion Temple in Philadelphia. In an interview aboard the train to New York with Louis Effrat of the *New York Times*, USC coach Sam Barry might have offended eastern partisans when he admitted he knew absolutely nothing about LIU and hadn't scouted the Blackbirds. He mentioned that several of the Trojans were nursing minor ankle injuries and colds, but was confident that his club, sparked by captain and guard Gail Goodrich, would put on a good show, if they didn't get caught up in sightseeing and stargazing. Barry also mentioned that if plans to build a new arena in Hollywood—a project backed by Bing Crosby and Pat O'Brien, among others—went through, he hoped it could become Madison Square Garden West, with teams from around the country brought in to play the Trojans.

In the real Garden, the starstruck and travel-weary Trojans were abominable, and so was the game. They fell 33-18 to the Blackbirds in a game that wasn't anywhere near as exciting as the opener of the doubleheader, a St. John's 39-37 victory over Colorado. Arthur Daley claimed LIU made the Trojans "look like P.S. 9 on a bad night."

Whizzer White, who played for the Buffaloes in the inaugural invitation tournament nine months earlier, had accepted the Pittsburgh Steelers' "ridiculous" offer and had just finished his rookie season in the NFL. He came to the Garden to watch and root on his alma mater against St. John's, but his support didn't bring the Buffaloes luck. He and 18,000 others saw CU blow a nine-point lead in the final minutes and lose.

---

3. Now Western Illinois.

*   *   *

After heading from the Midwest to northern California, the Web-foots on New Year's Eve met Stanford in San Francisco's Civic Auditorium, theoretically a neutral site away from the Stanford campus. Even the Associated Press story on the game noted that the Webfoots were "obviously weary from a barnstorming tour, played tired ball and did not have the pep needed to beat the fresh Indians." Stanford had lost Hank Luisetti and several other play-ers off its PCC championship team of the previous season, but was good enough to beat the Webfoots 50-46. It wasn't all bad news for Oregon, though. Wintermute looked to be healthy again, scoring 10 points, and Gale tossed in 19.

The tally for Oregon's barnstorming: seven wins, three losses. Validating Hobson's faith, the trip made a $4,400 profit after Or-egon received its cut of the gate receipts. Despite the troublesome defeats to CCNY and Bradley Tech, his team wedged its way into the national consciousness, drawing attention for its front-line height and its high-paced style, plus its talent.

"We learned to adapt to varied living and playing conditions," John Dick said. "We learned to travel and change living accommo-dations daily and to travel up to 96 consecutive hours by train with no opportunity to practice or even get any meaningful exercise. We learned to adjust quickly to a variety of playing styles, techniques and systems, some of which were rarely seen in our home area. Per-haps most importantly, we learned to adapt quickly to officiating differences and differences in rule interpretations that varied widely from one area to another."

After fooling around a bit with lineups on the trip, and not only because of Wintermute's injury, Hobson seemed on the verge of inserting John Dick into the starting lineup.

*   *   *

Ohio State struggled on its six-game West Coast trip, losing four times—at Washington (43-41 and 51-37) and California (49-35 and 45-42). The Buckeyes did manage to twice knock off the Southern Division's worst team, the dreadful UCLA Bruins, 46-38 and 59-57. At least they got to spend Christmas in sunny Los An-geles before facing the Bruins for the first time the next night. The Buckeyes, 3-4 for the season when the trip ended, chalked it all up as a positive experience, both as tourists and basketball players, and set their sights on the Big Ten season.

* * *

It was on to league play for the Webfoots, too, and they were favored to again win the PCC's Northern Division. There, the schedule was two home and two road games against the division's other four teams—Oregon State, Washington, Washington State, and Idaho.

Two months later, with Dick established as one starting forward, the division title came down to a two-game, regular-season-ending showdown against the Washington Huskies in Seattle. Oregon was 12-2 in the division, with the losses coming to Washington State in Eugene on January 7 and to Oregon State 50-31 in Corvallis on February 17. The decisiveness of that score would have been inexplicable if it hadn't been established long ago that inexplicable things often happened in the Webfoots-Beavers rivalry, and it was one of those nights when nothing went right, with Gale and Dick scoring only three points apiece and Wally Johansen going scoreless.

Washington was 11-3, so a Huskies sweep of the two games against the Webfoots in Seattle would give them the division title and advance them to the league's championship series against the Southern Division winner. The Webfoots needed only a split, but two losses would end their season. So the series in Seattle for all intents and purposes was the start of their championship run.

* * *

In Columbus, the Buckeyes got righted in the Big Ten season, losing only twice, on the road to Illinois and Indiana. The problem was that Indiana, with only one loss, was in control of the race as the stretch run began. Then on February 27, the Hoosiers fell 45-34 at rival Purdue, and Ohio State easily won 42-28 at Michigan. That left the Hoosiers and Buckeyes, who had split their two meetings, deadlocked at 9-2 with one game remaining for each.

Ohio State's coach, Harold Olsen, occasionally tended to duties as the NCAA tournament chairman, checking in with the committees in the eight districts and making sure all were prepared to select the teams in the tournament. Since his original announcement of vague plans in December, the schedule and sites had been changed and firmed up. The four-team Western championships were scheduled for San Francisco's Treasure Island on March 20–21, in conjunction with the Golden Gate International Exposition, which had opened in mid-February. That was the 1939–40 world's fair, and the games were going to be played in the 12,000-seat, multi-use pavilion—officially, the Golden Gate International Exposition Coliseum—built for the fair. The Monday and Tuesday dates for the Western games were designed to lessen competition with the weekend crowds and attractions at the fair.

The Eastern and Western champions would head to Chicago and meet in the NCAA's national championship game on March 27 at Northwestern's Patten Gymnasium. The theory was that Chicago was centrally located and likely would be suitable neutral ground for the two finalists—especially if the teams, as seemed entirely possible, were from the opposite coasts.

And suddenly, there seemed more of a chance that one of the teams competing in the tournament would be Harold Olsen's Ohio State Buckeyes.

* * *

On the last day of February, on the Blackbirds' home floor at the Brooklyn College of Pharmacy, LIU improved to 20-0 with a 65-25 win over the John Marshall College of Law of Jersey City. As ridiculous as the Blackbirds' home schedule was, their victories in the Garden legitimized them. After beating USC, they also had knocked off Adolph Rupp's Kentucky Wildcats 52-34, Marquette 41-34, Toledo 46-39, and Duquesne 48-31 in their other appearances in the Garden. Yet they had played a grand total of zero road games. The neutral-site game against New Mexico A&M in Chicago had been canceled, and the Blackbirds were set to close out the regular season against La Salle in Philadelphia. They seemed to be overcoming the loss of 6-foot-7 starting center Art Hillhouse, the team captain the previous season, who left the squad after a January 27 home game against Geneva because the term was ending and he was graduating. He had been honored before his final game, and after his departure, senior Myron Sewitch and sophomore Si Lobello were both getting playing time as his replacements. Another big man, William "Dolly" King, who later would be honored by Bee with the *Hoop Crazy* dedication, joined the team for the new school term.

Bee's team was closing in on another undefeated season.

*   *   *

As was the case at most state-supported schools, the U of O required two years of military training for all able-bodied men to graduate. Most of the Webfoots got it out of the way as freshmen and sophomores. "We used old World War I uniforms and rifles," John Dick recalled. As the tensions heightened around the world, the Webfoots still hoped they'd never have to call on what they had learned.

*   *   *

From coast to coast, Americans tore off calendar pages.
It was March 1939.

II

MARCH

10.

White Smoke

Wednesday, March 1
NEWSREEL

BERLIN—Field Marshall Hermann Goering boasts in a speech to the German nation that the strength of his air force was crucial in causing Great Britain and France to cave in at the Munich Conference. "The German air force is the terror of our opponents, and it will remain so," he declares.

CHICAGO—Before his speech to the Chicago Association of Commerce, Assistant Secretary of War Louis A. Johnson discloses that the war department is asking airplane manufacturers to move their plants from the east and west coasts to the nation's midsection. He points out that the current locations leave the plants susceptible to air raids. He doesn't say from what country.

MADRID—The Nationalist rebel forces of Generalissimo Francisco Franco wait out the remaining Loyalist troops holding a besieged Madrid. Residents are demanding that the Loyalists—losing the fight to save the Spanish Republic—either surrender or find ways to feed the starving populace.

You'd think Howard Hobson would have more power or be more insistent on the sanctity of the powerful Webfoots' basketball floor in The Igloo as the Northern Division–deciding games in Seattle against Washington approached. But on the previous Saturday night, the university's students staged a dance in The Igloo, and the jitterbugging and waltzing left the precious basketball floor in such pitiable, slippery shape that Hobson realized he risked player injuries if he sent his boys out there for practice. He summoned workers to apply layers of varnish to make it safe again, and the Webfoots

77

had to practice in the men's gym for a couple of days. When they finally were back on their own floor, Coach Hobson emphasized to the boys that they had run up an amazing 115 points in the two victories over Washington in Eugene a month earlier, and that while Washington also was known as a "fast-break" team, it sure looked to him as if the Huskies couldn't handle the dizzying pace in those games. So Hobson told the Webfoots they would need to repeat that approach, and he passed along to the players the rumors that Washington's Hec Edmundson, the longest-tenured coach in the Pacific Coast Conference, was preparing a new countering strategy, getting ready to use his reserves far more than usual.

The Oregon coach didn't make a major issue of the fact that the Huskies' best player, forward Dick Voelker, missed the first game against the Webfoots in Eugene because of an upper respiratory infection and still was weak and ineffective when he bravely played in the second. The Webfoots were aware of that and were determined not to take the Huskies lightly, especially in Seattle. They also tried not to allow their heads to swell because Edmundson had said after the series in Eugene: "That's as good a team as we've played against since I've been coaching. Yes, sir, it ranks with the very best."

Coach Hobson ran the boys hard through the practice and a long scrimmage, while having the extra squad members not on the traveling squad imitate the Huskies. The Webfoots seemed sharp and even lobbied to keep going, but Hobson was satisfied with the frantic pace and called a halt to it early. That was the other revolutionary thing about these boys: they *enjoyed* turning the game into something other than a leisurely stroll.

Hobson was thrilled that Wally Johansen, who missed the two games the previous weekend against Oregon State because of mysterious injuries, looked to be ready to go. Rumors were circulating about the nature of Johansen's injury. Dick Strite, Johansen's former YMCA coach, finally disclosed that he had been told that Johansen had injured his back in a collision in one of the weekend games against Idaho two weeks earlier. Previously, the reports had vaguely attributed his absence from the floor for three games to "body injuries." Not lower body injury. Not upper body injury. Just "body injuries." The less their opponents knew, Hobson believed, the better. He was ahead of his time on that, too.

Strite took great pride in his daily column, labeled "High Climber." He didn't own a car and rode his bike to the office and, whenever possible, to the games he covered. His entertaining column was his way of getting things off his chest and filling space in a section that was pretty much his baby. His latest offering passed along the results of a poll of over 200 U of O students about the basketball season. The sampling indicated that a majority of the students—and this might have been the biggest upset of the season—believed the officiating at least to that point had been fair. That rankled Strite, briefly a referee himself. He often used his space to rate the work of the men in striped shirts and speculate on who might be assigned to wear the whistles at upcoming games and what effects the choices might have on the Webfoots' chances. Among the small number of students labeling the work of the officials to be "partial," the most frequent reason cited was the "protection of star players." Heck, if something weren't done about that, the protection of star players might diminish the game in ensuing years! Even more decisive than the evaluation of officiating, though, was a 95 percent affirmative response to the Webfoots' fast-breaking style of play. The students were buying into it and begging for more, especially if it translated into winning basketball games and perhaps even a conference championship.

Strite also enjoyed informing his readers that when the diplomatic Hobson told scribes that Washington was a fine team and a worthy challenger, Anet overheard and piped in with: "Yeah—the second-best team in the division." The boys laughed. They were used to this now from the ebullient Anet, a business major they all expected to do well because of his charisma, leadership, and self-confidence—none of which crossed the line to the intolerable.

In Astoria, Wally Johansen's father, Arthur, let it slip to the local paper that Charles Anet, Bobby's father and the Johansens' across-the-street neighbor, never had seen the Webfoots lose a game during his son's career at Oregon.

The staff of the campus student paper, the *Oregon Daily Emerald*, among others, started a campaign to make sure Charles was in Seattle the next weekend.

* * *

The ASUO, Oregon's student-body organization, staged an assembly forum featuring retired Navy Commander Stewart F. Bryant, a lecturer in international relations at Stanford. He spoke about the world situation and most notably directed his comments to the U of O students in the audience who were involved in the campus peace movement and the national advancement of a "students' plan for peace." Bryant clicked off the crises, including what he believed to be the increasing influence of the Japanese Navy on that nation's moves and policies. He decried that military build-ups seemed to be getting more attention than peace formulas. The development of air power and advancements in science tied to flight would be one of the best means to keep the peace, Bryant maintained. He also told the students: "Washington's formula is to build up peace by building up military power to ensure victory in case of war, but this will not fundamentally solve the problem. The fundamentals of the students' formula for peace lie in leadership in human thought."

* * *

In another Madison Square Garden doubleheader, Villanova knocked off CCNY, the Webfoots' conqueror in mid-December, 37-30. Leading up to the game, speculation was that a win would lead to a national invitation tournament berth for Villanova. The Wildcats had managed to stay afloat despite not having their star forward, George "Duke" Duzminski, for a significant stretch of the season because of a knee injury. With him out, the Wildcats' coach, Al Severance, tinkered with the offense, perhaps plotting between classes as he also served as a professor of business law. Duzminski was back in the lineup, but neither he nor his team-mates were headed for the national invitation tournament. The word at the Garden after the victory over CCNY and in the *Times* the next morning was that the Wildcats instead had "qualified" for the NCAA's Eastern championships, which still were more than two weeks off.

Thursday, March 2

VATICAN CITY—The conclave to select a successor to Pope Pius XI, who died on February 10, ends on its second day. The new pope is Eugenio Pacelli. He takes the name Pius XII to signal his admiration for his predecessor and his intention to continue his policies—policies Pacelli influenced as Papal Secretary of State. Pacelli had been involved in negotiating the *Reichskonkordat*, the 1933 treaty with Germany that in theory safeguarded the rights of the Catholic Church in that nation, but which critics decried as further emboldening and even dangerously legitimizing Germany and Hitler.

HOLLYWOOD—With the eagerly anticipated epic *Gone With the Wind* five weeks into its filming, movie critics and followers are speculating whether it was wise to cast a British actress, Vivien Leigh, in the role of Scarlett O'Hara. Declares the International News Service: "If she clicks, she'll be one of the stars made overnight. If her performance fails to hit par, she'll be lucky if she ever gets another role of any kind in an American production."

Among the *Oregon Daily Emerald*'s sportswriters was junior George Pasero, the son of Italian immigrants who lived in St. Helens, Oregon. The shortest of the Webfoots towered over the 5-foot-3 Pasero, who was hoping to parlay this experience into a newspaper career. He enrolled as a freshman at Oregon State in 1935, hoping to study chemical engineering, but left and worked in a St. Helens paper mill until enrolling at Oregon in 1937. At the *Emerald*, he worked with John Biggs, Jim Leonard, and Milt Levy, often scrambling to produce as much staff-written copy as possible to fill the eight columns allotted to the sports section.

Like other state papers, the *Emerald* also often ran copy that came straight from the U of O's Athletic News Bureau and the energetic publicist Bruce Hamby. In the *Oregonian*, it usually was labeled "EUGENE (Special)—," while in other papers, there often wasn't any attribution at all.

In Hamby's preseason "Duck Dope" preview of the 1938–39 season, he included brief bios of each player and Hobson, plus statistical information, and also two stories newspapers could run, one on "The Flying Finns" and the other on Laddie Gale. Each story came with blanks to fill in. The one on the Astoria boys began: "Oregon's giant basketball team, which plays _____ in _____ on _____, might easily be named the 'Flying Finns' instead of the Oregon 'Webfoots.'"

By March, those stories had run in various papers, most notably during the barnstorming trip. But Hamby's updated daily copy also appeared in the Oregon papers. The papers used wire-service copy for game stories most of the time when the Webfoots were on the road. All of that meant that on many days, the same material about the Webfoots ran in several newspapers, including the *Emerald*.

On the morning of the team's departure for Seattle, Pasero quoted Hobson in the *Emerald* as saying: "The kids have shown improvement this week over their play in the last three games. I think that they are nearer their peak than at any time this season."

The lead picture on the front page of the student paper that morning was of student Bob "Smokey" Whitfield sitting on a campus building stairway, holding a book and smiling at the camera. The headline over the picture: "Our Boy Smokey." The caption noted that Whitfield, one of the university's few "Negro" students, was starring in the campus production of Eugene O'Neill's *Emperor Jones*. The word on campus was that movie talent scouts already were dangling offers in front of him and encouraging him to head to Hollywood after graduation.

*   *   *

After a loud send-off at the Eugene station, the Webfoots boarded the Cascade train and headed for Seattle. Despite the crucial nature of the series against the Huskies, they were surprised to note that the Monday Morning Quarterbacks booster group and Rally Squad had organized the rally at the downtown station, complete with the university's portable "Victory Bell" that was brought out only for special occasions. Yell King Bob Elliott tried, but failed, to convince the U of O administration to cancel one hour of Friday morning classes for an on-campus rally, so the gathering at the train station was going to have to do.

Hobson's opposing coach in the crucial games, Edmundson, had coached the Huskies long enough—since 1920—that he had seen Hobson as an opposing player in an Oregon uniform. In the 16 seasons that the PCC had been playing in two divisions, Washington had eight outright titles and one other shared.

As a Northwest boy, too, Hobson had a natural bit of awe when competing against the man who was one of the top all-around athletes in the region when the Oregon coach was a young boy. An Idaho native and one of the first athletic stars at the University of Idaho, Edmundson was best known for track and field. In the 1912 Olympic trials, he won the 800 meters and was the runner-up in the 400, qualifying to the U.S. team in both events.

At the Stockholm Games, his teammates included decathlon men Jim Thorpe and Avery Brundage, by 1939 the unchallenged czar of both the United States Olympic Committee and the Amateur Athletic Union. In those 1912 Games, Edmundson didn't win a medal, finishing sixth in the 400 and eighth in the 800, but his reputation in the Northwest wasn't diminished. Before he arrived at Washington, his coaching stops included Idaho and a brief stint at Texas A&M. He might have been even better known as a proponent of the fast break than Hobson, in part because he had been coaching longer. Both he and the sportswriters loved to play up his past as a trackman and portray the Huskies' style as owing homage to that sport.

In his *Register-Guard* advance story, Dick Strite noted that basketball fever had hit Seattle. He wrote: "The boot blacks, the cafeteria waitresses, and the elevator operators, are all talking basketball—and talking it in a positive victorious lilt." He predicted that the games in Seattle, at least stylistically, would be similar to the two breakneck games in Eugene. "The blistering pace the two fast-breaking quintets use will no doubt be duplicated," he said.

When Edmundson repeatedly said that the Huskies needed to be zealous about avoiding running out of gas against the Webfoots, it was high praise. "For the third year," John Dick recalled, "we were challenging the Huskies' long-held claim that no other team could keep pace with them in their fast-break, up-tempo offense and pressure man-to-man defense."

The Webfoots traveled to the on-campus UW Pavilion for a light practice. Oregon annually played a two-game series in Seattle, so the players were familiar with the Huskies' floor in the multi-purpose arena. But it irked L. H. Gregory, who wrote: "It's a peculiar floor, not a true court at all in the usual basketball sense. Just sections of plywood fir floor laid flat on supporting cross-timbers that rest on the dirt bottom of the combination field house-pavilion. No spring in it whatsoever, and this deadness troubles teams playing there the first time."

After the practice, the Webfoots went to the Edmond Meany Hotel, new and palatial, towering above all the other buildings in the University District. It was as nice, or better, than any of the Webfoots' lodgings on their cross-country swing earlier in the season. Because their choice of hotel was published in the papers, and was predictable, anyway, Washington fans greeted them and told them what havoc the Huskies might wreak over the next couple of nights.

In Seattle, Coach Hobson told Strite and other reporters: "We'll win. We beat them twice in Eugene and we'll do it again here. My boys are ready, they've played good basketball, and we're in top condition. At our best, as we are now, I think we have the all-around strength to win."

Edmundson wasn't as decisive. "The boys are as high as they'll ever get," the Huskies' coach declared. "They'll give their level best and I hope that's good enough to win."

* * *

Reading newspapers on the train and in Seattle, the four Astoria boys on the trip—Bobby Anet, Wally Johansen, Ted Sarpola, and Earl Sandness—found mentions of their hometown. As the Second Sino-Japanese war continued, Chinese women and children, most of them from among the approximately 150 Chinese residents of the Oregon fishing town, congregated at the Astoria docks to protest the shipping of U.S. scrap iron to Japan. Dockworkers refused to cross the picket lines and participate in the loading of the 21 railcars of scrap iron onto the Japanese freight ship *Norway Maru*. Federal arbitrator Samuel F. Weinstein, representatives of the National Labor Relations Board, and longshoremen's union officials all were in Astoria to deal with the dispute. Harry Bridges, head of the international longshoreman's union, also was on the way to town. The squabble was getting considerable national attention as a test case, with many assuming the protest might spread to other West Coast docks and affect even more significant American commerce with Japan.

Also, Astoria was part of a widely publicized Boeing strategy to avoid charging for Washington sales tax in the sale of planes to airlines. Oregon had no sales tax,[1] so as the Webfoots rode to Seattle, a new 74-passenger Boeing Yankee Clipper made the trip from Seattle to Astoria, landed, was "sold" on Oregon soil, and was turned over to representatives of Pan-American Airways. Then, officially part of the airline fleet, it took off again.

---

1. As of this writing, it still doesn't.

11.

Cayuse with a Saddle

Friday, March 3

WASHINGTON—U.S. Army Air Corps brass disclose they're going to send at least 600 prospective airplane mechanics to "rush" training at Lowry Field in Denver, adding to the bustle at the facility where the Air Corps technical school already is overflowing and overtaxed.

ST. PETERSBURG, Fla.—Young Yankees outfielder Joe DiMaggio agrees to a $26,500 salary for the season and is said to be on his way to Florida. Less trumpeted is the fact that second baseman Joe Gordon, the former Oregon Webfoots star who is coming off a 25-home run rookie season, arrives in St. Petersburg after a cross-country drive from Oregon and immediately comes to terms with the Yankees, too. He attended classes at Oregon through the winter term, completed requirements for his physical education degree, and enjoyed attending Webfoots basketball games.

In Eugene, the chairman of a police committee charged with investigating whether prostitution and gambling were problems in the college town announced that to the best of his knowledge, they were not. But he added that the investigation would continue. That drew quite a few laughs around town as the sports fans prepared to follow the game in Seattle that night.

*　*　*

Fight!

While closing out their regular season with their 21st consecutive victory, a 28-21 win over La Salle in Philadelphia's Convention Hall, the Long Island Blackbirds were drawn into or—depending on who was doing the telling—started a fight that turned ugly. LIU was ahead 19-14 with nine minutes left in the game when jostling under the La Salle bucket evolved into a full-scale brawl, with players coming off the bench to join the fray and spectators coming to the edge of the court to at least get a better view. Milton Gross later wrote that Clair Bee was seen "wading like a waterfront brawler through the free-for-all." Police officers rushed into the melee, trying to help restore order, and when the fighting stopped, both teams were sent to their locker rooms and fans ordered back to their seats. The delay lasted eleven minutes. When the teams were brought back out to the floor, the rest of the game was uneventful.

Stories about the game and brawl also confirmed that the Blackbirds, who had just played their first and only genuine road game of the season, had accepted a bid to the national invitation tournament. That had been a foregone conclusion for weeks, though.

*   *   *

Washington didn't sell reserved seats for the Oregon games, and UW officials regretted that decision once it was clear the two-game series would decide the Northern Division championship. With fans poised to scramble for the best seats the second the doors opened, a huge mob was waiting outside the Pavilion as the Webfoots approached in a caravan of cabs. They had to stop well short of the arena, and then get an escort from security officers through the anxious fans.

In front of the overflow crowd of more than 10,000, the Webfoots overcame a rough start and went on to easily handle the Huskies 39-26. A Slim Wintermute tip-in gave the Webfoots an 8-7 lead, and they stayed in control the rest of the way. The Huskies' fans were primed to go into the night, celebrating a victory that would have set up a Saturday night showdown for the Northern Division title, but instead they left disappointed.

"Oregon virtually ran the Huskies into the checkerboard sections of the court to end the desperate championship drive of Hec Edmundson's 'racehorse' hoopsters," Dick Strite wrote in the *Register-Guard*. John Dick later said neither team played well in the game, disputing Strite's claim that the first half was "one of the greatest exhibitions of modern basketball."

In the *Oregonian*, L. H. Gregory allowed that the Webfoots had played better games, but showed considerable grit and poise throughout. He was especially excited about one of Wally Johansen's baskets in the first half, noting he took a pass from Wintermute on the move and tossed the ball in the hoop backward, over his head, without looking. Occasionally, Strite's affinity for his former Astoria YMCA players showed through.

It was another night when Anet, running the show on the floor and as the decision maker, made it a matter of pride to avoid calling the first time-out of the game. That was a familiar Anet strategy, one that usually was fine with his teammates and with Hobson. The Huskies caved in first, calling the first time-out halfway through the opening half.

Gregory wrote that the Webfoots made 14 of their 67 attempted shots from the floor, the Huskies 10 of 66. And he couldn't resist adding: "It was the best officiated game of the year, the officials letting the petty stuff go."

Laddie Gale had a team-high 11 points, and he at least helped provide some sort of suspense for the Saturday night game. With 172 points in the 15 Northern Division games, he was 15 short of tying the record for a 16-game division season set in 1936 by Oregon State's Wally Palmberg, who hailed from Astoria and was a hometown hero to several of the Webfoots.[1]

The potential problem for Oregon was that Anet fell and aggravated a hand injury that had troubled him off and on for several weeks. This time, he suffered one dislocated and two sprained fingers, and when Hobson noticed him getting treatment from trainer Bob Officer after the game, he decided to hold Anet out of the game the next night. The coach remembered how Anet had insisted on staying in the lineup when the hand was troubling him in the final rivalry game of the season against Oregon State. In that game, he used only one hand, and his left hand at that, in making a close-in shot off a drive, then chirped to his own bench: "How'd you like that?" But Coach Hobson could afford to rest his ace guard on the second night against Washington and hope to have him well for the league championship series.

Saturday, March 4

WASHINGTON—Addressing Congress on the 150th anniversary of its first gathering, President Roosevelt brings up America's sympathy for those who have lost much of

---

1. Again highlighting the haphazard nature of the scorekeeping process, Gale's Northern Division point total was listed differently in the Oregon papers during the Washington series. The figures here are what everyone seemed to agree on later, after final tallying.

their freedom under totalitarian regimes in Europe. He proclaims: "With many other democracies, the United States will give no encouragement to the belief that our processes are outworn, or that we will approvingly watch the return of forms of government which for 2,000 years have proved their tyranny and their instability alike."

The Astoria boys again followed news that had their hometown in the national spotlight. The Chinese picketers at the Astoria docks "won" a minor victory. They agreed to step aside and allow the union longshoreman to load the Japanese freighter with scrap iron, but they also exacted the promise from port authority officials that no similar shipments would be allowed. The Astoria case was the frame of reference and the precedent as similar protests spread to Portland. About 800 Chinese women and children picketed at the Portland docks near a Greek freighter scheduled to take on scrap metal for transport to Japan. The thinking, of course, was that the scrap metal would be used in armaments manufacture for the Sino-Japanese War, and little or no thought was given to the possibilities beyond that conflict. America's attention mostly was on Europe.

*   *   *

Indiana's collapse was complete. The Hoosiers lost 53-45 at Michigan, while Ohio State manhandled Purdue 51-35 in front of a record home crowd of 11,184 in Columbus. Buckeyes captain Jimmy Hull scored 20 points and claimed the Big Ten Conference scoring title with 169 points in the 11 games he played in, for a 15.3-point average. He finished 18 points ahead of runner-up Pick Dehner of Illinois, who appeared in one more game. The results left Ohio State, a game out and in trouble only a week earlier, the undisputed champions of the Big Ten at 10-2, a game ahead of the Hoosiers. "Undisputed league champions" sounded a lot better than "co-champions," and the Buckeyes had their rivals, the Michigan Wolverines, to thank for it. To those who had been paying attention to Olsen's role in the NCAA tournament process, it seemed obvious that the Buckeyes still had some games to play—and a national championship to seek.

*   *   *

Surreal in the contrast it presented to the wild atmosphere in the Seattle arena the night before, the Saturday Oregon-Washington game drew only 5,500 fans, and even that official figure might have been charitable. Distraught over the loss that had cost the Huskies any chance at the Northern Division title, many of the Washington fans had better things to do. A few of the UW students probably even studied.

With Anet watching from the bench, Ford Mullen, Matt Pavalunas, and Red McNeeley all got significant playing time in the backcourt as Gale just missed in his quest for the 16-game Northern Division scoring record. He finished the night with 14 points, leaving him (after final tallying) with 186 in division play, one point short of Palmberg.

The Huskies' George Ziegenfuss said going in that his goal was to shut down Gale, and he also got a lot of help, with the Huskies sagging on the Webfoots' star. Still, Gale had 10 points in the first half and seemed in good shape, but the Huskies continued to act as if it would be an affront to have the record set against them and Gale had trouble getting off shots in the second half. When he scored with 3:10 remaining in the game, making a running, whirling one-hander from 20 feet out, he was within one of tying Palmberg. But he couldn't get the ball in the basket again. Gregory was chagrined that only Wintermute seemed determined to get Gale the ball and the record, but it was a nip-and-tuck game, the Webfoots took what was available to them to get the victory, Gale was fine with the strategy, and the scribes seemed to be more concerned with the record. Gregory also noted that Ziegenfuss blocked one close-in Gale shot, saying the Husky "rode the ball as if it had been a Cayuse with a saddle on it." (It's a low-quality horse or pony.) The Webfoots ended up winning 54-52, with Wintermute leading the way with 18 points.

After the game, a scribe perhaps sarcastically asked Edmundson if he would stand by his previous statement that this was the best Washington team he had ever had. Four of the Huskies' five losses in the division had come to the Webfoots. "It still goes. Oregon was just better," he responded.

Almost as an afterthought, writers pointed out that Gale had scored 249 points in division competition the previous season, but the schedule had been 20 games for that one season alone.

Montana had given the league a one-season try, gone 3-17, and dropped out. Strite claimed to have figured out that he had scored 194 points in the 16 games that season against Washington, Washington State, Oregon State, and Idaho, and he accused the big-city scribes in Portland of manufacturing a Gale quest for a 16-game season record he already held. It was a bit surprising, though, that anybody noticed the point totals at all, because the newspapers generally only ran individual box scores and didn't get around to publishing cumulative statistics until the season was over. Also rare was any mention of a player's scoring average. In fact, when the "official" Northern Division statistics for the 1938–39 season were released, Gale and Wintermute, with 174 points, finished 1-2. It was a slight improvement over the season before, when they were first and third. If anyone took pencil to paper and did the math, their scoring averages in division play were 11.6 and 10.9, respectively. All 11 members of the Webfoots' regular traveling squad scored in conference play.

Also on the final night of conference regular-season play, Southern California hammered rival UCLA 56-27 and California defeated Stanford 43-32, leaving the winners tied atop the Southern Division. A single-game playoff would break the tie.

The final PCC standings:

NORTHERN DIVISION	W	L	Pct.
Oregon	14	2	.875
Washington	11	5	.688
Washington State	8	8	.500
Oregon State	6	10	.375
Idaho	1	15	.063
SOUTHERN DIVISION	W	L	Pct.
California	9	3	.750
Southern California	9	3	.750
Stanford	6	6	.500
UCLA	0	12	.000

The ineptitude of one horrible team in each division, Idaho in the North and UCLA in the South, inflated the records of the other teams.

Sunday, March 5

BERLIN—Deutches Nachrichten Buro, a German news agency considered a semi-official voice of the regime, responds to President Roosevelt, saying: "After misrepresentations and curious opinions, Roosevelt turns to flat lies. He lied when he said that in states governed by the people, religion is being persecuted." The news agency claims that Roosevelt citing the vaunted freedom of the press in America was hypocritical because U.S. public opinion was controlled and influenced by newspapers that "are under pressure from powerful factors which permit them to publish only a distorted picture of the true situation."

It was the Northern Division winner's turn to play host to the Southern Division champion in the PCC's best-of-three series. The original schedule called for games on Friday, March 10; Saturday, March 11; and, if necessary, Monday, March 13. (Playing on a Sunday was out of the question.) To stick to that, the Southern Division playoff game would have to be played during the week, and neither USC nor California wanted to do that.

The early speculation was that the championship series might be moved back a full week, with a possible Game 3 on Monday, March 20. Quickly, though, Hobson and others pointed out the potential conflict with the March 20–21 NCAA Western championships in San Francisco. If that was the playoff schedule, an NCAA spot couldn't be held open for the PCC winner. After citing the NCAA tournament as a goal all season, Hobson and the Webfoots couldn't stand for that.

12.

Maneuvers

Monday, March 6

BERLIN—Third Reich officials issue a clarification: Although the government has mandated that Jews turn over anything of value to the state, they *don't* have to give up wedding rings, small pieces of jewelry, or gold in dental work.

TOKYO—Japanese cabinet and military officials announce five-year programs to upgrade the nation's navy and air forces, and a four-year program to improve armaments production. Much already is being thrown into the war against China.

WASHINGTON—The Senate votes to support the Army Air Corps' addition of 6,000 new planes as part of the $358-million air defense bill. The stunning aspect is that the House earlier had approved the acquisition of "only" 5,500 planes and the fear was that Senate Republicans might balk at even that number as excessive.

Southern California athletics head W. O. Huntington sent a telegram to Oregon officials announcing three things: One, a coin flip had determined the USC-California Southern Division playoff game would be played in Berkeley. Two, it wouldn't be played until the next Saturday, March 11, minimizing the academic disruption during the week, especially for the traveling Trojans. And three, "faculty" at California and Southern California had granted permission for the Southern winner to play in the series in Eugene . . . beginning Thursday, March 16, and including games on the next two nights, if both were necessary. While that would get the series over before the Western championships, Oregon officials insisted it was cutting it too close and refused to agree to that schedule.

The students working on the 1939 edition of the U of O's yearbook, *Oregana*, reached their official deadline. The rush to have the ambitious volume out by the end of the 1938–39 school year meant that the latest information sports editor Hubbard Kuokka could have in the five pages devoted to the basketball team in the main body of the yearbook was that the Webfoots beat Washington in two straight games to win the division championship.

What the staff sent along to the printer about the basketball team at this point was both fun and reverential in spots. The Webfoots were labeled both "The Maple Courtiers" and "The Lanky Boys" in headlines. Candid shots showed the five starters.

The captions:

- LADDIE GALE, 6'4" FORWARD, WAS THE BEHEMOTH-HANDED HIGH SCORER OF THE NORTHERN DIVISION.
- JOHN DICK, 6'4" FORWARD, WAS THE ONE STARTING JUNIOR IN THE TEAM OF SENIORS, MADE SCORES WHEN THEY REALLY COUNTED.
- URGEL "SLIM" WINTERMUTE, 6'8" CENTER, PULLED THE GAME OUT OF THE FIRE MORE THAN ONCE WITH HIS HIGH ALTITUDE PLAYING.
- SMILING WALLY JOHANSEN JOKED HIS OPPONENTS INTO A MUDDLE. A BALL-HAWKING GUARD, HE CANNED LONG ONES.
- CAPTAIN BOBBY ANET, SPEEDBALL FROM ASTORIA, WAS ON THE BALL ALL THE TIME: FREQUENTLY OUTJUMPED THE TALLER BOYS.

The early deadline also meant the material sent to the printers about the spring sports—baseball and track and field—came from the 1938 seasons. The '38 baseball team picture included Coach Hobson and three reserves on the 1938–39 basketball team—Bob Hardy, Ford Mullen, and Matt Pavalunas. The Webfoots track team, in its 36th season under legendary Coach Bill Hayward, had done well, and the lead picture showed a black athlete, Mack Robinson, in an Oregon uniform breaking the tape in a meet against Washington. The caption labeled him a "speedball," also, and noted: "This dusky sprinter was largely responsible for

Oregon's victory in every dual meet of 1938 track season." It didn't note that Robinson, from Los Angeles, had won a silver medal at the 1936 Berlin Olympics, finishing second to Jesse Owens in the 200 meters, before coming to Eugene. There was no reason to note this, but Robinson also had a 20-year-old brother who was about to graduate from Pasadena Junior College and was planning to enroll at UCLA in the fall.

Mack Robinson's brother was named Jackie.

*   *   *

The national invitation tournament organizers—the Metropolitan Basketball Writers—announced that Roanoke College of Salem, Virginia (21-1), unheralded but with just the single loss to Villanova, would join the LIU Blackbirds in the six-team field.

Two teams in, four to go.

Schools considered for the other spots were said to be independents Loyola of Chicago and Bradley Tech, plus Southwestern (Kan.), Warrensburg Teachers (Mo.), Texas, Missouri, Oklahoma, and Colorado. St. John's wasn't mentioned, but the consensus was that the Redmen would end up in the local tournament, too, if they beat St. Francis in their final regular-season game. The lack of mention of Villanova seemed to confirm that the Wildcats were ticketed for the NCAA Eastern championships. Loyola, coached by former Chicago Cardinals end Lenny Sachs, was undefeated. Yet the New York scribes didn't seem to note that Roanoke College and at least two of the other schools on the list of prospective invitation tournament invitees weren't considered among the nation's elite and hadn't played big-time schedules.

Tuesday, March 7

WASHINGTON—President Roosevelt makes it clear he believes the 1937 Neutrality Acts, the latest and adjusted versions of the measure first passed in 1935, no longer are realistic. They are to lapse in May but are expected to be renewed. Also, Colorado Senator Edwin C. Johnson, a former governor who already is assertive in his first term in Washington, boldly introduces legislation that calls for the various U.S. armed forces to train and stockpile 100,000 pilots in active service and reserves. It follows similar legislation proposed in the House by U.S. Rep. John McCormack of Massachusetts.

Oregon's turn: The athletic board announced that the Webfoots would refuse to participate in the league championship series if it was scheduled any later than March 11, 13, and, if necessary, 14. Given that Game 1 would have been only four days away, and the Southern Division playoff game was slotted for March 11, that challenge to move that game up or to determine a representative another way was unrealistic—and the U of O folks undoubtedly knew it. But they were re-emphasizing a common Northern Division viewpoint: that the California schools too often acted as if the "other" division was their minor league and tried to push around the folks in the Northwest.

John Bunn's NCAA tournament district selection committee would have faced a major challenge if neither side budged and the PCC championship series was scrubbed, leaving the league with two division champions but not a league winner. Oregon had better credentials than either California or Southern California. But with Bunn operating out of the Bay Area and at a Southern Division school, and mindful that California would have been a far better draw in the four-team Western championships in San Francisco, the choice likely would have been the winner of the Southern Division playoff.

The rhetoric heated up. California athletics graduate manager Kenneth Priestley scoffed and said: "It looks to me as if Oregon just doesn't want to play."

As they waited, the Webfoots continued to reap the benefits of their division title. Hobson and most of his players were introduced and got a free lunch at the Tuesday meeting of the Eugene Rotary Club. Then they got to listen to the previously arranged guest speaker, an Oregon professor whose speech was billed as "The Creative Aspects of Chemistry."

The boys thought they were back in class.

Meanwhile, the speculation about the possible NCAA field continued. The issues were multi-fold. Which teams would draw invitations? And which teams would accept? There were eight spots available and eleven recognized "major" leagues. Plus, of course, there were the geographic issues involved in filling the field with one team from each of the eight districts. Five of the leagues already had determined their champions, whether through simple regular-season play or tournaments. The known solo champions were Ohio State in the Big Ten, Texas in the Southwest Conference, Colorado in the Big 7 (also known as the Mountain States Conference), Clemson (16-8) in the Southern Conference, and Kentucky (16-4) in the Southeastern Conference. Clemson was the biggest surprise, since the Tigers had gone only 6-6 in league play, tying for ninth among 15 teams, before winning four straight in the league tournament.

The Colorado Buffaloes had gotten over their loss to St. John's in Madison Square Garden. They easily won their league with a 12-2 league record, beating out (in order) Utah State, Utah, Wyoming, Denver, Brigham Young, and Colorado A&M. The Buffaloes were the obvious NCAA tournament choice in the Rocky Mountain district that included the states of Colorado, Wyoming, Utah, Montana, and New Mexico.

CU officials announced that they would conduct a vote among the players and take the result under advisement. With the Buffaloes' season over and no league playoffs, Colorado's players knew they would have two weeks to rest up for the regional—or, to put it another way, their season would be extended at least two weeks if they accepted the bid. These were mostly the same fellows who the previous year had traveled by train cross-country to play in the first national invitation tournament, and then made another trip to New York in December. Would they be up for more travel, first to San Francisco, then possibly to Chicago? For a new tournament?

The Buffaloes' decision was announced Tuesday.

No, thanks.

Colorado's athletic committee said that it had consulted with Coach Frosty Cox and the players, and the decision was based on the fact that the Buffaloes were banged up, tired, and even sick. CU's star center, Jack Harvey, was hospitalized three times during the season and missed the final three games because of illness, and two other starters had spent time in the hospital, also. Without naming the national invitation tournament, the committee said CU wouldn't consider taking part in any other tournament, either. The Buffaloes were going to stay home.

The next day, the head of the NCAA Tournament's Rocky Mountain district selection committee, Wyoming coach Dutch Witte, said his group had recommended to Harold Olsen that Big 7 runner-up Utah State—coached by the respected Dick Romney, a former multiple-sport star himself and a member of a prominent Utah family—get the NCAA bid. Harold Olsen went along with that, and Utah State's athletic council quickly accepted the invitation.

The haphazard nature of the selection process became even more obvious when the District 5 committee, also charged with selecting one entrant for the Western championships in San Francisco, announced it would hold a three-team playoff in Oklahoma City to determine its choice. Drake and Oklahoma A&M, co-champions of the Missouri Valley Conference, would play first, and the next night the winner would play Big Six co-champion Oklahoma. The Sooners and Missouri had both finished 7-3 in the league standings, but the Tigers (12-6 overall) declined an invitation to join the Sooners and make it a four-team play-in competition. The official word was that Missouri "faculty representatives" had nixed that, citing academic concerns.

13.

RSVP

Wednesday, March 8

LONDON—British War Secretary Leslie Hore-Belisha tells the House of Commons that the plan is to send 300,000 British troops to France if war breaks out. There will be no sitting by as others take up the fight against Germany.

ARCADIA, Calif.—Thoroughbred trainer Tom Smith announces that the great Seabiscuit, conqueror of War Admiral in a match race the previous November that captured coast-to-coast attention, won't race again for at least a year—and might not race again, period. He is recovering from a ruptured suspensory ligament.

The Metropolitan Basketball Writers Association continued to fill out the field for its second national invitation tournament, announcing that undefeated Loyola of Chicago accepted a bid. Although the Ramblers' independent schedule also was suspect, they had beaten a few decent teams, including Santa Clara, DePaul, Villanova, Drake, Michigan State, Toledo, and CCNY. That night, St. John's beat St. Francis in front of 14,818 in the Garden and the scribes said that the Redmen (17-2), as expected, had agreed to join LIU as a local host and draw.

Four selections down, two to go.

In the NCAA tournament, meanwhile, Ohio State was confirmed as another choice for the Eastern championships in Philadelphia. Despite Harold Olsen's role as the national committee chairman, nobody second-guessed the selection of the Big Ten champions. The players, though, later said the whole thing surprised them.

Olsen told his boys, in effect: *Congratulations, boys, you have some more games to play in this new tournament!* It's impossible to believe that the man who had been chairman of the NCAA tournament committee for nearly a year didn't ever mention the tournament to his players. Yet that's the way some of them said they remembered it years later. One possible explanation could be that since it required an Indiana collapse in the final two games for the Buckeyes to overhaul Indiana and win the Big Ten title, Olsen didn't think it would be an issue and didn't say *much* about it. But the "new" NCAA tournament was mentioned in many stories that season, including when the Buckeyes' *own* coach announced the specific format and plans in December in Columbus and accounts were carried from coast to coast. The Buckeyes of that season undoubtedly believed what they said as they looked back in later years, yet it had a bit of revisionist history feel to it. The tournament wasn't a secret, and especially not in the home city of the tournament chairman.

"What in the world is the NCAA tournament? That's what we wanted to know," Jimmy Hull said later. "Vote? No, we did not get to vote on it." On another occasion, he added, "We didn't even know what it was all about. Two or three of the players didn't even want to go. The state high school basketball tournament was going on, and we wanted to see that. We were tired. We had reached our goals."

But the Buckeyes were in the tournament . . . and Kentucky, surprisingly, was out. It had been a strange season for the Wildcats. They lost four of five in the January stretch that included the 18-point rout at the hands of LIU in Madison Square Garden, a loss to Notre Dame in Louisville, and then SEC defeats to Tennessee and Alabama. But Kentucky didn't lose again, finishing a sparse 5-2 in the league and winning the regular season title, and also beating Mississippi, Louisiana State, and Tennessee to take the league tournament at Knoxville. They were on a roll. Yet that night, Adolph Rupp announced that the Wildcats had turned down an NCAA invitation. The Associated Press story stated: "After playing a difficult schedule . . . Rupp said the team needed a rest."

Wait a minute. During Kentucky's visit to New York for a Madison Square Garden doubleheader back in 1935, didn't Rupp draw considerable attention by proposing that college basketball decide a national champion with a national tournament? His idea had been for a round-robin format at one site, but this was at least a reasonable facsimile.

The Wildcats would have had nearly two weeks off between the end of the SEC tournament and their first game in Philadelphia.

Some suspected the Wildcats were angling for another trip to New York, but like the Colorado Buffaloes, Kentucky didn't end up in either tournament.

* * *

As law student Wally Johansen and the other Webfoot seniors approaching graduation looked ahead to the potentially extended basketball season, they at least could take comfort in the fact that the Western championships in San Francisco would be played in the early stages of spring break, and if the team headed off to the title game in Evanston, that travel also would come during the break. But the game itself and several days of travel back would take them out of a week of classes. They decided they could live with that . . . if it happened. Johansen also had his student-body treasurer duties to be concerned about, but president Harry Weston was a track team star and would be tolerant if Johansen missed a meeting or two.

* * *

Laddie Gale and Slim Wintermute were named to the Northern Division's first-team all-star squad, the result of voting by the players on the five teams' traveling squads conducted by Washington athletic officials. The other first-team choices were forward Roy Williamson and guard George Ziegenfuss of Washington, and guard Al Hooper of Washington State. The only real eyebrow-raising part of that was the omission of Bobby Anet from the first team. It probably was a way to spread out the honors, and perhaps an indication that the brash little guard had made some enemies. However, he and Johansen both were named to the second team, along with Washington forwards Dick Voelker and Pat Dorsey, and Oregon State center Frank Mandic.

Thursday, March 9

PARIS—A Paris newspaper publishes details of what it claims is a German plan to invade Holland and Switzerland in mid-March. The plan is on hold, the paper reports, but still is under consideration.

WASHINGTON—Several senators are among the sponsors of a constitutional amendment to require a national referendum to approve a declaration of war unless a Western Hemisphere nation has been attacked. Two of them, Robert La Follette Jr. (Prog.-Wisconsin) and Joel Clark (D-Missouri), are assured in a judiciary subcommittee meeting that it will be brought up for a vote in the Senate at the current session. The proposal, the brainchild of Indiana Congressman Louis Ludlow, has been rejected several times, including in 1938. The Roosevelt administration opposes it.

Pacific Coast Conference officials, tiring of the volleys back and forth between the California schools and Oregon, conducted a vote of the member schools and announced the championship series would be played March 16 and 17, plus, if necessary, on March 18. Oregon reluctantly went along with a schedule it had rejected earlier. At least it allowed participation in the Western championships in San Francisco. But if the series went three games, the winner could end up playing five games in six nights.

As the Webfoots waited, Gale was named to the Newspaper Enterprise Association's first-team All-America squad, joining LIU's Irv Torgoff, Illinois center Pick Dehner, Colorado guard Jim Wilcoxon, and Indiana guard Ernie Andres. NEA writer Jerry Brondfield wrote that the choices were "based on recommendations by coaches and sports writers from all sections of the country." Wintermute was among those on the honorable mention list. The story, accompanied by a picture with head shots of the first-team choices arranged in a circle and the list of those honored, ran in many newspapers coast to coast.

*　*　*

The New York basketball scribes met at the Hotel Lincoln and emerged to announce that New Mexico A&M (20-2) and Bradley Tech (17-2) were the final choices for their tournament.

The field was set.

The scribes also made sure all knew that Bradley Tech—which had beaten Oregon and lost to California—turned down a bid to the NCAA tournament, too, preferring to make a return trip to New York. Because the Braves' credentials were legitimate and Loyola was undefeated, the invitation tournament's boosters had cause to brag about having those teams in the bracket. Both were given byes in the March 15 quarterfinals, enabling them to delay their travel in from the Midwest. On that first night, LIU would play New Mexico A&M and St. John's would face Roanoke. Even before the teams arrived in town, though, the New York scribes seemed ridiculously eager to build up New Mexico A&M and Roanoke into bona fide national powers. Despite their impressive records, they weren't.

The lack of agreement on what to call the tournament continued. Various wire stories that week called it both "the second annual invitation basketball tournament of the Metropolitan basketball writers" and the "New York Basketball Writers Invitation tourney." The New York *Herald Tribune*, whose writers were among the writers association's ringleaders, generally called it "the second annual intercollegiate invitation tournament." Another reason for the inconsistent use of capital letters in references to both tournaments was that some wire services transmitted copy in all capital letters and it was the job of copy editors at newspapers to underline the letters that should have been uppercase in print. So you might see just about every upper- and lowercase variation possible over the course of a week in the names of the two tournaments.

Friday, March 10

LONDON—Concluding that the rush to military buildup was going to bankrupt Europe, British Prime Minister Neville Chamberlain leaks word that he is planning on proposing that European leaders convene a conference to seek disarmament agreements. London papers generally cheer the strategy and speculate that the United States could become involved in the negotiations, too. Reports indicate that despite heated rhetoric in public, back-channel discussions along those lines already have taken place between Germany and Great Britain. That is said to be in part a response to Hitler's January 30 speech to the Reichstag, in which he declared that his nation had no desire to acquire British or French territory and that his nation's goal should be to develop its export trade, not add lands. Chamberlain and his government are continuing to send confusing, mixed, and even contradictory messages.

Another crisis: John Bunn took note of the PCC series schedule and said the NCAA district committee might have to bypass the league champion. He claimed that while the PCC series would be over on time to allow the winner to get to San Francisco, the league champion would be too tired to be a formidable entrant in the regional against representatives from the Southwest, Midwest, and Rocky Mountain districts. Incredibly, Bunn suggested the choice to represent the West Coast might have to be PCC Northern Division runner-up Washington or the loser of the Southern Division's one-game playoff, California or Southern California. It was obviously he was mainly attempting to leave open the option of inviting California to the Western championships as a virtual "host" team on Treasure Island if the Golden Bears *lost* the Southern Division playoff game to USC the next night.

It was a trial balloon that didn't fly, and Hobson reacted quickly.

"If we should win the conference title, we will attempt to enter the NCAA tournament," the Webfoots' coach declared. "We have played as many games on successive nights in our Northern Division, and games on our eastern trip were as closely crowded as the situation that may be present in the conference and NCAA playoffs."

Saturday, March 11

MIDDLETOWN, Conn.—The former commander of the U.S. Marine Corps displays shocking disdain for his nation's commander in chief at a Wesleyan University conference on foreign policy. Major General Smedley Butler says he will attempt to make sure that President Roosevelt's son, James, is quickly on the front lines "if his father starts another war." Butler angrily declares: "If we're going to send boys out to fight every twenty years for democracy, what's the use of keeping democracy?"

MOSCOW—Soviet leader Joseph Stalin addresses the Communist Party Congress and asserts that the United States, England, and France were reacting passively to world aggression because they hoped Germany or Japan might be emboldened to attack the Soviet Union.

Arthur Daley was among the New York writers protective of their tournament. In a *Times* preview piece, he called it "the national invitation tournament that the Metropolitan Basketball Writers conceived and staged for the first time a year ago." And he added: "Six teams have been invited to the tournament by the scribes who have refused to allow themselves to be entranced by 'name colleges,' but have insisted on getting teams of undisputed class. Two games is the most any tournament quintet has lost."

If anyone at the *Times*, or any other New York paper, was self-conscious about the obvious conflict of interest that led to exaggerating the credentials of some teams in the tournament and the overall field, the coverage didn't reflect it. Daley's story went on to label the 1938 tournament "a tremendous success. Everything worked almost as though it had been planned that way."

That raised the obvious question: *Well, hadn't it?*

*   *   *

California was going to be the Webfoots' opponent in the PCC championship series. Before an overflow crowd in Berkeley, the Golden Bears beat Southern California 42-36 in the Southern Division playoff game. California led for most of the game, but seemed on the verge of letting it slip away when the Trojans pulled ahead 36-34 with three minutes left in the game. But USC didn't score again, the Bears ran off eight points, and they had punched their train tickets to Eugene. Slick center Bill Ogilvie led the way for California with 17 points.

Hobson scouted the game and managed to refrain from commenting to the nosy scribes. California coach Nibs Price declared that his Bears had "more than equal chance" of knocking off the Webfoots in the series that would begin five days later in Eugene. "The boys have been coming up fine after two weeks of looking pretty dull and tonight, they played their best in two weeks," Price said. He added: "I've been too doggone busy trying to get the kids into the Southern Division championship to pay much attention to Oregon. All I know is that they're tall in three forward spots and that they use a zone defense system with those three big fellows, Slim Wintermute, Laddie Gale and Bob Hardy, in the back line."

Price likely was being honest about not spending much time worrying about or scouting the Webfoots. He hadn't noticed that by then, John Dick was the third starter up front, replacing Hardy.

14.

Jumping Either Way

Sunday, March 12

ROME—Many Americans are aghast that the U.S. ambassador to Great Britain, Joseph Kennedy, not only was present at the coronation of Pope Pius XII, but the Catholic businessman from Massachusetts also was an official representative of President Roosevelt and the nation. It was the first time a U.S. president sent an official representative to a papal installation, and many saw it as violating the principle of separation of church and state. Adding to the controversy, Kennedy calls the ceremony "overwhelming in its solemnity, in its magnificence, in its universal appeal. But above all the pageantry, ceremonies and cheers stood the figure of his holiness. It seemed to us no longer the figure of a man, but more a Godlike figure." Kennedy's son John, 21, is in the early stages of a long tour of Europe to research his senior honors thesis at Harvard. He and seven of his eight siblings join his parents to witness the coronation.

Hoping it would be inspirational for the Webfoots, Oregon athletic board officials began making arrangements to bring in Coach Dean Walker and the players on the 1919 PCC champion Webfoots for a 20th reunion in conjunction with the series against California. It wasn't a massive undertaking: that team had only six players. The Webfoots swept the league title series with California in two games—and in Berkeley, no less. The six to be feted in Eugene were Ned Fowler of Astoria, Herm Lind and Franz Jacobberger of Portland, Nish Chapman of Eugene, Eddie Durno of Medford, and Carter Brandon of San Francisco.

Oregon writers also brought up the infamous 1926 PCC championship series, when the Webfoots and captain Howard Hobson lost to the Golden Bears in two games after their star, Swede

Westergren, ran afoul of ptomaine poisoning after the dinner with Hobson and the other players. Hobson didn't say if he'd ordered the Webfoots to stay away from Crab Louie all week.

*   *   *

Athletics always opened doors to fraternity membership, at Oregon and virtually everywhere else. In Eugene, the houses were especially excited about the outlook for the team and their members in the second consecutive appearance in the league championship series, this time at home.

Slim Wintermute was a member of Phi Delta Theta, his coach's former fraternity.

At the Beta Theta Pi house, young reserves Matt Pavalunas and Red McNeeley, plus squad member Wellington "Wimpy" Quinn, all got encouragement from studious older fraternity brother and law student Wendell Wyatt.

Bobby Anet, Wally Johansen, John Dick, Ted Sarpola, and squad members Toivo Piippo and Stanley Short were getting pats on the back at the Sigma Nu house.[1]

Sophomore reserve Earl Sandness was the only player at Phi Gamma Delta, and the boys treated him as if he already were a star—assuming, among other things, he would continue the Astoria tradition and be a mainstay on the team in ensuing seasons.

Monday, March 13

WASHINGTON—Senator Homer Bone (D-Wash.), reiterates to the Naval Committee his long-standing support for the constitutional amendment to require a national declaration of war referendum. "No force stands between the man in the White House and plunging this country into a bloody war," Bone says.

ROME—Pope Pius XII receives Ambassador Kennedy and his family. The youngest of the Kennedy children, Edward, 7, receives his first communion from the new pope.

Oregon officials continued to publicly assume the winning team in the PCC series would be the league's representatives in the Western

---

1. Years later, much of the movie *Animal House* was filmed inside Sigma Nu. Yes, Webfoots were members of what at least stood in for the infamous Delta House and where John Belushi one day would ask: "Was it over when the Germans bombed Pearl Harbor?"

regional in San Francisco. But they were nervous. John Bunn still wasn't guaranteeing that. Now that California was in the series, the major alternative seemed to be that the Bears—in advance, or win or lose—would get the invitation, especially if it could be publicly justified in any way other than blatant box-office considerations.

Oklahoma and Oklahoma A&M, which had beaten Drake in a Western elimination game, were set to meet in Oklahoma City to determine one representative in the San Francisco field, and Texas (19-4) also was locked in to join Utah State.

*   *   *

Scribes around the country were shaking their heads about this sudden proliferation of post-season tournaments, pointing out that two older events remained in play—the National Intercollegiate tournament at Kansas City, which James Naismith had started in 1937 for smaller schools, and the AAU national tournament. Plus, some noted that a forerunner of the Kansas City tournament was played in 1922 in Indianapolis. Called the National Intercollegiate Basketball Tournament, its field was lackluster—Mercer, Grove City (Pa.), Wabash, Illinois Wesleyan, Kalamazoo College, and Pacific Coast Conference champion Idaho. The Moscow, Idaho, school had won the PCC with a 7-0 record, but lost in the tournament quarterfinals to Kalamazoo. Wabash beat Kalamazoo in the title game.

The AAU tournament in Denver mainly was for company-sponsored teams made up of former college players, but college teams routinely were among the entrants. LIU had made several appearances. In 1939, the huge AAU field included ten college teams, mostly from smaller teachers schools, and the favorites to win the championship were the hometown Denver Nuggets.

Tuesday, March 14

PRAGUE—Headlines around the world scream: With Germany pulling the strings, Slovakia officially secedes from Czechoslovakia. It's ominous because it seems a next step in the continuing shredding of the Versailles Treaty, and German troops are poised to invade, if Hitler deems it necessary.

The first two games in the PCC championship series in Eugene were nearly sold out, but Oregon officials begged fans who had reserved tickets before the series was pushed back to reconfirm their intentions by mail or phone, or the tickets would be released. That created chaos at the ticket office as the series approached, and the biggest fear was that fans would show up to pick up and to pay for tickets, discover they had been reallocated, and throw fits.

Meanwhile, the Webfoots prepared for the Golden Bears.

"I've only seen California play in one game," Howard Hobson said after Oregon's practice. "But judging from that one game, we have a better club and should win it if we play up to par."

Bunn finally backed off his ridiculous position and agreed that the winner of the PCC series would get the district's berth in the NCAA tournament—if it wanted it. By then, all indications were that both teams did. Finally, the Webfoots were certain that they wouldn't be a league championship team bypassed for the series loser or for a "rested" PCC team.

The division-clinching results in Seattle represented the first step of the Webfoots' championship run.

The second step was the belated confirmation that they would be in the NCAA tournament if they beat California.

They had their fate in their own hands.

Meanwhile, the NCAA's Eastern field was all set. Carnegie Tech won on the final night to pull into a tie with Georgetown in the Eastern Intercollegiate Conference, but neither school was inclined to continue to play beyond the regular season. Dartmouth, which won the Eastern Intercollegiate Basketball League with a 10-2 record, one game ahead of Columbia, was of like mind.

So in Philadelphia, Ohio State was going to meet Wake Forest (18-5), which had won the 15-team Southern Conference's regular-season title, besting such teams as Maryland, North Carolina State, Duke, North Carolina, Virginia Tech, and South Carolina before losing to eventual surprise league tournament champion Clemson in the second round of the tournament in Raleigh.

In the second game in Philadelphia, Villanova (19-4) was matched with fellow independent Brown (16-3). Villanova would be playing in its hometown, but the Wildcats later said they were disappointed not to be getting a post-season trip to New York and a chance to follow up on their victory over CCNY. Although the references after that game in the Garden seemed to indicate the Wildcats were headed for the NCAA tournament, and perhaps even that school officials considered it a commitment, the players had hoped for something different. "We didn't see how they could pass us up, but they did," Wildcats guard Mike Lazorchak said later. "When we heard we were going to the NCAA tournament, we didn't think too much about it."

One of the reasons Wake Forest got the berth despite its league tournament loss was the high regard for the Demon Deacons' coach, whose résumé was similar to Hobson's. Murray Greason earned 12 letters in football, basketball, and baseball at Wake Forest from 1922 to 1926, and he was in his fifth season of coaching at his alma mater.

* * *

Once they were in Manhattan, the New Mexico Aggies—LIU's quarterfinal opponents in the national invitation tournament— willingly played the hicks from the Wild West, dressing the part in their first meeting with New York scribes. In his "Sports of the Times" column in the *Times*, John Kieran described the wardrobe of the boys from Las Cruces: "Ten-gallon hats, cowboy boots, fawn-colored corduroy pants, crimson jackets and cerise shirts! What a sight!" Wearing those outfits and holding basketballs, the five starters appeared in a *Times* picture. Several other New York writers had fun writing about the Aggies, making them sound as if they had just come off the ranches and farms, or right out of Zane Grey novels. They pointed out that the star of the team was 27-year-old Francisco "Kiko" Martinez, who played for Mexico's bronze-medal team at the 1936 Summer Games in Berlin.

Martinez explained that his nickname really was "Quico" and that he lived on the U.S.-Mexico border. "I can jump either way in a hurry," he said. "I jumped the other way just for the fun of going to Berlin."

Those Berlin Olympics weren't much of an advertisement for the sport in Europe, considering the games were played outside on tennis courts and rains turned the championship game into a muddy mess. The U.S. beat Canada 19-8 in that gold-medal game, while Martinez and Mexico knocked off Poland 26-12 to take the bronze. The National Association of Basketball Coaches pooled contributions to send Dr. James Naismith to the Games, and he had presented the medals.

In New York, young Associated Press sportswriter Drew Middleton quoted Martinez as saying of the city: "No grass, eet tightens up the legs to walk on thees stone." And this about Long Island U.: "All basketball teams can be beaten. Thees Blackbirds can be licked, too. You see."

Winners of the seven-team Border Intercollegiate Athletic Association for the third consecutive season, the Aggies scored an eye-popping 64 points a game, with Martinez averaging 14.3.

Another AP story setting up the national invitation tournament took what by then was becoming a familiar approach, noting the first round included "four teams who thought so much of the little tournament sponsored by the New York Basketball Writers association that they chose to play in it rather than in national tourneys of more impressive size." That seemed to recognize that the NCAA tournament involved more than the eight teams in the Eastern and Western championships.

*　*　*

Finishing up the three-game mini-tournament in Oklahoma City to determine the District 5 spot in the four-team San Francisco field, the Oklahoma Sooners played an uncharacteristic slowdown game and knocked off Oklahoma A&M 30-21. The Sooners were only 11-8 overall, but the Big Six co-champs earned their advancement, after co-champ Missouri declined the invitation to join the Sooners in the play-in field. So it was down to Oregon or California for the fourth berth in the West.

Either way, the PCC was going to be sending a "tall" team to the Western regional. The Bears' (official) average height in the starting lineup actually was slightly higher than that of the Webfoots, with California having only one starter, Walt Bickerton, under 6 feet. The other Bears' starters ranged from Ivor Thomas, at 6-1, to Bill Ogilvie, at 6-6.

Wednesday, March 15

PRAGUE—The next shoe falls. On the same day Germany declares Bohemia and Moravia to be protectorates under its control, essentially annexing them, German troops march into Czechoslovakia—at least what had been considered Czechoslovakia—and into Prague. Many residents of the historic capital city greet the German soldiers with the disdainful European "*Pfui*" taunt. It accomplishes about as much as had appeasement.

LONDON—A shaken Neville Chamberlain tells the House of Commons that he "regrets" Germany's moves. He adds, "Hitherto Germany has only incorporated into the Reich people of German race, but now they are taking military occupation of places where there are people with whom they have no racial relation." He is insistent he will not give up trying to maintain peace through agreements.

WASHINGTON—On the House floor, Rep. George Bender (D-Ohio) is one of the first to speak up on the latest developments, saying: "We are now living in a world gone mad. Here in America, it is our duty to do everything we can to defend the principles for which Czechoslovakia has been destroyed." At a press conference, Secretary of State Sumner Welles says he had conferred with President Roosevelt about the events in Europe, but adds the situation is fluid and thus the administration wouldn't yet comment on the developments or on Chamberlain's remarks in London.

As expected, and as the sponsoring Metropolitan Basketball Writers had hoped, the local clubs took care of business in the national invitation tournament's first two games, with a crowd of 14,443 watching the doubleheader in the Garden. LIU beat New Mexico A&M 52-45 and St. John's routed overmatched Roanoke 71-47, advancing the winners to the semifinals the next week.

In the opener, LIU raised concerns about whether Clair Bee's club would be affected by the loss of center Myron Sewitch, who had suffered an injured hand in the next-to-last regular-season game. He sat out the semifinal and was hoping to at least get in the championship game. Irv Torgoff had 14 points and guard John Bromberg pitched in with 13 for the Blackbirds. But the Aggies, shocking the New York fans with their onslaught of successful *one-handed* shots from long range, stayed with the Blackbirds until the final five minutes before running out of gas as Bee's more frequent substitution, deeper roster, and his instructions to make sure that one guard always was hanging back to stymie fast breaks, paid off. One of the keys to the win was containing Kiko Martinez, who had only eight points for the Aggies. Arthur Daley said the game "had the crowd in ecstasies of delight for its entire duration." The Aggies felt something else—stinging eyes and sore throats. By the late stages, they were asking the referees if something couldn't be done to thin out the cigarette smoke in the Garden. And, of course, there wasn't.

In the second game, Bill Lloyd led St. John's to the easy win over over-hyped Roanoke, breaking the Garden scoring record with 31 points. The fans that stayed through both games at the smoky Garden left chortling about how Joe Lapchick's Redmen had run up 71 points, and eagerly looked forward to their semifinal matchup against the undefeated Loyola Ramblers, the invaders from Chicago.

* * *

During the regular season, California had beaten Bradley Tech and Stanford, the teams that accounted for two of the three Oregon losses on the December barnstorming swing. But with the Webfoots playing at home and having the experience of playing in the PCC title series the year before, Oregon was favored going into the championship series. The issue of where the game was played also involved the officiating, since Northern Division officials would be used. Economy and travel convenience outweighed all else. "It will be the same as we have had all season," said California coach Nibs Price. "The interpretation of the rules in the Southern Division has been different in nearly every game."

Another of the advantages to having the home court was that the Oregon "Rally Squad" was renowned for getting the crowd going. Made up of nine men and six women wearing trademark white sweaters with lemon-yellow O's on them, the squad members caught the attention of visiting teams, too, with their effervescence and Yell King Paul Cushing's innovative gymnastics-style acrobatics after the cheers. Previously, Yell Kings were supposed to holler through megaphones or cupped hands and then turn and watch the game. The squad was pulling for the Webfoots to win and advance to the Western championships and to the national title game, of course, but there never was any serious consideration to the Rally Squad making the trips, too.

The Oregon athletic department put 1,600 general admission tickets on sale for each of the two California games guaranteed to be played. Tickets were 85 cents for the corner bleachers on the main floor and $1.10 for the center bleachers.

15.

Spotlights

Thursday, March 16

PRAGUE—German Foreign Minister Joachim von Ribbentrop delivers a radio broadcast of an official Hitler proclamation that advances his justification for sending his troops into Czechoslovakia. It is both ominous and delusional, citing "the law of self-survival that the German Reich is determined to intervene decisively again to erect the foundations of reasonable central European order." The entire translated proclamation runs in many U.S. newspapers, with stories also summarizing it, so Hitler dominates the news from coast to coast.

The California Golden Bears traveled on the Southern Pacific's 16-hour overnight run from San Francisco to Eugene, arriving at 9 on game-day morning and heading to McArthur Court to stretch their legs and try to get a feel for an arena none of them ever had seen before. Oregon's most decisive advantage in the series would be in the first game. With all three, if necessary, ticketed for Eugene, an opening-game loss wouldn't be complete disaster for the Webfoots. But it would be a major lost opportunity.

"We were two of the tallest college teams and for the first time all season, neither of us would have a size advantage over our opponent," noted John Dick. "We both preferred up-tempo, fast-break basketball, so slowdowns and stalling would not be a factor." He also said the Webfoots understood that if they won the series, they "faced an overnight 19-hour train ride to San Francisco for the first game of the Western regional on Monday, March 20, so it was important to close out the PCC championship in two games. If we could do this, we would only have to win four games in six nights instead of five in six nights to qualify for the final game in Evanston and you'd get a little rest around your train ride to San Francisco."

* * *

Members of the Metropolitan Basketball Writers Association were genial hosts at a luncheon honoring the teams that had played at Madison Square Garden the night before. LIU players Dan Kaplowitz and George Newman were a hit with their performance of "On a Puerto Rican Night," the song they wrote on the team's September seven-game pre-season tour of Puerto Rico.

New Mexico A&M and Roanoke seemed to have made travel plans based on the assumption—or at least the hope—that they'd win their quarterfinal games. A "consolation" game matching the two teams was added to the March 20 session, making it a triple-header. It also gave the scribes more material during the delay between the quarterfinals and semifinals. The boys in the cowboy hats still were going to be on the town, raising hell!

Joseph M. Sheehan's *Times* story about the day's events closed with a reminder: "With a lull here over the weekend, the Eastern spotlight shifts to Philadelphia, where the NCAA sectional play-offs get underway at Penn's Palestra."

* * *

Suddenly, it seemed possible that Howard Hobson and Clair Bee might soon be coaching against one another in the PCC.

In the wake of the resignation of longtime coach Pierce "Caddy" Works, UCLA officials let it be known that they were tired of the Bruins being the doormat in the PCC's Southern Division. The *Los Angeles Times* reported that they were "considering" the LIU coach for the opening.

The report was ignored in New York.

* * *

In Eugene, with The Igloo overflowing and tension high for the opening game of the PCC series against California, the Webfoots left their locker room in the basement and headed up the stairs that led to the street level and the court. Before passing through the concourse to get to the floor, they had a stop to make. They waited as Bobby Anet went to a back door, leading to the baseball field. He opened it, letting in three familiar kids whom the Webfoots had come to consider their good luck charms. In January, knowing the approximate pre-game timing and the path the Webfoots took to go to the floor, the three boys had knocked on the back door when

Howard Hobson, a former Webfoots player and captain himself, was in his fourth season as the head coach at his alma mater in 1938–39.

Bobby Anet, the Webfoots' pacesetter, emotional leader, and team captain, graces the cover of the makeshift press guide. Although they officially were the Webfoots, the alternative nickname was on the verge of coming into vogue.

DUCK DOPE
ALL THE DOPE THAT'S FIT TO PEDDLE

1938-39 BASKETBALL SEASON
UNIVERSITY OF OREGON

Forward Laddie Gale, the Webfoots' leading scorer from tiny Oakridge, Oregon, displays his unique ability to palm the laced ball of the era at a practice. Laddie Gale & Dale Lasselle (not-pictured), 1938–39, University Photographic Collection, UA_ATHB-SKTF0017, Special Collections & University Archives, University of Oregon Libraries, Eugene, Oregon.

Center Slim Wintermute was listed at 6-foot-8. That wasn't true. He was at least an inch taller. Hobson called him the best defensive center the coach had ever seen, and he also was able to keep up with the Webfoots' fast-paced offensive approach.

Guard Wally Johansen, Bobby Anet's running mate and teammate since their childhoods together in Astoria, Oregon, already was studying law.

Forward John Dick, from The Dalles, became the only non-senior in the Webfoots' starting lineup early in the season and took advantage of the opportunity.

The Webfoots had a strict dress code for road trips. Here, Bobby Anet, John Dick, Slim Winter-mute, and Wally Johansen wave good-bye as the Southern Pacific train leaves Eugene and heads for San Francisco and the Western championships. They wouldn't return to Eugene for nearly two weeks. Tall Firs, 1939, University Photographic Collection, UA_REF_3, UA_ATHBSKTF0035, Special Collections & University Archives, University of Oregon Libraries, Eugene, Oregon.

Against Ohio State in the first-ever championship game, Webfoot John Dick (18)—the game's leading scorer—defends against a Buckeye at the hoop. Laddie Gale (28) and Bobby Anet, right, look on. AP/Wide World Photo.

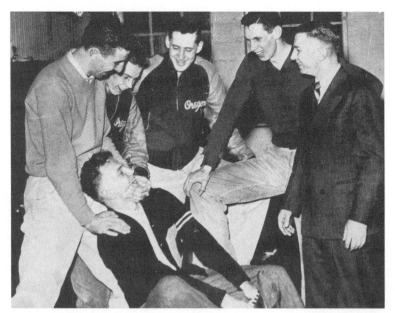

Commemorating the Pacific Coast Conference championship, and going to press before NCAA play began, the alumni magazine *Old Oregon* featured the Webfoots on its March 1939 cover. Slim Wintermute, Wally Johansen, John Dick, Laddie Gale, and Howard Hobson get a laugh out of the boys picking on Bobby Anet. Courtesy of *Oregon Quarterly*.

Between beaming teammates Wally Johansen and Laddie Gale, captain Bobby Anet clings to the broken championship trophy in the locker room after the title game.

Years later, the players would remember their welcome back to Eugene, and the image of one fan climbing the light pole to get a better view stuck with them, too. Home from championship game at railroad station, 1939, University Photographic Collection, UA_ATHBSKTF0001, Special Collections & University Archives, University of Oregon Libraries, Eugene, Oregon.

The nattily attired 11-man traveling roster poses with the championship hardware. Back row: Bob Hardy, Red McNeeley, manager Jay Langston, Ford Mullen, Matt Pavalunas, trainer Bob Officer, Ted Sarpola, Earl Sandness. Front row: Wally Johansen, Slim Wintermute, Bobby Anet, Coach Howard Hobson, Laddie Gale, John Dick. 1939 basketball national champions, 1939, University Photographic Collection, UA_ATHBSKTF0036, Special Collections & University Archives, University of Oregon Libraries, Eugene, Oregon.

Clair Bee's 1938–39 Long Island University Blackbirds in a pre-season team photo. Back row, standing: Joe Shelly, Ken Ehlers, George Newman, Irv Torgoff, Ossie Schectman, Irving Zeitlin. Middle row, seated: Dan Kaplowitz, Myron Sewitch, Arthur Hillhouse, Henry Lagerenberg, John Bromberg. The three players in front (two unidentified) were reserves at the start of the season, but one of them—sophomore Si Lobello, holding the ball—was playing by the end of the year. At the semester break, Hillhouse graduated and left the squad, and William "Dolly" King joined the team.

the team was coming up the stairs. It was a long shot, but Anet had opened the door and heard the kids say they didn't have any money and thus couldn't afford to pay their way in. They beseeched the players to help them see the game. The kids rushed in, the Webfoots won that night, and after that, Anet let them in every game.

It worked again in Game 1. The Webfoots got the tone-setting victory over the Bears, 54-49. The 1919 championship team had been the last Oregon squad to defeat California—the teams didn't meet in the regular-season play of split divisions—so scribes compliantly blew up the presence of the Webfoots of yore into an inspirational move of genius.

Oregon was down by one point late in the first half, but Wally Johansen lobbed in a 30-footer with 10 seconds left to put the Webfoots up 20-19 at the break. After coming back from the locker room, the Webfoots surged into a 41-25 advantage a little over eight minutes into the second half. Anet and Johansen dashed and slashed through the Bears, setting a frantic pace and then finding open teammates. "We got our fast break rolling and the Bears were unable to keep pace," Dick recalled. "But the Bears kept battling. We may have rested on our oars a bit and they slowly closed the gap. The 16-point gap was too much for them to overcome, however."

Laddie Gale, often working from the low post, finished with 18 points. "We got the ball to Laddie, because for some reason they didn't double team him," Dick said. "He was by far the best post player I had ever seen, and I knew that from experience because I had to guard him at practice."

Slim Wintermute was the other Webfoot in double figures, with 11, and Oregon became the first team all season to run up more than 50 points on the Golden Bears.

The *Oregonian*'s L. H. Gregory again evaluated the officiating, saying referees Emil Piluso and Frank Heniges "did a beautiful job. . . . There were only 23 personal fouls in the lively 40 minutes of play. . . . They achieved that nice balance where they kept the game under control, yet let the players go, and the spectators saw lots of fiery action."

The diminutive Piluso was one of the best-known referees on the West Coast, with a demonstrative style that some considered showboating. Yet he was widely respected. The regional nature of the officiating pools, though, created problems of perception, and in this case, Piluso was from Portland and also worked as assistant manager of the Multnomah Athletic Club, and his partner, Heniges, worked at the Hop Gold Brewery in Vancouver, Washington, across the river from Portland. At one point during that season, Buck Buckwach of the *Oregon Daily Emerald* caught up with Piluso and Heniges after a game and asked about their reactions to the bitter criticism from fans. "As long as they don't boo the figures off our paychecks, we won't care," Piluso said. He also noted: "A person might know the rules and regulations backward and forward, but when a whistle is put into his mouth, still be a flop. You just have to have it."[1]

Hobson never seemed to be as concerned about the work of the referees as were the scribes who covered his team, and he focused on the Webfoots' continued improvement. "We played our best ball in the second half, but we believe we can play better ball than we showed tonight," he said. "California has a fine ballclub, one that stays going and one that the opponent can never coast with."

That could be filed under the heading of: *Don't rile up your opponents . . .*

Oregon athletics head Anse Cornell threw a party at his house after the game and invited the California athletic department delegation, too. Nibs Price showed up and needled Hobson. "Listen, we'll stop those big horses of yours tomorrow night," he declared. "Wait and see!"

Hobson just smiled.

The Webfoots were within one win of making the first NCAA tournament.

Friday, March 17

BIRMINGHAM, England—Drawing cheers for his belated defiance, Neville Chamberlain declares that Hitler again broke a promise made at Munich to not attempt to add more territory to the Reich, and poses the question that so many believe he should have been asking himself earlier: *How can anyone trust a word Hitler says?* The prime minister says that Great Britain will resist "to the utmost of its power" any German threat to its freedom. Yet he also tries to rationalize his previous appeasement.

---

1. Clearly, Piluso was one of the forerunners of such later famous officials as Irv Brown, who worked several Final Fours and was renowned as the best of his craft, yet still claims to have never read the rulebook; and the NBA's Earl Strom, always a showman and always respected.

"I have never denied that the terms I was able to secure at Munich were not the terms I would have desired," he says. "But I was dealing with a problem that had existed ever since the Treaty of Versailles—a situation that ought to have been settled long ago. After all, the first objective of my visit was achieved. The peace of Europe was saved and if it had not been for those visits hundreds of thousands of families would now be in mourning for the flower of Europe's manhood."

St. John's coach Joe Lapchick, whose pro career had ended only a couple of years earlier, already was getting tired of being asked about Loyola's giant center, Mike Novak. The Rambler star was 6-9 and, unlike the Webfoots' Slim Wintermute, willing to admit to being at least that tall. After Loyola's regular-season victory over CCNY, losing coach Nat Holman had said the only way to score on the Ramblers was to get down the floor with the ball before Novak could get back and get set under the basket. Otherwise, he maneuvered under his own basket, and then often leaped and swatted away shots as they were about to drop into the hoop. But after watching the Ramblers again at a practice, the writers in attendance were convinced that there was more to this team than Novak, who continued to be touted as the sport's pre-eminent "goaltender."

Meanwhile, Lapchick shrugged off any suggestions that his Redmen had looked so good against Roanoke, they had assumed the favorite's role in the tournament. That also might have been the scribes' attempt to build interest in the semifinals, too.

* * *

In Philadelphia, the Ohio State Buckeyes trailed 25-19 at halftime in their Eastern championships semifinal against Wake Forest. The Buckeyes shook their heads, saying they didn't see this many one-handed shots in the Big Ten and that Wake Forest's Jim Waller was a wizard. Waller, a senior forward who also was Wake Forest's student-body president, was only 5-11, but always seemed to manage to get his left-handed hook shot over larger men in traffic. He had led the Southern League in scoring for three straight seasons, and the Buckeyes got a crash course in how he pulled it off. His other big shot was a two-handed, underhanded sweep-type shot, and one of the tricks was that he often was fouled when he lifted his arms into those of the defender. Against the Buckeyes, he had 14 points with 11 minutes left, but drew his fourth foul and was done for the night. Ohio State ran off seven consecutive points, gained the lead, and won 64-52. Despite their slow start, the Buckeyes had just shattered by 11 the record for most points by one team in the Palestra, and Dick Baker's 25 points for Ohio State also was an arena record.

The second game was horrible, with Villanova beating inept Brown 42-30. Brown had only seven points in the first half, and it would have been even more embarrassing if Villanova hadn't let up in the final minutes, looking ahead to the Eastern title game the next night. Guard John Krutulis had 14 points for Villanova, and he later joked that he made three hook shots from the corner that exasperated his coach, Al Severance. "I think he covered his eyes on every one, but it was one of those nights where everything was going in," he said. Krutulis, from North Braddock, Pennsylvania, near Pittsburgh, was 27 years old and was known as "Pappy" to his teammates. He had worked in a steel mill and in the Chrysler factory and also held other jobs until Villanova football coach Harry Stuhldreher, the former Four Horseman quarterback at Notre Dame, visited him and said he was in the area recruiting and had agreed to look up Krutulis on behalf of Severance. "Who could say no to one of the Four Horsemen?" Krutulis said. "Not me." And that led him to college—and the starring role in the first Eastern championships. (Soon after landing Krutulis for the basketball program, Stuhldreher left Villanova to become coach at the University of Wisconsin.)

At the Palestra, the disappointing part of the evening was the attendance—announced as only 3,500, not even half filling the seats in the 12-year-old arena on the University of Pennsylvania campus.

Executives of the National Association of Basketball Coaches, on the hook for any losses, started to sweat. And if the truth be told, more of them probably turned into fans of the California Golden Bears, hoping they could come back and win Game 2 of the PCC series that night, and then Game 3, to give the NCAA tournament a box-office draw in the Western championships in San Francisco early the next week.

16.

Moving On

Friday, March 17

WASHINGTON—Without getting into specifics, President Roosevelt says that the latest events in Europe again prove the need for Congress to revise the Neutrality Acts. Later in the day, Sumner Welles, making it clear he is speaking for Roosevelt after a careful assessment of the situation, condemns Germany's moves. Welles calls the takeover and invasion of Czechoslovakia "wanton lawlessness and arbitrary force threatening world peace and the very structure of modern civilization."

When California's Bill Ogilvie drove under and past the basket, then stepped out and made a short shot nearly six minutes into the first half, the Golden Bears led the slow-starting Webfoots 9-3 in Game 2.

The crowd of 6,500 was a school record and that might even have been understated to keep the fire department happy. But the sold-out, overflowing Igloo was eerily quiet.

The gloomiest of the Oregon fans already were saying, well, the bright side was that maybe the host team's share of the gate receipts for the third game the next night would help out the athletics board and the programs.

Then John Dick and Slim Wintermute hit consecutive buckets from the key to get the Webfoots going, and with nine minutes left in the half, another Dick one-hander broke a 12-12 tie and put Oregon up for good. It was no runaway, since the Webfoots led only 25-23 at the half, and the Webfoots' lead peaked at only eight points midway through the second.

After the Golden Bears fought back to within 43-41 with a little over six minutes remaining, Dick returned to the lineup from a rare two-minute respite and scored the next six Oregon points, the first off a nice feed from Laddie Gale and all of them off physical battles inside. The Webfoots went on to claim the 53-47 victory that secured the two-game sweep and the school's first league championship since the ironman squad of 1919.

They pulled it off on a night when the Webfoots' biggest star, Gale, didn't have a basket.

Nibs Price had tried to confuse the Webfoots with alternating man-to-man and zone defenses, and either way the goal was to shut down Gale. In fact, L. H. Gregory said Gale's big Game 1 "caused him to be guarded like a prisoner of war" in Game 2. California captain Bob Chalmers had the primary responsibility, but he had a lot of help. In one way, it worked: Gale made six free throws and nothing else. But the focus on him came with a price, as both Dick and Wintermute had 16 points, and both credited the unselfish adjustments from the Webfoots' star player and leading scorer. "In the second game, they did double-team [Gale]," Dick said. "But Laddie didn't complain or force shots. He just kicked it out to the open man. We just wanted to get the ball in the hole and didn't care who put it there."

The team in green had won on St. Patrick's Day.

Shaking hands with Howard Hobson when the game ended, Price brought up his promise to slow down Oregon's big men. "I told you, we stopped 'em," the California coach said. "But I didn't say anything about those little so-and-sos in your backcourt. Their drive killed us."

Bobby Anet was walking around with bandages on his feet not long after the game because, as often happened with the speedy guard, the soles of his basketball shoes had virtually disintegrated. He had scored only four points, but again hit the accelerator in the crucial moments, and his Astoria running mate, Wally Johansen, had 11 important points, including three of his trademark two-hand set shots from long range.

The post-game ceremony saluted the Webfoots as league champions, but it was more geared to honoring the seniors—Gale, Wintermute, Johansen, Anet, and Bob Hardy—who had just played their final collegiate game in McArthur Court. The fact that the Webfoots had just won the league title was a bonus. Dean Walker, coach of the 1919 team, lauded them as champions during the ceremony, and he clearly meant it to go beyond the scoreboard. Hardy had transferred in after his sophomore season at Southern Oregon, but it was pointed out that the Webfoots had gone 41-16 in conference games during the three varsity seasons of the other four seniors, and they never had lost a four-game Northern Division season series. Most important given the bitterness of the intrastate rivalry, they had gone 10-2 against the Oregon State Beavers in their varsity careers as Webfoots.

Although their home-court careers were over, they had more basketball to play.

When speaking with the scribes a little later, Price saluted the Webfoots, too. "Greatest basketball team we ever played," he said. "If Southern California instead of us had won the right to this playoff, I don't see how the shorter Trojans would have a chance against the height of these Oregons."

John Dick reflected: "Coming from a coach who'd spent the three previous years struggling to beat the great Hank Luisetti-led Stanford teams, that was high praise indeed. These were two exciting, crowd-pleasing games between two evenly matched teams. The difference? I thought we had an edge in speed and quickness across the board and our big men may have played taller than their advertised heights."

Hobson tried to return the praise. "I've said all season that Bradley Tech, which beat us in the east, was the best team we met," the Webfoots coach said. "I take that back. California gave us by far the most trouble. Nibs has a wonderful basketball team, and they were a great pair of games."

The Oregon coach, in fact, seemed more relieved than ecstatic. "Well, we got what we went after," he said. "It was a tough season and the fellows played fine ball. We aren't through yet."

The *Register-Guard*'s Dick Strite made several references during the series to the California manager's comment about Oregon not wanting to play the series at all. He sniped in his game story that the Webfoots now were "looking for bigger game besides the rather tattered Golden Bears." Strite also gave Dick credit for playing the "most brilliant game of his career."

Even before the final buzzer, U of O athletic officials were beginning to firm up travel plans for the trip down to San Francisco for the Western championships, beginning three nights later. The official invitation came in a wire from John Bunn that arrived shortly after the game ended.

Attention was divided in Oregon because the state high school tournament, a popular event, was going on in Salem, and the Salem Vikings and Medford Pearpickers won that night in the semifinals to advance to the championship game the next night. (Eventually, the Pearpickers would become the Medford Black Tornado, officially adopting another L. H. Gregory–coined nickname.) At least there wouldn't be a Game 3 in the PCC series to steal the state tournament's final-night thunder.

17.

Suitcase Test

Saturday, March 18

BERLIN—German officials profess to be shocked and dismayed over the U.S. treasury department's announcement of an imposition of 25 percent duties on German goods, effectively shutting off the American market to products from the Third Reich. The German ambassador to London, Dr. Herbert von Dirksen, is recalled to Berlin.

HONG KONG—U.S. officials are upset after Japanese bombing of targets in central and northwest China destroys a hospital run by American missionaries and an American-maintained refugee camp. No Americans are killed, but both facilities had been clearly marked with U.S. flags. A little over a year since what will become known as the Rape of Nanking, it's another instance of barbaric Japanese conduct in the war.

TAMPA—Rookie outfielder Ted Williams, coming off a huge 1938 season with Minneapolis of the American Association, is likely to be installed in right field for the Boston Red Sox when the 1939 season begins. "Just think," he says at spring training, "I'm going to see cities like New York and Chicago. That'll be an education in itself, even if I wasn't making money. Hell, a fellow always can pick up a dollar."

John Bunn supervised a drawing procedure in the Bay Area and announced Monday's semifinal pairings for the Western championships: Utah State would play Oklahoma in the first game at 8 p.m., with the Webfoots meeting Texas at 9:15. An International News Service dispatch on the pairings declared: "Experts predicted that the Webfoots loom almost certain winners unless the University of Texas proves a surprise. Advance reports on Utah State, Rocky

Mountain representatives, and Oklahoma, Big Six co-champions, the other two teams in the tournament, indicate they have neither the height nor the speed to cope with Oregon."

*   *   *

Ohio State manhandled hometown favorite Villanova 53-36 in the Eastern championship game in Philadelphia, again in front of a small crowd. Dick Baker's Palestra individual scoring record lasted only 24 hours, with teammate Jimmy Hull pouring through 28 against the Wildcats. He outscored Villanova by himself in the first half, getting 15 points to the Philadelphia boys' 10. With the Buckeyes up by 20 in the second half, Harold Olsen emptied his bench. By then, Hull was out of the game, anyway. He later recalled that he played 28 minutes before suffering a sprained right ankle and being carried off the floor. John Krutulis came back to earth for the Wildcats, scoring only five points, and Paul Nugent led Villanova with 16.

Olsen addressed the Buckeyes after the game and surprised them by saying, "Gentlemen, this is a little embarrassing to me."

OSU center John Schick was puzzled. "What do you mean, embarrassing?" he asked. "We just won you an Eastern championship of the United States."

"Well, gentlemen," Olsen responded, "I'm the chairman of the tournament committee and here my ballclub wins."

With an eight-day break until the title game, the Buckeyes at least could go home to Columbus for a few days.

The four teams preparing to play in the Western championships at San Francisco knew that the winner from among them would face Ohio State in the title game. Also, Oregon representatives already were reminding one another that California and Washington, the teams the Webfoots had just beaten twice apiece, both had beaten Ohio State twice in December.

*   *   *

With townspeople and students showing up to send them off, the Webfoots boarded the train for the overnight trip to San Francisco. If they didn't win the Western championships on Treasure Island, they would be gone from Eugene only a few days. But if they won twice, they would head directly across country, to Chicago for the national championship game.

Slim Wintermute's mother, Ivie, a second mother to many of his teammates, had packed the big center's suitcase for him. When Slim checked it out, he noticed she had packed only three shirts. "That won't be enough to take me all the way to Chicago and back," he told his mother.

She threw in more clothes.

The 11-man traveling squad was the same as for all the conference road games. The boys all wore coats and ties and again, as was their pattern, looked like dapper businessmen on the train. Bobby Anet, Wally Johansen, John Dick, and Wintermute stood outside the last car and waved to the crowd as the train departed.

*   *   *

In Denver, the biggest tournament of all, the week-long AAU tournament, ended with a crowd of 7,000 watching the championship game in the downtown municipal arena. The Denver Nuggets knocked off the Phillips 66 Oilers of Oklahoma 25-22 to win the title in a slow, chess-match type of a contest that nonetheless seemed to thrill those in attendance. The players in many cases were pseudo- or semi-professionals recruited for company teams. The Nuggets, a first-year operation, had been founded to pick up the pieces and many of the players after the Safeway grocery store dropped sponsorship of the local powerhouse team. The management retained and recruited players with the lure of being able to continue to play basketball, plus make a living wage in jobs the Chamber of Commerce helped line up with Denver companies, including the Public Service power company, the Brown Palace Hotel, and car dealers. The Nuggets' star was player-coach "Jumping" Jack McCracken, who had played under coach Hank Iba at Northwest Missouri State Teachers College.

Considering the shaky state of professional basketball, AAU ball was a far more realistic and even desirable post-collegiate option for most of the nation's best players. There had been several attempts to get pro leagues off the ground and the best-known in 1939 was the National Basketball League, a fledgling Midwest-based operation that for the most part then still was made up of corporate-sponsored teams, such as the powerhouse Akron Firestone Non-Skids. Although some players, including Joe Lapchick, had made decent money playing for barnstorming teams or short-lived pro operations in the past, even the best players in the college game realized they couldn't count on making a living in the sport and that the AAU program, with jobs provided, at least could allow them to continue to play for a while.

The way some folks were talking in Eugene, there seemed a chance that some of the Webfoots might be playing for an Oregon-based team in the AAU tournament in 1940. Eugene Lumber Sales already had announced that it hoped to sponsor an AAU team the next season, taking advantage of the hoop-mania the Webfoots were generating. The company said it hoped to land the five Web-foot seniors as the core of the AAU roster. With Bob Hardy, the trick likely would be convincing him he could play basketball for a while in the winter before reporting to a pro baseball organization's spring training.

Sunday, March 19

BERLIN—After touring portions of his newly acquired territories, including Prague, Hitler returns to the German capital and is hailed as a hero who, without his troops firing a shot, added 10 million subjects and considerable mineral and other resources to the Reich. Newspapers around the world are running maps of Germany and its empire almost daily, attempting to keep up with the changes, both in terms of boundaries and resources. The question most are asking, of course, is: *What's next?*

Following his team's arrival in San Francisco, Howard Hobson decided not to hold a practice and to give the Webfoots another day off. One of the reasons was that the Golden Gate International Exposition Coliseum on Treasure Island wouldn't be available to the teams until Monday, game day, because of the other events taking place at the world's fair. So any Sunday workout would have been in another gym. The other three teams in the field did that, and also scheduled game-morning workouts in the arena so they could familiarize themselves with the pavilion.

Hobson also passed on that chance to have the boys on the pavilion floor on Monday morning. "I figure the boys have played on enough floors and thrown at enough baskets in games this season from Eugene to Madison Square Garden and back not to need a workout," the Webfoots coach said.

Hoping to get a respectable crowd into the 12,000-seat arena, organizers announced that they would price one-third of the seats at only 25 cents apiece. Yes, for two bits, fans could see two games involving at least two of the nation's top teams—Oregon and Texas, unfortunately matched in the first round. It was pointed out that Colorado had won Utah State's league and turned down the bid, but the consensus was that the Buffaloes, playing in a league of Rocky Mountain–region teams, were a notch below Texas and Oregon, anyway. But that always was going to remain an unanswered question. Utah State was making its second appearance in the Bay Area of the season: the Aggies also had lost to California in Berkeley as part of a barnstorming tour.

The Longhorns and Webfoots both were at the Hotel Whitcomb on Market Street in downtown San Francisco, and a nodding familiarity developed among the players. Another reason for Hobson passing on scheduling a practice either on the day before or on the morning of the game was that the Oregon coach realized his players could get exercise as tourists and walk up and down Market Street or beyond. The Longhorns were impossible to miss because they made sure to wear the cowboy boots and cowboy hats that fans presented them before they left Austin. They looked a little like the New Mexico A&M Aggies, still on the town in New York as the national invitation tournament continued. L. H. Gregory, who had made the trip to San Francisco, joked in his *Oregonian* story that the Longhorns' tallest player was only 6-foot-4, and that if Slim Wintermute donned a cowboy hat and boots, he'd look like the Statue of Liberty.

Like Oregon, Texas had an alumnus as its coach, and the Longhorns' Jack Gray—a former football and basketball star—had been even more successful as a player than Hobson. Less than five years earlier, in the fall of '34, Gray, who played left end, had recovered a fumble that set up the game-winning touchdown for Texas in the Longhorns' stunning 7-6 upset of powerhouse Notre Dame. It was the biggest football victory in school history up to that point and built momentum for the Longhorns' program. Playing for the basketball team, he was another of the pioneers of the one-handed "push" shot, and in 1935, he was UT's first basketball All-American. Two years later, he was the Longhorns' head coach, at age 25. So as he prepared the Texas squad for its first NCAA tournament game, he still was only 27 and could pass for a player in the Whitcomb lobby. Scribes routinely called him the "Kid Coach."

The Webfoots also got another ringing endorsement from California's Nibs Price, who was back in the Bay Area. He said the differences in the PCC series were Anet and Johansen. "They were just too fast," he said. "That drive—whew! They kept messing up our plays so that we never had a chance to set. In other words, this Oregon crew isn't a one-man or two-man or even a three-man team, but a great five-man club. When we stopped Gale, Dick and Wintermute, Johansen came through with three long ones in the pinch and Anet kept driving in and spoiling our plays. . . . I expect them to win at Evanston. They have what it takes to be national champions."

The coverage in the Bay Area every day more strongly labeled the Webfoots, the conquerors of the local-favorite Golden Bears, as the Western championships' favorites—both to win the games and to serve as a local surrogate for box-office purposes. Coach Hobson told his boys not to sound overconfident. "We were asked not to comment," recalled John Dick, "but privately we all agreed with the headlines."

In Eugene, residents were assured that San Francisco radio station KGO was broadcasting both sectional games, and that all they had to do was tune in to 790 kHz to hear the Webfoots continue their quest for the national championship. Presumably, KGO's signal traveled a long way.

The *Emerald*'s student journalists put together an advance package on the Western championships for the next morning's paper. George Pasero's advance story declared: "Picked by the Southern casaba favorites to top the NCAA's Western cage championship, Oregon's coast champion hoopsters will open their quest for the nation hoop honors tonight at Treasure Island." A second piece, minus a byline, noted that total attendance for the Webfoots' games to that point of the season was roughly 350,000. It told the student readership: "Imagine 350,000 pairs of eyes watching every move you make, picking out faults, noticing the way you part your hair, and the mole on your shoulder. Imagine 350,000 voices hooting and cheering you, calling you by name, and you have a conception of what Gale, Wintermute, Anet and Johansen have been through the past three years. What price a basketball player's glory?"

The story didn't answer that question.

18.

Eighth Avenue

Monday, March 20

WASHINGTON—President Roosevelt nominates William O. Douglas, the 40-year-old chairman of the securities commission, to succeed the retired Louis D. Brandeis as a Supreme Court associate justice. Many westerners bristle that while Douglas lived for a time in Washington state and graduated from Whitman College in Walla Walla, he is a former Yale law professor with longtime ties to Connecticut and hardly provides what many had been lobbying for—a Western voice and perspective on the high court. Douglas is Roosevelt's fourth nomination in his second term. His first-term frustration with the court after it scuttled aspects of the New Deal, and his subsequent ill-advised and much-derided attempt to "pack" the Court through the Judicial Reorganization Bill of 1937, now seem moot. That bill would have given him the right to appoint a new justice for each sitting justice over the age of 70.

After the tripleheader in Madison Square Garden, the national invitation tournament had its dream matchup in the finals—undefeated Long Island vs. undefeated Loyola of Chicago. The crowd of 18,206 was the third-largest basketball crowd in Garden history, and the box office stopped selling tickets just as the consolation game—New Mexico A&M beat Roanoke 55-52—was ending. Then the serious business began. The fans saw LIU hold off Bradley Tech 36-32 and then Loyola pull out a thrilling 51-46 victory in overtime over St. John's. The sponsoring writers would have been fine with either result in the second game, since a matchup of locals LIU and St. John's in the title game would have been an easy sell, too. But this way they had one New York team and an undefeated "invader," adding to the intrigue and perhaps combating the image that their tournament was, first and foremost, about New York and not a truly national event.

In the *Herald Tribune*, Everett B. Morris noted that the overflow crowd reacted emotionally both when the "Star-Spangled Banner" was played before the first semifinal, and when Dr. James Naismith was introduced and went on the floor to toss the ball up for an opening jump.

After that, in the first semifinal, Clair Bee's Blackbirds built a 23-11 first half lead, largely on four long set shots from guard John Bromberg. Bradley Tech, the club that had so decisively beaten the Webfoots in Peoria in December, made it interesting in the second half, suffocating the Blackbirds with a scrambling defensive effort, but it couldn't quite recover. Bradley Tech's undoing was its lack of depth, since the Braves used only six players and hit the wall in the comeback attempt after twice getting within three points.

The loss was the Braves' first since the 12-point rout at the hands of SMU in Peoria, two nights after the victory over the Webfoots. Charles Orsborn had 9 in a losing cause for Bradley Tech. Bromberg's 12 points led the Blackbirds, who managed to win despite getting only 4 from star forward Irv Torgoff.

The Blackbirds scrambled to shower, get dressed, and watch as the second semifinal determined their opponent in the finals two nights later.

They saw a tense game that was billed by Arthur Daley, Morris, and others as one of most thrilling, exciting games ever played. It was close and tight, yet not particularly well played. The New York coverage went over the top, going beyond its usual superlatives for the college games in the Garden, to sheer and ill-concealed boosterism. Morris labeled the two games "a tremendous show in every way. . . . The games were exciting, vigorously fought and brimming with spectacular shooting and brilliant playmaking."

Loyola had a seven-point halftime lead and increased it to ten early in the second half, but St. John's fought back and pulled into a 43-43 tie on guard Dutch Garfinkel's long shot with 2:45 remaining. Each team scored only one basket the rest of regulation, and St. John's guard Howie Vocke hit a shot from the corner to tie it 45-45 with 1:20 left. That still was the score at the buzzer, after Loyola center Mike Novak successfully goaltended a last-second shot to force the overtime.

In the five extra minutes, the Redmen could only get one free throw and suffered the disappointing defeat.

The scribes were impressed with Loyola's towering Novak. Daley, in fact, labeled him "the altitudinous center." He made a crucial hook shot in the overtime, and that was the only hoop of the extra five minutes, since the Ramblers' other three points came on foul shots. More important, the informal tally was that Novak batted away at least nine shots, including the one in the final seconds of regulation, that would have gone through the net if he hadn't gotten to them as they were on the way down. He also scored 20 points himself, but the consensus was that speedy guard Wibs Kautz was the Ramblers' most talented player, and he had 16 points. Wrote Daley: "Kautz was not just a stooge for Novak by any means. Outside of Hank Luisetti, he seemed the best all-around college performer ever to show in the Garden. He could dribble, shoot, and pass, and was so fast and so clever that a tent hardly could have kept him under cover."

The scores from the Garden made their way to the other coast, on the wires. There, the scribes and maybe a few coaches attending the Western semifinals took note. But the Webfoots, set for the second game that night at the world's fair, had more important things on their mind than what was going on in the other tournament.

19.

Treasure Island

Monday, March 20
WASHINGTON—The U.S. ambassador to Czechoslovakia, Wilbur J. Carr, is ordered to leave Prague and return to America. In the U.S. House, first-term Republican
Congressman Lewis Thill reacts to the European news on
the floor. He says he wouldn't vote to "embroil the United
States in the coming European war. Hitler's seven league
boots will lead to another European conflagration." And
he declares the U.S. must decide "whether she will stay
neutral or not." His view is considered a mainstream Republican stance, not extreme.

The Golden Gate International Exposition had been open a month
on the 400-acre island, man-made from material dredged from the
bottom of San Francisco Bay and attached to Yerba Buena Island
near the new San Francisco-Oakland Bay Bridge. The fair was a
celebration of the American ingenuity involved in constructing the
massive bridge, dedicated in 1936, and the Golden Gate Bridge,
which opened the next year.

One of the problems for potential basketball fans was that anyone attending games at the Golden Gate International Exposition
Coliseum would be caught up in the traffic and crowds heading to
Treasure Island for other fair exhibits, attractions (including 100
restaurants), and events. Fans could get to the island either by ferry
or, more likely, by automobile. Spotlights shone up from the island
and were visible from all around the Bay Area and even beyond.

As the dates for the Western championships approached, it
didn't take a genius—say, a bridge architect—to figure out why fair
organizers and tournament officials, including John Bunn, had been
hoping for California or Stanford to win the Pacific Coast Conference and make the four-team field on Treasure Island as a "host"

team and draw. That likely would have been more helpful than having Villanova in the Eastern championships in Philadelphia. But the Webfoots upset those plans, and the fallback plan was the attempt to portray the PCC representative as the gallant conquerors of the Golden Bears who would make the two local-league teams look better if they won the Western championships and perhaps the national title game.

When the Oklahoma-Utah State game tipped off at 8 p.m., the small crowd in the coliseum left organizers with only one hope—that the seats would fill in when the Webfoots took the floor later. By halftime, some paying customers might have been tempted to leave the pavilion to tour the nearby Court of the Seven Seas or the Court of Flowers and then return for the second game, if they returned at all. The opener was tied 10-10 before forwards Garnett Corbin and Jimmy McNatt got hot for Oklahoma, and the Sooners pulled away. They were up 25-14 at the half and never in trouble in the final 20 minutes, also playing their reserves much of the way to rest up the starters for the matchup the next night. The final was 50-39 and could have been a lot worse. Corbin and McNatt each finished with 12 points.

Back in Boulder, the Colorado Buffaloes—sick, banged-up, tired, whatever—wondered how they would have done against Oklahoma if they had accepted the Big 7 bid, rather than letting it trickle down to Utah State.

In the second game, the Webfoots continued to take advantage of opponents deciding that the way to try to beat Oregon was to focus on containing Laddie Gale. The Webfoots' star struggled offensively, especially in the first half, because of the man-to-man attention from Texas forward Oran Spears and the considerable help he got from his teammates, including sagging guard Bobby Moers. But the other Webfoots responded, and they also throttled Texas with strong defensive work of their own. The Webfoots were up 8-1 after seven minutes, 10-2 midway through the first half, then 16-5 after 13 minutes. By then, John Dick, driving to the hoop or converting off his pivot moves, had eight points and Slim Wintermute six.

The Longhorns rallied, and it was 19-16 at the half. At that point, Gale still didn't have a field goal.

Texas closed to within one point on three different occasions in the second half, the final time when a Moers bucket for Texas made it 23-22. Then Dick hit consecutive hoops to put the lead back up to five and a 9-0 run a couple of minutes later put it away. The Webfoots led by as many as 19 points late and claimed the 56-41 victory that moved them into the Western championship game.

Dick and Wintermute ended up with 14 and 13 points, respectively. Wally Johansen, featured in the Associated Press Wirephoto of a scramble for the ball that ran in many papers from coast to coast, again hit long-range shots that complemented the Webfoots' inside game and finished with seven points, as did Gale. The touted matchup between Anet and Moers, also a Longhorns star third baseman in baseball and a halfback in football, was a standoff. Moers had six points before fouling out late, while Anet had four for the Webfoots. Hobson was able to empty his bench in the final minutes, and given that the Western championship game would be Oregon's fourth in six nights, that was an advantage.

"Kid Coach" Jack Gray ended up using nine players for Texas, and one studious reserve majoring in zoology, Denton Cooley, checked in with three points.

L. H. Gregory opened his *Oregonian* story by calling the winners "the tall-fir Oregon boys."

Even as the Webfoots were within one victory of reaching the national championship game, the 1938–39 team's ultimately famous nickname didn't yet merit capital letters, not even from the man who coined it.

As good as the victory looked on paper, especially given the final 15-point margin, the Webfoots realized they hadn't been sharp, especially not offensively, and it was far from their best game. They knew if they'd played this way against either Washington or California, they might not have gotten this far. In a way, though, that was a ringing endorsement for PCC basketball. They also again wrestled with overconfidence, knowing that most considered Texas a far better team than Oklahoma.

No, the seats hadn't filled in for the second game. An official figure wasn't announced, but Gregory pegged attendance for the doubleheader as 3,000, the Associated Press reporter had it at 5,000, and Hobson later wrote it was 6,000. So even the most generous figure meant the building was no more than half-filled.

Most of those who did show up, at least for the second game, seemed to have gone along with the implorations to adopt the Webfoots as the Pacific Coast's team or had some sort of affinity for the Oregon boys in the first place, whether as alumni or former Oregon residents. In that sense, although the Webfoots were 525 miles from Eugene, they felt a bit at home.

20.

How the West Was Won

Tuesday, March 21

PARIS—French Prime Minister Edouard Daladier declares the 60-hour workweek, previously imposed in many defense-related industries, will be the standard for railways and mining, too. Additionally, he states that any potential workers on the relief rolls who refuse to go to work in defense industries will be ineligible for aid for a year.

LOS ANGELES—Works Progress Administration officials sheepishly announce that German-made rails in a line built as part of $1.6 million storm drain project tied to the 1932 Los Angeles Olympics will be torn out and replaced. U.S. materials were supposed to be used in the entire project, and the gaffe was noticeable because "GERMANY" was stamped on the rails.

In Eugene on the afternoon of the Western championship game, residents flipping through the *Register-Guard* before or after reading news of the Webfoots in the sports section came across a letter to the editor from Martin F. Simon of Eugene. Simon protested the U.S. sending Ambassador Kennedy to the papal coronation as an official emissary. He called for readers to protest to the Oregon congressional delegation, because if they didn't? Gasp: The U.S. might even have an official ambassador to the Vatican—and vice versa.

He wasn't identified as such, but Martin F. Simon was the pastor of Eugene's Grace Lutheran Church. He had a ten-year-old son, Paul—the same Paul Simon who would go on to (briefly) write sports under Dick Strite at the *Register-Guard*. Young Paul later wrote that he and his brother Art "followed athletic scores and the sports pages faithfully, particularly anything to do with the University of Oregon." Unlike his father, Paul probably was more concerned about the Webfoots' progress in the NCAA tournament than he was about whether Roosevelt dispatched an official emissary to the papal coronation.

* * *

Speculation continued that Clair Bee and Howard Hobson soon might be coaching against each other in the Pacific Coast Conference. The *Berkeley Daily Gazette*'s story on the Western semifinal games of the night before on nearby Treasure Island was next to a King Features Syndicate caricature feature on Bee, and it ran in many other papers nationally. Above his likeness, the headline read: "He Seeks U.C.L.A. Job." The copy accompanying his caricature noted, "This season's team is one of Bee's masterpieces and is rated one of the best college quintets developed in the East in many moons." The cartoon feature did nothing to establish whether Bee truly was going after the job, or that the speculation was anything but wishful thinking on the part of Bruins partisans.[1]

* * *

For the second straight game on Treasure Island, Hobson was going up against a coach who had similar credentials as a former star at his school. Oklahoma coach Bruce Drake was an All-American in 1928–29 and was finishing up his first season as the school's head coach.

Oklahoma hung with the Webfoots for the first 15 minutes, actually taking a 14-11 lead. Hoops from Slim Wintermute and John Dick fueled a run that produced the final 10 points of the half and a 21-14 Oregon lead. The Sooners tried to run with the Webfoots to get back in the game, but that played right into Oregon's hands. Also, Oklahoma rarely could get the ball inside, with the Oregon front line intimidating the Sooners. The Webfoots also switched from a zone to a man-to-man, and with the boys following the orders Hobson had drilled into them at practices, they kept their arms up and were surprised when Oklahoma continued for a time to attack the defense as if it were a zone.

It turned out to be a laugher, with the Webfoots winning 55-37.

Jimmy McNatt was the only Oklahoma player in double figures, with 12 points.

---

1. Soon, UCLA hired Wilbur Johns, who lasted nine years before John Wooden succeeded him. It would have been interesting to see if Bee's approach would have worked in Westwood.

It seemed strange that Dick hadn't even been in the starting lineup at the outset of the season, because his 14 points led the Webfoots and he had scored in double figures in all four post-season games—the two against California and the Western championships contests against Texas and Oklahoma. Laddie Gale added 11 points and Wintermute 10, and Coach Hobson was able to get four of his reserves in the game for significant playing time, even though the Webfoots now wouldn't play again until the championship game in Northwestern's gym on March 27. Bobby Anet had six points for the Webfoots and then went on the KGO radio broadcast—the one that reached Eugene—after the game to declare, among other things, that the Webfoots in the national championship also would be playing for their league and region. "We will win it for the west," he said.

After the 15- and 18-point victories in San Francisco, the Webfoots walked away thinking their top PCC opponents were better than their challengers so far in the NCAA event. "We were head and shoulders above [Texas and Oklahoma], but not so with Washington and California," Hobson said.

The Eastern championships hadn't held a third-place game, but the West did, with Utah State, most likely because it was more excited about playing another game after being eliminated from championship contention, surprising Texas 51-49.

Legendary Kansas coach Phog Allen, who was at the Western championship game as an NABC representative and observer, selected the all-Western championships team—the Webfoots' Dick, Wintermute, and Gale, plus Oklahoma's McNatt and Herb Scheffler.

Again, though, the attendance was disappointing, with estimates once more ranging from 3,000 to 6,000. That high estimate this time came in the United Press "PM" version of the game story, the one that declared that Pacific Coast fans who had seen the Webfoots play in San Francisco, and also seen California whip Ohio State twice in Berkeley early in the season, considered Oregon a lock to win the national title. But even then, one of the points that seemed to be underplayed was that the NCAA tournament—or any tournament, for that matter—came down to which team was playing the best at the end of the season, and that early season results were, if not irrelevant, at least secondary.[2] The

---

2. That point would become obvious as the NCAA tournament's tradition built, with teams peaking at the right time, sometimes even producing "flukish" results.

steeling experiences of the testing pre-conference schedule, the league season, and then the playoff against California indeed had made the Webfoots better.

All along, Hobson was committed to heading to Chicago, regardless, since the title game was being played in conjunction with the NABC convention. But the victory meant he was going to have a lot of company on his trip.

A lot had happened in the year since the coaches batted around the idea of their own national tournament at the '38 gathering.

It was coming down to Oregon vs. Ohio State for the first national title.

21.

49th Street

Wednesday, March 22

KAUNAS, Lithuania—As expected, Lithuania agrees to relinquish to Germany the Baltic port of Memel. The port was German territory until the Treaty of Versailles and most of the 150,000 residents are German-speaking. Lithuanian officials concede they were "forced" into the move and threatened with invasion if they didn't buckle under.

In the "advance" story in the *Herald Tribune* about the upcoming Loyola-LIU title game in the national invitation tournament, Everett B. Morris noted: "Although the Metropolitan Basketball Writers' Association makes no national championship claims for its tourney, you will have to stretch your imagination more than somewhat to find a more likely pretender to the throne of collegiate court king than the survivor of the competition which ends [Wednesday night]. Every team in the tournament possessed a record of unusual excellence, both in the matter of games won and lost and the caliber of opposition encountered."

For several of the teams, the part about the caliber of schedule was shaky at best.

Morris didn't mention in his story that he was the MBWA president.

* * *

Writing after the game that night, the *Times*' Arthur Daley labeled the Long Island Blackbirds "the Wonder Team from Brooklyn" in his game story about the national invitation tournament's championship game.

There was a lot to salute: The Blackbirds routed previously unbeaten Loyola 44-32 in front of 18,033 in Madison Square Garden. Clair Bee's genius, or at least his flexibility, was on display.

The wizard of the 1-3-1 zone defense had his boys surround the Ramblers' big man in the middle, Mike Novak, keeping him away from the basket and then also pressuring him when he got the ball, preventing him from effectively feeding unattended teammates for easy shots. Novak had only one point for the Ramblers.

At the other end of the floor, the Blackbirds' strategy to avoid the "goaltending" work of Novak wasn't unprecedented, but still a bit unusual. In the early stages of the game, the Blackbirds, on Bee's orders, increased the trajectory and length of their shots, carrying over Novak's outstretched arm, and tried to carom them in off the backboard. Enough of them went in for the Blackbirds to take a lead, and Novak, unaccustomed to the helplessness and frustration, decided he was wasting his energy and switched to a strategy of going to the board to try and get the rebound, if it came. Noticing that, the Blackbirds went back to shooting conventionally. They also used more screens than usual, trying to confuse Novak.

Irv Torgoff led the Blackbirds with 12 points, with Dan Kaplowitz and Ossie Schechtman adding 9 apiece. When it was over, they were celebrating both the tournament championship and the school's second undefeated record in four seasons. They were 24-0. Yet as smart as they played and as astute as Bee's leadership was, it still was hard to get a feel for just how good the Blackbirds were. For the first time, the wire-service stories on the New York tournament seemed to address which post-season event would produce a national champion. One dispatch to national papers came right out and said the Blackbirds "claimed the mythical national championship" and cited the handful of major opponents they had beaten—Bradley Tech, New Mexico A&M, Southern California, Kentucky, Marquette, Toledo, and Duquesne. But what it didn't mention was that this was a Brooklyn-based team that wasn't in a league and played all of its major opponents in its quasi-home arena, the Garden, and had only one game all season out of the New York area. It wasn't out of line to wonder how California, for example, would have done playing all but one of its games in the San Francisco Bay Area against any opponents that could be rounded up, from the second-rate to the major.

The *Herald Tribune*'s Irving T. Marsh broke from the norm to speak with Loyola coach Lenny Sachs for his reaction after the game in the Garden's Dressing Room No. 30. Sachs had been Loyola's coach since 1923, and he juggled both coaching the

Ramblers and playing in the NFL for the first three years as he wound down his football career. "What can you do with a team like Long Island?" Sachs asked. "They were hot. We were off. We cracked wide open; they were magnificent. We were inferior; they were superior. There's the story of the ball game. I'm sorry it had to end like this after twenty-one straight, but there's nothing I can do about that now." Marsh also reported that next door, in Dressing Room No. 31, the Blackbirds' celebration was raucous—and that Bee, for a change, was speechless.

Bradley Tech beat St. John's 40-35 in the third-place game.

*   *   *

After a quiet day in San Francisco, the Webfoots boarded a 9 p.m. train and headed toward Chicago.

22.

Destinies

Thursday, March 23

MEMEL—German troops enter the port city and Adolf Hitler arrives in the pocket battleship *Deutschland*. In an eight-minute speech to a welcoming crowd, Hitler offers a hedged pledge that his territorial grab is over. "I believe that now, in the main, we have arrived at the end of this unique process of reparation," he says. The Treaty of Versailles is in tatters.

The Webfoots were determined to at least make modest attempts to stretch their legs and get *some* exercise on the train ride, but they suspected they'd be stiff and rusty by the time they disembarked in Chicago on Saturday. This would be their third game of the season in Illinois, and a slight part of their motivation was to demonstrate what a fluke the decisive loss to Bradley Tech in Peoria was during the marathon trip in December. Howard Hobson also reminded them that the NABC convention was going on at the same time in downtown Chicago and most of the nation's coaches would attend the championship game.

As the team was in its early stages of the trip to Chicago, Ivie Wintermute departed Eugene. Her benefactor and employer, department store owner Carl Washburne, asked her if she wanted to go to the game and, after getting her excited reaction, made it happen. He presented her with a train ticket and a promise to take care of her expenses, including her stay at the Sherman Hotel. A crowd of about 100, including Slim's fraternity brothers at Phi Delta Theta and her co-workers, saw her off and presented her with gifts as she boarded the Southern Pacific train to Portland. Because it was spring break, the Phi Delta boys arranged for other members to meet her in Portland and help her transfer to the Great Northern Line's Empire Builder, bound for Chicago.

Interviewed before her departure, Ivie said Slim's height was especially surprising because her late husband had been barely over 6-feet tall, and she was of average size herself. "He was always a tall boy," she said of Slim. "When he was 12, he was about as tall as I am. When he was about 14 or 15, he shot up nine inches in a year and he attained his present height when he was 17. But he has always been healthy and athletic and has never been sick a day."

She said she had wired both Slim and Coach Hobson, and they had promised they would meet her at the Chicago train station. "The trip will be education for me," she said. "I've never been out of the two states of Oregon and Washington."

*   *   *

In Columbus, the Buckeyes made travel plans for their trip to Chicago.

They were going to make the 360-mile trip in cars.

Jimmy Hull later said that his sore ankle prevented him from practicing between the Eastern title game in Philadelphia and the national championship game in Evanston.

*   *   *

The Chicago papers began trying to re-introduce the Webfoots, who had run up a 60-45 win over Western Illinois Teachers College in Chicago three months earlier, to their readers in advance of the team's arrival. The *Chicago Tribune* noted that Oregon had "rolled up an amazing total of 835 points, an average of 46 points per game. . . . Oregon's high scoring is attributed to its use of the fast-break offense, which consists of outrunning the defense in a dash for the goal."

*   *   *

At a Hotel Lincoln luncheon, the sponsoring Metropolitan Basketball Writers presided and had Dr. James Naismith officially award the national invitation tournament team trophies and then the most outstanding player award to Bill Lloyd of St. John's. The LIU players were presented 21-jewel watches; the Loyola runners-up got 18-jewel versions.

That night, with their official collegiate seasons over, the LIU Blackbirds split into two squads for additional play. The seniors on Bee's team immediately formed a pro team for a barnstorming schedule. Among the many ways they were billed over the next few weeks were the LIU All-Stars, the LIU Blackbirds, the Long Island All-Stars, and the Long Island Blackbirds.

Also, the five underclassmen on the New York tournament champions, plus six freshmen, headed to upstate New York to play in the Saratoga Invitational AAU tournament. They were referred to as LIU's 1939–40 varsity.

Friday, March 24

NEW YORK—In his "On Broadway" column syndicated to nearly 2,000 newspapers worldwide, Walter Winchell preaches: "In the last year, two republics have fallen before the advance squadrons of the Nazis. They died—not by bullets, but by infection. For the new and deadly weapon is propaganda. The two fallen nations teach a great military lesson to America. Their fate proves that unless guarded, a nation's soul is more vulnerable than its coastline."[1]

The nation's coaches began to arrive in Chicago, and they were looking forward to watching basketball in addition to talking about it. If so inclined, and this was going to be their official story whether they followed through or wandered off to sample the Chicago nightlife, they could watch a tournament matching several barnstorming professional teams. Loyola center Mike Novak had already joined one of those pro teams. Also, the coaches could see the finals of the national Catholic high school tournament on Sunday night, then head to the Oregon-Ohio State game on Monday night—the culmination of the tournament their organization had created.

The coaches also anticipated spirited discussions on whether to abandon what some of them considered a failed two-season experiment. Notre Dame coach George Keogan, among others, advocated returning to the center jump after every basket. His rationalization for that was that the game's increased pace had made it too strenuous and potentially dangerous to play, with the players running as much as *four miles* during a full game. Clair Bee was going to be running sessions as the chairman of the rules recommendation committee, and he was known to share Keogan's view that the

---

1. According to Lynne Olson's *Those Angry Days*, the Anti-Defamation League's New York counsel, Arnold Forster, sometimes wrote passages for Winchell. I'm wondering if this was one of them.

restoration of the center jump would be good for the game. Opponents liked the flow of the "new" game and pointed out that the old system put a premium on having a tall center to win the jump ball after every basket. Slim Wintermute was about to finish his time with the Webfoots, so Oregon wouldn't have him for jump balls if the old rule were restored the next season. But that didn't affect Hobson's opinion. He wanted to stick with taking the ball out of bounds after every basket. The coaches also were going to consider whether to somehow discourage deliberate fouls in the final minutes and whether to divide games into quarters instead of halves.

*   *   *

Young *Oregonian* reporter Charles Buxton, who likely kept it quiet that he was an Oregon State graduate, was aboard the train with the Webfoots. He spoke with Hobson and filed a story from a stop in Grand Island, Nebraska. "The train ride apparently won't hurt the boys a bit, and they should be raring to go," Hobson said. He confidently declared that the Webfoots should be able to whip Ohio State unless they were "completely off."

John Bunn, who had issued the official NCAA tournament invitation to the Webfoots, was on the same train. Buxton noted that Bunn asked of a group of several players: "Aren't you fellows tired of basketball yet?"

"No, sir," Bobby Anet declared. "Not until next Monday night."

In Eugene, business leaders and members of the Monday Morning Quarterbacks Club began putting together plans to fete the team after its return the next week. They said the celebration would go on as planned, even if the Webfoots lost in Evanston, because they would be the champions of the West.

*   *   *

At the AAU tournament in Saratoga, LIU's 1939–40 varsity defeated the Hudson Falls Iroquois of Vermont 58-30 in the opening round. Unfortunately, the famous horse track wasn't open in the spring, so nobody could combine basketball with placing $2 on a thoroughbred's nose.

Saturday, March 25

MILAN—In the newspaper owned by Italian ruler Benito Mussolini, Field Marshall Hermann Goering promises that

Germany will stand behind Italy in all things—including, he makes clear, its aspirations to add territory in the Mediterranean and Red Sea areas to Mussolini's rule. "The Berlin-Rome axis is unbreakable," Goering says. He expresses scorn for Great Britain, comparing it to a pesky, barking dog that won't bite. Many suspect it will further embolden Mussolini to emulate Hitler in the rush to add to his empire. Hitler also telegrams Mussolini with similar assurances. This all comes on the eve of Mussolini's speech commemorating the 20th anniversary of the founding of the Fascist combat squads.

NEW YORK—With it still unclear whether Franklin Roosevelt will defy tradition and seek a third term, New York Mayor Fiorello LaGuardia responds to speculation that he would be a candidate. He says he doesn't care who is elected "if he has a brain, a heart and a soul, and is ready and able to deal with the real issues before the nation." Reporters attempt to find a yes or no in there.

When the Webfoots arrived in Chicago, they received a pleasant surprise—spending money. Oregon fans passed the hat, so to speak, for money to wire to the Webfoots, giving the players expense money during their stay. The athletic board hadn't planned on the Webfoots getting that far and was flying by the seat of the pants on everything, and most of the players had run out of spending money in San Francisco.

Also, concerned that the Webfoots were facing a disadvantage because Ohio State would be playing much closer to home, likely with more fans, the Eugene Moose Lodge decided to try to make it a little more like a game at McArthur Court. They hooked up with organizers of an accomplished 100-member children's band of Mooseheart, Illinois, and arranged for it to represent Oregon at the game on Monday in Evanston.

The children went through a crash course, learning how to play "Mighty Oregon," the fight song. If fans were inclined, they even could sing along:

> *Oregon, our Alma Mater,*
> *We will guard thee on and on,*
> *Let us gather 'round and cheer her,*

Chant her glory, Oregon!
Roar the praises of her warriors,
Sing the story, Oregon,
On to vict'ry urge the heroes
Of our Mighty Oregon!

Radio station KEX in Portland announced that it would pick up a "national" broadcast of the championship, noting that the man at the microphone would be an "eastern sports announcer." Quickly, arrangements were made to transmit the signal from the Portland station to KORE in Eugene.

* * *

The Buckeyes journeyed over from Columbus—Hull remembered riding in an old Packard—and went through a light workout at Patten Gymnasium. Newspaper stories reported that the Webfoots did, too, but didn't provide any details, and John Dick's recollection was that Hobson decided it was too late for a productive practice and scrapped it. Regardless, Hobson went over a scouting report of the Buckeyes with the Webfoots in a "chalk talk," and they got the impression one or more Big Ten coaches had pitched in with information about Ohio State's strengths, weaknesses, and strategies.

* * *

The coaches' convention got underway, and they were excited to learn that Dr. James Naismith was going to attend the championship game on Monday night. (The good doctor got around.) In his honor, Northwestern's team agreed to be part of an exhibition preliminary game, shooting at peach baskets and using the original rules—with nine players per side, including a goaltender, and with the center jump after every basket.

* * *

In Saratoga, LIU beat the Stillwater Collegians 50-38 on the second night of the AAU tournament.

Sunday, March 26

ROME—Benito Mussolini's speech is a masterful walking of a fine line, blustery enough to convince his followers he will continue to seek much territory now under French control, including Tunisia, the port of Djibouti, and the Suez Canal, but conciliatory enough to convince French officials and others that there is room for negotiation and discussion. It's clear that Hitler's success in acquiring territory is additionally emboldening *Il Duce*.

Slim Wintermute met his mother at the train station, saw to it that she got to her hotel, and then joined the Webfoots for their practice at the Northwestern gym. Dick recalled that the session wasn't very productive. "It degenerated into an interview and photo op session for the media types who also showed up," he said. "We didn't want to spoil our perfect record of no practices on our season-ending odyssey."

*　*　*

At the coaches' convention in downtown Chicago, Clair Bee's rules committee decided *not* to recommend the restoration of the center jump after every basket. Instead, the LIU coach announced that the committee report, to be presented to the NABC membership the next day, suggested that:

- On fouls ruled to be deliberate, the team fouled would regain possession after the single foul shot.
- The college game should be divided into quarters instead of halves.
- The three-second rule in the free-throw circle should apply only to a player with the ball.
- Goaltending—or deflecting the ball while on its downward flight—should be illegal, rather than saluted as a tradition of the game dating back to the peach baskets. On plays judged to be goaltending, the shooter's team should get credit for a basket.

Banning goaltending was a monumental potential change, but, curiously, most stories summarizing Bee's report treated it as an afterthought. If passed, the recommendations would be sent along to the NCAA. Most considered the proposal a direct response to how Loyola successfully utilized center Mike Novak to do little defensively but stand at the basket and try to goaltend shots. Bee's Blackbirds had overcome it, but others were worried about it becoming a way to reward giants who couldn't do much else.

It was a tribute to the Webfoots that while Slim Wintermute was considered a giant, he could do a lot more and wasn't part of the discussion about the need to put what the coaches labeled "restrictions" on big men. At some point over the weekend, in fact, Hobson was able to see Novak play in the pro tournament in Chicago, and later told Dick Strite that Wintermute was a much better all-around player. Hobson was prejudiced, of course, but he also was right.

* * *

Bee's Blackbird underclassmen kept up the winning habit, taking first place in the Saratoga AAU tournament with a 38-29 victory over the Amsterdam American-Lithuanians. Dolly King had 12 points for the Redbirds, Joe Shelly 7, and Ossie Schechtman and Si Lobello 6 apiece.

The same day, the seniors—this time billed as the "LIU Blackbirds"—beat the seniors from St. John's 38-31 in New York as their professional schedule continued.

* * *

Hobson took the Webfoots out to dinner in downtown Chicago and after the team arrived back at the hotel, he told them to get a good night's rest. Most likely jokingly, he told them to sleep until noon.

Monday, March 27

MADRID—The Spanish Civil War had seemed on the verge of ending, but after surrender negotiations break down, Franco's Nationalist troops renew offensives against Republican forces on several fronts and are on the verge of entering Madrid.

As a group, the coaches' convention rejected most of the Clair Bee–led rules committee's recommendations. The only rule change the NABC endorsed to forward to the NCAA was a tweaking of the intentional foul proposal that came out of the committee. Instead of a free throw and possession, the fouled team would have the option of taking a free throw *or* retaining possession and taking the ball out of bounds. The thinking was that it would make deliberate fouls a futile gesture if the fouled team could just keep the ball. What it overlooked, of course, was that getting the ball inbounds could be challenging, too. Marquette coach W. S. Chandler, finishing his term as the NABC president, explained: "This was the only recommended change, the general sentiment being to leave the rules alone."

In the debate among all the coaches, Notre Dame's George Keogan, upset that restoring the center jump after every basket wasn't seriously considered either by Bee's committee or the membership as a whole, suggested a compromise: the return of the jump after every basket in the final five minutes of each half. That idea was shot down, too.

Goaltending remained legal.[2]

After the session ended, the coaches rushed out to Evanston to see the championship game.

---

2. The sentiment was building. Goaltending finally became illegal in 1944.

23.

Broken Trophy and All

Monday, March 27
WASHINGTON—Senator Key Pittman (D-Nevada), chairman of the Senate Committee on Foreign Relations, is gathering support for his proposal to modify "cash and carry" aspects of the neutrality laws. Since 1937, the sale of non-war materials to nations at war on that basis has been allowed, but armament sales still are banned. Pittman wants to expand the "cash and carry" provisions to arms sales. This follows a fiery weekend speech from isolationist Senator William Borah (R-Idaho), who again declares that the U.S. has no business providing support for European democracies or getting involved in European squabbles.

Regardless of when the coaches or fans arrived to Patten Gymnasium, they found that plenty of good seats still were available. Official attendance was 5,000 in the 9,000-seat arena on the Northwestern campus, and many thought that was being charitable. Charles Buxton of the *Oregonian* guessed 4,400—including the 400 coaches.

Part of subsequent myth would be that the tournament was little noticed in the nation's newspapers and other press outlets. That's partially true. Leading up to the championship game, most papers ran only three- or four-paragraph wire stories about the Western and Eastern championships and didn't give them splashy play. The advance coverage and then stories about the national championship game tended to get more space and better play. But it was relative: outside of New York, the national invitation tournament got similar—or worse—play. On the national front, boxing, horse racing, and baseball spring training were the big stories, and local papers supplemented that with tales of the area sports teams. The NCAA tournament, while not given mega-coverage, wasn't ignored, and the stories about the championship game got more space. That said, though, there was no denying the fact that at least at the box office, the NCAA tournament hadn't caught on. So as the first NCAA championship game began, the atmosphere was a mixed bag, with the nation's coaches in the stands; with a stand-in band playing "Mighty Oregon" whenever it had the chance; with a radio broadcast; yet with many empty seats. Most important, the Buckeyes and Webfoots stepped onto the mid-court circle for the opening jump ball knowing they were playing for a national championship . . . and the right to be the first national champions. The championship and runner-up trophies were sitting at courtside, balanced on the scorer's table. The Buckeyes' own coach was the head of the NCAA tournament committee and one of those most responsible for the founding of the event in the first place. If he didn't communicate that he believed this was the time for true competitors to step up, he wasn't a good coach. And he was a good coach.

For his part, Howard Hobson later reconstructed his pre-game discussion with Bobby Anet. The coach was worried that the train rides had left his boys tired.

"Bob," Hobson said, "run 'em to death if you can. Make them call the first time out. Make them say uncle first. Whatever you do, don't call time until you're all in."

Said Anet: "Okay, coach."

Thirty seconds into the game, Anet ended up with the ball after the carom of a Webfoots miss and tossed it into the hoop to open the scoring. On the next possession, he was fouled and made a free throw, putting the Webfoots up 3-0. John Dick added a free throw, and Wally Johansen's bucket made it 6-0.

The Webfoots were on their way.

Jimmy Hull finally got the Buckeyes on the scoreboard with a free throw three and a half minutes into the game.

The Buckeyes seemed befuddled about how to attack the scrambling Ducks' defense, couldn't get the ball inside, and settled for long—and bad—shots. And the coaches in the stands who hadn't seen the Webfoots before realized what they had heard was true, that they were *both* extraordinarily big along the front line but also a mobile and speedy outfit, with the big men able to keep up with

Anet and Johansen, the guards from Astoria. That was what made this team both so good and so different.

Although the Buckeyes were playing in a Big Ten building, they ultimately appeared to be out of their league.

At the half, balanced Oregon was up 21-16. Johansen led the way with six points and Anet, Gale, and Dick all had five. Slim Wintermute had yet to score, but was intimidating defensively and effective on the boards.

Coach Hobson later said that as the teams headed to the dressing rooms at halftime, he overheard Hull telling his teammates: "We'll run them into the ground in the second half."

Johansen remarked to his coach, "I wish they'd run a little but so we could work up a sweat. They play like they're pooped."

The Buckeyes indeed tried to pick up the pace and come from behind, and for a minute or two, it worked. Hull scored twice after the break to cut the lead to 21-20. Then Wintermute hit two baskets (for his only four points of the game), and Dick and Anet also scored in the run that put the Webfoots back up 29-20, still with over 17 minutes to play. Again, the Webfoots' defensive strategy fooled their opponents, as they went from a zone to man-to-man, but Ohio State didn't recognize it as such in time. From then on, the Webfoots never were in trouble.

At one point, Anet charged after a loose ball and fell over the press row while attempting to save the ball from going out of bounds. The little guard knocked over the championship trophy. "He clipped off the figure of the basketball player that was on the top of the trophy," Dick said. "He ended up in the seats with the reporters."

Later, his daughter, Peggy, asked him about the trophy.

"He said, 'Well, I was just going for the ball and it was on the table there and I knocked it over,'" she says. "I know he would have gone for the ball under any circumstances."

When Anet came out of the game late, he got a standing ovation. Hobson later said his major regret was that he got only two reserves—Matt Pavalunas and Ford Mullen—in the game and thus didn't get all 11 boys memorialized in the box score of the first championship game. They were far enough ahead that he could have pulled it off.

Final score: Oregon 46, Ohio State 33.

Oregon never called a timeout.

Ohio State called five.

After the game, Hobson asked Anet why he hadn't at least called one with the Webfoots holding a big lead in the second half. "You told me not to call one until we were tired," Anet told his coach. "Hell, we're not tired."

Dick, who led the Webfoots with 13 points, never pretended that the game was well played. "Both teams shot poorly," he said. "I blamed our poor shooting on the lack of practice. We hadn't had a real practice since the day before the first Cal game, twelve days earlier. I felt their poor shooting stemmed from their inability to penetrate our team defense. In spite of our poor marksmanship, with our strong defense and control of the boards, we slowly built our lead. Our big size advantage was a major factor in our success, as was the speed and quickness of our guards, which they couldn't match."

The unofficial tally was that the Webfoots made 17 of their 63 shots from the floor, the Buckeyes 14 of 83. Anet and Gale both finished with ten points for the Webfoots, and Johansen added nine.

The Buckeyes in later years would assert their hearts weren't in the game, and Hull said his ankle still was troubling him. "My leg just felt terrible," he said. "I had more pain in it than you can imagine, and more tape on it than stores have on their shelves. And my accuracy just wasn't there." Still, he led the Buckeyes with 12 points. And they were blown out by a team that hadn't been home in ten days, had spent much of that time on trains, and came to generally scoff at the Buckeyes' alleged indifference about the game as excuse-making, even if the Buckeyes came to believe it all themselves.

Anet, wearing his warm-up jacket with the duck on the shoulder, accepted the broken championship trophy in two pieces. Hull, next to him, held the runner-up trophy. Nobody rushed the court, not even the Oregon alumni in attendance. The celebration was more about handshakes and pats on the back than exultation. The Webfoots were thrilled and gratified, but they didn't realize what this would mean.

They were the first champions.

"In the final 12 days of our season, we had won five games, four of them in one six-day period," Dick said. "We had won the championship final game against the well-rested Big Ten champion playing close to home on a Big Ten court, with Big Ten referees and an overwhelmingly Big Ten crowd."

Anet again was interviewed on the makeshift radio broadcast after the game. Anet gave credit to his teammates, and the radio man pressed him: *What about you? You played pretty well, too!* Anet laughed, shrugged, and said something along the lines of: *Huh?* He was cocky and self-assured on the court and usually away from it, too, but at least this time, the microphone turned him into a cliché-spouting milquetoast. Since reporters rarely interviewed and quoted players, mainly because the print scribes believed their job was to provide the facts, opinion, and perhaps a narrative, Anet didn't have much practice at speaking for the record or on the air. None of the Webfoots did, as a matter of fact.

Asked later to assess the game, Laddie Gale said: "Ohio State was really a setup for our kind of basketball. It used a fast break, which was right down our alley. Then Ohio State had never seen our kind of zone defense, I don't think, because the Big Ten team took 40 long shots of its entire total. It couldn't break through. Our height helped a lot because we could dominate the backboard."

In the dressing room, with photographers jammed in, too, the Webfoots made no moves to undress and shower. With Astoria pal Wally Johansen next to him, Anet leaned against a hall in one corner and held the trophy—the broken championship trophy—as if he never was going to let it out of his sight. Gale held a basketball against his rib cage, grinning as he watched Anet.

* * *

In their quick dispatches from Evanston, the two major wire services phrased it carefully.

The Associated Press dispatch began: "The University of Oregon, displaying superior ball handling and shooting ability, defeated Ohio State tonight, 46 to 33, on the Northwestern Court in the final for the basketball championship of the National Collegiate Athletic Association."

The United Press dispatch at least acknowledged the elephant in the room—or on the floor. It opened with: "Oregon's rangy sharpshooters, new champions of the National Collegiate Athletic association, entered a claim to the national intercollegiate basketball title today, and it's as good a claim as any other." It gave the final score and said the result "left no doubt of their superiority. . . . The national championship, however, still is a muddle. Long Island University, victor in Manhattan's invitational tournament, is a popular eastern choice for the title and Southwestern Teachers of Winfield, Kan., won a similar tournament at Kansas City."

The mention of the small-schools Kansas City tournament, while perhaps polite, was ridiculous.

Let's recap: On the way to finishing with a 29-5 record for the season, Oregon won its three NCAA tournament games by 15 over Texas, 18 over Oklahoma, and 13 over Ohio State. In an era when getting into the 50s was considered high scoring, those were astounding margins. At least among the teams that had earned and accepted bids to the NCAA tournament, the Webfoots were by far the best. By the end of the season, they were playing great basketball, hardened by their early-season marathon trip to the East Coast and back. They had much tougher times with their PCC rivals, Washington and California, and they were convinced that even in the year after the great Hank Luisetti finished his career at Stanford, the best basketball in the country was being played on the West Coast. The fact of the matter, too, was that while Ohio State deserved much credit for its late-season rally to the Big Ten title, it took an Indiana collapse for the Buckeyes to pull that off. While some of the Buckeyes' downplaying of the significance of the NCAA tournament later was retroactive and seemed a bit lame, it's undoubtedly true that the Webfoots were happier to be in Evanston. But, as Dick noted, even at the end of another grueling trip, the Webfoots routed the Buckeyes.

Many of the coaches watching imagined what a game between the LIU Blackbirds and the Webfoots would be like. It would be wrong, though, to portray this as a debate raging at lunch counters from coast to coast over the next few weeks. Even among sports fans, it came down to the fact that LIU and Oregon each had won a tournament with "national" in its name and that Oregon's tournament involved teams from all parts of the country.

Ned Irish was at the NCAA title game, too, and he broke the ice with Coach Hobson by congratulating him and lamenting that, wow, if Hobson thought the East Coast officiating was bad, what about these guys? Hadn't the Webfoots had to overcome the Big Ten refs, too?

Irish already had an LIU-Oregon game in mind for the Garden the next season. With only John Dick returning from among the Webfoots starters, and with LIU set to be similarly depleted, such a matchup wouldn't provide a retroactive answer about which team was better in 1938–39, but Irish was thinking box office.

* * *

In Eugene, after the game and the radio broadcast ended a little after 8 p.m., Oregon students spilled out into the streets, and the *Register-Guard* the next morning would say they "took the town like Hitler took Czechoslovakia." They mostly went up and down Willamette Street, going in and out of establishments and theaters, loudly celebrating the victory and saluting the Webfoots. The Yell Kings led a spontaneous rally on the stage at the Heilig Theater, where *Love Affair* with Irene Dunn and Charles Boyer was playing, and also burst into the McDonald Theater before the doorman at the nearby Mayflower, where the feature was *I'm From the City*, got wind of what was going on and locked that theater's doors as the movie played. Eugene police turned off the traffic signals and allowed Willamette Street to become a pedestrian mall with the cars stuck. Jennie Hobson, Howard's wife, even joined in. The celebration was spontaneous and raucous, and it seemed to be likely that many students would skip their morning classes on Tuesday, although it would be only the second day back after spring break. University President Donald Erb, who had been in office barely a year, still was only in his late 30s, and was Hobson's neighbor and friend, had made it clear that he wouldn't cancel classes and that Friday would be the official day of celebration, after the team returned. But the students partied as if they had nothing against doing it twice. On 11th Street, fraternities brought out radios and staged impromptu dances. Students pulled a dead tree that had been chopped down, but not hauled away, into the street to block it, creating a safer and bigger dance floor. The large group of male students greeted police officers trying to keep an eye on things by hoisting them on their shoulders, which the officers handled with good humor and aplomb, and then dropped them and suggested they dance with the co-eds to "Flat Foot Floogie with a Floy Floy." By 10:30, the tree was dragged off the street, the dance broke up, and the men continued on down the streets to the sororities, where they stood outside and sung for the girls. The only real over-the-top behavior was the tossing of eggs near the end of the celebration.

President Erb sent a telegram to Hobson, saying: "Congratulations to you and the boys from 3,000 university students, a million Oregonians and me."

*　*　*

From the expense money kitty, each player was allotted about $2, and Anet and several of his teammates took a late commuter train into downtown Chicago and did some mild celebrating. "I think some of us had a couple of Heinekens or something," Anet said later. "It was quite late and none of us were big on bars or things like that, mainly because nobody ever had any money."

They toasted their championship.

The very first one.

24.

Ride Home

Tuesday, March 28

MADRID—Republican forces in Spain's largest city surrender. The Spanish Civil War, in its 32nd month, for all intents and purposes is over. Celebrations break out in the Madrid streets, and not necessarily because the celebrants are Franco's Nationalist sympathizers. What's important now is that the long siege and bombardments will end. Franco is expected to enter the city by the end of the week. Fears of the war acting as a spark for additional European conflict prove to be unfounded, but by now there are other worries.

CHICAGO—In another Chicago championship basketball game, the New York Renaissance—better known as the Rens—wins the professional tournament of mostly barnstorming teams, defeating the Oshkosh All-Stars 34-25. The AP story notes the Rens are "a fancy ball-handling and shooting Negro team." The Harlem Globe Trotters take third place with a 36-33 win over the Sheboygan Redskins.

The Webfoots' victory, and Charles Buxton's story, made the front page of the *Oregonian*'s main section, a rarity for a sports event. The headline and secondary "decks," over and next to the picture of Bobby Anet accepting the broken trophy, were:

Oregon Steamrollers Buckeye Five 46 to 33 to Take National Title

TALL FIRS HOLD
LEAD ALL ROUTE

Basketball Contest Thrills
4000 Fans and 400 Coaches
Two Speedy Teams Pitted
in Test of Skill

Beneath it:

Mighty Oregons Scramble Ohio State To Take Hoop Title of All America

In the *Register-Guard*, Dick Strite, who wasn't thrilled that he hadn't been sent to Chicago for the game, noted that Eugene residents were going through a hoops hangover, but otherwise his story was a summary of the Webfoots' season. A separate piece ran down the celebration on the city and campus streets the night before. The paper also published two wire-service stories from the game to give local readers a taste of the national reaction.

A *Register-Guard* editorial directly addressed the Webfoots: "Years from now, when your hair is thin and your bones creak, you will be hauled from your haunts and occupations to remind future generations of this Golden Age which you helped to create. . . . You have been 'the best.' You have not been merely 'almost' or 'second-best.'"

Plans continued for Friday welcoming festivities in Eugene. Organizers wouldn't have to settle for making it a celebration of a Western title. Because the Webfoots had won, it would be a grand salute to the national champions. Dean of students Virgil Earl met with student leaders. Together, they came up with a slogan: "No incident to mar the victory."

By the time the Eugene paper hit the streets that afternoon, the boys were on their way home.

As the state prepared for the Webfoots' return, President Erb made speeches in Portland and Salem, discussing the real and possible future economic impacts of the "European Crisis." He was an economics professor on the Eugene campus before leaving for a five-year stint at Stanford that set the stage for his return as president in March 1938. Also, the *Emerald* was one of 85 student papers pooling data and then publishing the results of a poll question: "Should the colonies taken from Germany after the World war be returned to her?" National results: 28.1 percent yes, 71.9 percent no. The *Emerald* story noted that college campuses provided many of the U.S. soldiers in the earlier war. The implication was that the same would be true if America was dragged into another world conflict.

Even this week, all was not about fun and games.

* * *

The *New York Herald Tribune,* the newspaper of the Metropolitan Basketball Writers Association's leaders and the unabashed cheerleaders for the national invitation tournament, ran a two-paragraph Associated Press story and a box score on the NCAA championship game. Squash matches got better coverage.

Wednesday, March 29

WARSAW—There is considerable concern among Polish officials in the wake of a quasi-official declaration published in the newspaper of Germany's foreign office. The piece urges Poland to stop listening to "foreign sirens." That refers to Great Britain and France's attempts to get Poland to join in a multi-nation denunciation of Germany's moves. To many, it comes off as a threat from Germany: *Behave, Poland . . . or else.*

LONDON—Neville Chamberlain announces plans to double the size of the British territorial field army, to 340,000 men, as part of the response to Nazi Germany's moves. His cabinet discusses instituting conscription and mandatory service.

On the Streamliner train headed from Chicago to Portland, the Webfoots' unassuming demeanor impressed the *Oregonian*'s Buxton. It was as if they didn't even know they had won the national championship. They received hundreds of telegrams at stops along the route, including from the governors of the two home states of players on the squad—Oregon's Charles Sprague and Washington's Clarence Martin.

Getting wind of sorority Sigma Delta Chi's "Dance of Champs" scheduled for McArthur Court on Friday night, Anet allegedly sent a wire to his fraternity brother Hank Nilsen. Whether Nilsen was pulling the leg of the student reporter or otherwise, the *Emerald* in bold print declared that Anet had asked Nilsen to line him up with a date for the dance.

Amid all the basketball talk, the campus's Youth Committee Against War met in Alumni Hall to make plans for a national day of protest on April 20 against the possibility of the U.S. becoming involved in another world war. The Oregon students praised and endorsed the stand of Oberlin College president Ernest Wilkins, who had come out against allowing the use of college campuses for part of U.S. military pilots' training. The students announced the speaker on the Oregon campus on April 20 would be University of Washington engineering professor F. B. Farquharson. A pilot in the Great War, he was shot down over Germany and held in a prisoner of war camp until the armistice. Farquharson didn't want his students to have to go through that kind of experience—or worse.

* * *

The LIU seniors suffered a 42-25 thrashing at the hands of the American Professional League All-Stars in Troy, New York. In Brooklyn, university officials were angry that no matter what the boys called themselves at any given moment, many newspapers simply called them the Long Island University Blackbirds.

Thursday, March 30

ROME—The ongoing territorial disputes between Italy and France take ominous turns. French Premier Daladier rules out negotiation, saying his nation will give up neither "a foot of our land nor one of our rights." Italy's Mussolini responds angrily, warning that France will regret that stance.

NEW YORK—Walter Winchell reports that engaged couple Clark Gable and Carole Lombard keep postponing their wedding each time a West Coast columnist gets wind of the plans and publishes a date. The movie stars want to make certain none of the gossips can claim to have been right. Later that day, Gable and Lombard are married in Kingman, Arizona. It's Gable's third marriage, Lombard's second, and it is front-page news from coast to coast— squeezed among the ominous word from Europe.

The yellow "City of Portland" train crossed from Idaho into Oregon in the middle of the night, and a few miles later, a small group of citizens at tiny Nyssa—the home of Webfoots trainer Bob "Two Gun" Officer—offered the first congratulations in Oregon for the boys.

The train didn't stop. The Nyssa folks yelled and waved.

Destined to arrive at Portland's Union Station at 8 a.m., the train entered the Columbia Gorge.

In the preceding days, residents of The Dalles, John Dick's hometown, aware the Webfoots would pass through at about 6 a.m., insisted that the train stop. Their mission was to cheer the local boy and present him with a deluxe $75 watch, purchased with 25-cent contributions from 300 residents. The Dallas citizens were told no, that it wasn't possible. Howard Hobson received Western Union wires telling him of the plans and asking him to intervene, and an appeal made its way to the Union Pacific president. He said no, too. Then he was told if the train didn't stop in The Dalles, the townspeople would block the tracks. Nobody really believed that— well, probably not—but the railroad president finally relented and consented to a brief stop.

It lasted 12 minutes. John Dick got his watch and congratulations. Most of his teammates slept through the proceedings. Others, curious and awakened, got up and watched. Those who did came away with an additional feel for the magnitude of their accomplishment, at least in the eyes of Oregonians. It was as if they had been quarantined for the past few days as they rode, only getting hints through the telegrams and the reaction of others traveling with them.[1]

At the Portland station, about 2,000 crammed into the terminal, and roughly 200 managed to get on the platform next to the track. The Oregon Duck Club and its president, Omar Palmer, had been beating the drums all week to get U of O alumni and fans to the terminal, and the effort probably wasn't necessary. Many gave up on trying to wedge their way in. Those who made it erupted when Laddie Gale was the first to step off, leading the stream of Webfoots out of the car. Police officers begged and then ordered

---

1. The Dalles watch presentation got a lot of publicity, and the other players' hometowns soon followed the lead. Most of the Webfoots ended up owning high-class watches of significant sentimental value.

the mob to let the boys through. Signing autograph books along the way, they made their way to a stage set up outside the station. Through a series of welcoming speeches, including from Portland mayor Joe Carson, the cheers kept coming.

Eager to get back to Eugene, the Webfoots instead spent the day in Portland. They went to breakfast at the Multnomah Hotel and to a luncheon with the Portland Executives' Club, before riding in a parade through downtown. Finally, they were honored at a banquet at the Portland Hotel, joining an affair originally set up to fete longtime Oregon track coach Bill Hayward. U of O President Erb and Governor Charles Sprague were on the scene to repeat their congratulations. Erb didn't mention that he and Hobson often walked home from work together.

* * *

The Metropolitan Basketball Writers held their annual awards dinner in the Hotel Lincoln, and the group's president, Everett B. Morris, announced the scribes' proposal to form a Metropolitan Intercollegiate Conference of the major New York schools. He declared it would turn haphazard and uneven scheduling among the schools into something more ordered, and transform those "mythical" New York league standings in the paper into something more formal. The suggestion wasn't as surprising as Morris's public offer to turn over the national invitation tournament rights to the new league, if formed, to help fund it.

The scribes presented the St. John's players watches for winning the *mythical* 1938–39 league. The LIU Blackbirds won the national invitation tournament and finished undefeated, but their single game against a major metro-area opponent—the win over lowly St. Francis—wasn't enough to qualify for the writers' consideration.

25.

Dance of Champs

Friday, March 31

LONDON—Even in the wake of his plans to expand the British Army, this still is a bombshell: Neville Chamberlain tells the House of Commons that Great Britain and France will lend Poland "all the support in their power" if Poland's independence is threatened. Characterized in many headlines as a pledge, it eventually becomes known as a "guarantee." It is clear: if Germany invades Poland, it will mean war with the British and French. President Roosevelt, vacationing in Warm Springs, Georgia, monitors the news and is in communication with French and British officials. The major question for Americans, of course, is if another war breaks out in Europe, as now seems likely, will the U.S. be drawn into it, too?

On the way down from Portland, the Webfoots' train made a ten-minute stop at Salem, the state capital, where Governor Sprague jumped on the rear platform and made a short speech of congratulation. Howard Hobson again introduced all 11 of his boys to the cheering crowds, and Bobby Anet was introduced to Jack Gosser, the captain of Salem High School's state championship squad. The stop at Albany, where about 2,500 waited, was barely long enough for the boys to wave.

As they neared Eugene, the Webfoots noticed citizens lining the tracks, waving and cheering. The groups became bigger as they neared the station. There, perhaps 10,000 folks waited, tightly packed at the Southern Pacific depot. Some of them were Eugene schoolchildren, dismissed from school and urged to attend the rally. It would have been a pickpocket's dream, but who would stoop that low at a celebration of the local heroes' accomplishment? Many of the players noticed and would remember for years a man hanging from a light-pole after climbing up for a better vantage point.

As the train pulled in at noon, bands from the university and the area high schools played "Mighty Oregon," and confetti flew, with students responding to the *Emerald*'s front-page plea to bring torn paper to the station and to "send it gracefully through the air like the Yankee Clipper." As the boys disembarked, the cheers were deafening, and the Oregon rally girls draped green and yellow Hawaiian leis around their necks. For the rest of the day, the Webfoots looked as if they were tourists in Honolulu.

Whether they had heard of the mess in Portland or just were using common sense, a group of Oregon football players appointed themselves the Webfoots' bodyguards and escorts, getting them from the train to the platform set up for their ceremony. The players signed autographs on anything thrust their way. During the ceremony, Mayor Elisha Large turned over the symbolic key to the city, and Hobson and all 11 players made brief speeches to the mob, with the ceremony carried on KORE.

Anet was genuinely affected. "We never imagined there would be anything like this," he said. "And we're just as glad to be home as you must be to see us."

Riding in open cars, the boys were escorted by the rally squad down Willamette Street. With the crowds spilling into the street and barely leaving room for the crawling cars, the Webfoots went past shuttered stores closed for the parade, townspeople and schoolchildren, and past rows of American flags and green and yellow banners. Student officers in the advanced ROTC program marched in front of and behind the cars. Eventually, after several turns, the cars let out the team in the area of the Commerce Building on campus. There, track runner and student-body president Harry Weston, not knowing that his successor would turn out to be one of the Webfoots, greeted the players officially on behalf of their fellow students. From the building steps, Hobson looked out over the throng and again offered his gratitude. The Webfoots again were overwhelmed, and Anet held up the trophy, not bothering to explain why it was in two pieces. Football coach Tex Oliver also congratulated the Webfoots, saying: "The sad part about this occasion is that the team is faced by a situation like that of

Alexander the Great, who sat down and wept because there were no more worlds to conquer."

* * *

Long Island University officials issued a statement with *harrumph* written all over it, declaring that the senior players were *not* representing the school in their pro games. LIU's dean, Tristram Walker Metcalfe, declared: "The athletic committee realizes that the boys are playing these games for money, and although it has no jurisdiction over such playing, wishes it known that the use of any name which has been affiliated with Long Island University is not authorized."

A few hours later, the LIU seniors, now billing themselves as "The Blackbirds Basketball Team," beat Kentucky State 37-33 at the State Palace in Harlem.

* * *

All week, Oregon fans had been wondering if the Webfoots would be able to hang on to Hobson. As Oregon's basketball and baseball coach, Hobson by then had advanced all the way to an annual salary of about $3,800.

After the rally at the Commerce Building, bandleader Art Holman and his 11-man orchestra set up on the tennis courts behind the building, and students were able to dance for free for three hours in a preview of the night's "Dance of Champs" at McArthur Court. Before that dance, the Webfoots were honored at another dinner at the John Straub Memorial Hall, organized by the Monday Morning Quarterbacks booster group. Students paid 75 cents, townspeople $1.50 to get in, eat, and join in the tribute. Hobson took the opportunity to let it be known he wasn't going anywhere. "We have things as good, and perhaps better, in Oregon as we have in any other part of the country," he said. "I feel that the team we will have here as long as I am connected with basketball will be largely Oregon boys. I am proud to be here at Oregon."

The Webfoots were getting weary of ceremonies. They managed to smile through them again. Anet served as the spokesman for the team and downplayed the Webfoots' accomplishment as "a bit of luck."

President Erb made a point of saying that the championship team could counter the often-heard criticism around campus, and around the country, that the emphasis on big-time athletics was getting out of hand in 1939. "Whenever an athletic program can set for a student body and academic life of a university an example of sportsmanship, scholarship and character, there is no more valuable part of a university," Erb asserted. He said the Webfoots' championship "helps to raise the tone and improve the tempo and morale of the entire institution." A much sought-after speaker, he knew the Webfoots' basketball accomplishment would give him something to talk about before getting down to more serious business of rallying support for higher education; for restoring high-level science courses at Oregon, which had been scrubbed; and for one of his pet projects, a much-needed new student union on the campus.

At Sigma Delta Chi's "Dance of Champs" in The Igloo, 15-foot-high banners with each player's picture were among the decorations as Holman's orchestra again played. All week, the newspapers, on and off campus, had been emphasizing that it was such a festive occasion, girls shouldn't be at all self-conscious about asking men to the dance, instead of the other way around, and it seemed to work. The highlight of the festivities was taking down the banners and presenting them to each player. Billed in *Emerald* ads as "Whoop!! With The Hoopsters" and a way to "honor the nation's best hoop squad," the sorority sold tickets for $1 and turned a nice profit. There was no follow-up story, but it's safe to assume that Bobby Anet found a date.

*   *   *

Dick Strite's *Register-Guard* column in the aftermath of the celebration made clear his feelings on the issue of which team deserved to be considered the best in the land. He wrote: "There was no hollow victory in winning the national championship as some might think, what with Long Island U. and the winner of the 'small-time' national tournament in Kansas City both claiming the title. Reports from the mid-west, recognized as the center of basketball for some years, unquestionably rank Oregon the greatest team in the nation."

Saturday, April 1
WILHELMSHAVEN, Germany—In a rant delivered while launching a German battleship, Hitler responds to the Brit-

ish and French guarantee to Poland. If they want war, he declares, Germany is ready for it. He says: "When today an English statesman opines that all problems must be discussed, that one must resolve them through open discussion and negotiation, then I would like merely to say to this statesman: There was opportunity for fifteen long years before our era for that!"

The die is cast.

Oregana sports editor Hubard Kuokka and his staff had a reprieve. After watching the Friday celebration, they rushed to put together a two-page spread to be wedged at the back of the 1939 yearbook, in a "Lemon Punch" section with all the book's advertising. There would be no reference to it in the Athletics section, and there was no table of contents, so it would require stumbling across it or being alerted it was there. The pages included six pictures of the Eugene welcome for the team.

The headline spread across the two pages captured the spirit.

. . . And the Boys Bring Home the National Basketball Championship!

III

CONCLUSIONS

26.

First, Always

As various organizations named their All-American teams for 1938–39, there were some surprising and even a bit strange variations. Laddie Gale, the Webfoots' best player and a first-team choice on the NEA All-American team, didn't end up on the NCAA's eventual and official consensus All-America list—which included first and second teams—for that season. After the tabulating, Slim Wintermute was designated the consensus first-team center, Bobby Anet a second-team guard.

While minor debates continued over whether Oregon or Long Island deserved to be considered the best team in the land, Webfoots fans were relieved when it was announced in mid-May that Howard Hobson had been granted a $1,200 raise, taking him all the way to $5,000 annually.

The Associated Press had a football poll at the time, but the wire service's basketball poll didn't come along until the 1948–49 season. In the aftermath of the 1939 tournaments, there were a few judgmental references, including by an Associated Press writer or two, to Long Island as national champion, ahead of Oregon. But that didn't come from an official poll. And, yes, as former New Yorker Dick Strite had implied, much of the pro-LIU sentiment seemed to come from the east. The Webfoots also had their advocates.

In 1942, when the Helms Foundation of Los Angeles began selecting its own national champions, it also retroactively went back to 1901 and declared its choices for each year. As part of that, it named LIU its 1939 basketball champion, and that distinction still is listed in such places as the Blackbirds' modern-era media guides.

The choice of LIU was (and is) defensible, of course.

The choice of LIU also was (and is) wrong.

Yes, the Blackbirds were undefeated, and their conquests included a handful of high-quality teams at Madison Square Garden.

Oregon and LIU played only two common opponents, Bradley
Tech and Canisius. The Blackbirds beat Bradley Tech 36-32 in
the invitation tournament semifinals in Madison Square Garden,
and the Webfoots fell 52-39 to the team from Peoria during the
marathon December road trip. Both teams handled Canisius by
12 points—the Blackbirds at home, the Webfoots on that eastern
trip. Then and since, many seemed to overlook the fact that the
Blackbirds played only *one* legitimate road game, weren't in a
conference, and played only soft touches in their "own" arena.
The Garden games were their only real tests. As impressive as
the Blackbirds were there, and as great of a coach as Clair Bee
was, the Garden was their quasi-home floor and the out-of-area
opponents often were weary from the marathon travel it took to
get to New York.

The Blackbirds were undefeated, but not completely tested.

There's an irony here, too, again involving Ohio State: the heroes of *Third Down and a War to Go*, football's 1942 Wisconsin
Badgers, defeated the Buckeyes 17-7 that season. The Buckeyes,
at the time, but also especially later, said they had gotten tainted
water on the trip and that many players were ill during their loss
to the Badgers. (Sound familiar?) Wisconsin finished 8-1-1, Ohio
State 9-1. AP voted the Buckeyes No. 1—*sportswriters!*—and the
Badgers No. 3. Just getting started in the business of naming champions of its own at the time, the Helms Foundation also selected a
football champion for that year, and it made the right call on this
one, making Wisconsin its national champion.

Today, it has become tiresome to hear the reflexive "East Coast
bias" argument advanced for everything from the minor—say, the
order of the highlights on SportsCenter—to the major. It's undeni-
able that there often is an East Coast *perspective* apparent in national coverage, but much of the talk is overblown. Still, think of
what it was like in 1939. Chicago and St. Louis were considered the
western outposts of major-league baseball. The Big Ten also was
known as the Western Conference. Some in New York probably
thought the Oregon Webfoots, isolated outside the major West
Coast cities of Los Angeles, San Francisco, and perhaps Seattle, tied
their horses at hitching posts when they went to class.

With the New York scribes often overlooking or completely
ignoring the quirks of the New York basketball scene, including

LIU's strange scheduling, evaluations could be skewed. There was no question that the Oregon press had been as partisan as were the New Yorkers arguing LIU's case. The laughable part of that, though, was that at least the folks in the Pacific Northwest didn't *pretend* to be completely objective.

Who would have won an Oregon-Long Island matchup in March 1939?

It depends.

If they played in McArthur Court, Oregon would have won, perhaps easily, in part because the Blackbirds would have traveled across the country and weren't accustomed to playing on the road at all. Oregon was playing its best basketball as the season wound down. The Webfoots were a different team than the one that passed through New York in December, and peaking at the right time was, and still is, a test of college basketball greatness, most notably in the NCAA tournament.

If Oregon and LIU played on a neutral floor—in, say, Evanston, Illinois, after the Blackbirds made it through the NCAA Eastern championships—Oregon would have won that one, too.

If they played in the national invitation tournament in Madison Square Garden, sure, LIU probably would have won.

Plus, of course, Ned Irish could have headed off much of the debate by matching Oregon against LIU instead of CCNY in the first Garden doubleheader of the season back in December. LIU would have had the home-court advantage and wouldn't have traveled, but it would have been difficult to argue against allowing a head-to-head matchup settle the debate over which post-season tournament champion was better that season. Judging by how poorly the Webfoots played against CCNY, they might have had problems with LIU, but there's no guarantee of that. Playing against a confirmed national power would have changed the dynamic for the Webfoots.

The bottom line: The Webfoots' tournament was part of a sincere effort to pick a champion from all regions of the country. League champions or co-champions that turned down bids to the regionals or play-in games—including Colorado and Missouri in the West and Kentucky in the East—and chose to end their seasons, had to live with those decisions. The only one of those three likely capable of challenging the Webfoots was Kentucky. The NCAA event began as a response to the national invitation tournament, absolutely, but its creation was inevitable with or without the NIT. Ned Irish and, secondarily, the Metropolitan Basketball Writers Association did the college game huge favors by providing the impetus, but it was going to happen sooner or later.

Before the Madness, Oregon was the first NCAA champion. They beat programs from three prominent schools and leagues with ease, and that came after virtual championship tournament atmospheres for their pairs of games against tough PCC opponents Washington and California helped toughen them.

They deserve their spot in history.

They *were* the first national champions.

In one way, though, the head-to-head matchup of the NCAA tournament and the national invitation tournament at first was a complete rout for the NIT.

That was at the box office.

Still designed to be a New York–centric event with invited guests joining the locals, the Metropolitan Basketball Writers' Association's tournament drew terrific crowds to Madison Square Garden. (It's possible that attendance figures were exaggerated, but even then, the true figures would have been impressive.)

The first NCAA tournament, at neutral sites—San Francisco, Philadelphia, and Evanston—with only Villanova as a "local" attraction in the Eastern championships, drew disappointing crowds.

So in the box-office sense, absolutely, the invitation tournament was "bigger" than the NCAA tournament in 1939 and for the next decade or so. At least at the outset, though, the NCAA tournament never was envisioned to be a box-office bonanza, but rather a competition to select a true national champion.

A couple of funny things happened after the 1939 tournaments, too.

In New York, as the offer to turn over the tournament rights in conjunction with the possible formation of a New York league hinted, the Metropolitan Basketball Writers Association was apparently eager to unload at least official control of the tournament. The New York–area basketball league wasn't formed, but the writers agreed to pass along the tournament to an association of New York basketball-playing schools. From 1940 on, the writers' stake in the tournament was indirect.[1] Absolutely, after the New York tournament expanded to eight teams in 1941, after the war years changed the picture considerably, and until a 1951 scandal led to a rearranging of the college basketball landscape, it was more reasonable to argue that the NIT was the better and more prestigious tournament. That argument was often overstated, and a countering one could be made for the NCAA tournament, but the point is, the New York tournament's alleged superiority in 1939 doesn't hold up to scrutiny.

In the wake of the 1939 tournament, the National Association of Basketball Coaches tallied up the ledgers for the first NCAA tournament and swallowed hard. The losses, which they were expected to cover as part of the deal for the NCAA's approval, were $2,531. But the NCAA agreed to pay that off in exchange for taking control of the event. In 1940, the NCAA tournament became truly the NCAA's tournament.

For $2,531 . . .

It was a better deal than $24 for Manhattan.

*   *   *

On September 1, 1939, under the pretense of reacting to a concocted attack from Polish forces, Hitler ordered his troops into Poland. Two days later, Great Britain and France declared war on Germany.

World War II had started.

---

1. In 2005, after several years of contentious litigation, the NCAA bought the rights to the pre- and post-season NIT for $40.5 million plus $16 million in legal fees. The NCAA now puts on those tournaments for both men and women.

27.

Coaches

Better late than never, Ned Irish decided. The New York promoter offered Howard Hobson a chance to return to Madison Square Garden in December 1939, this time for a game against LIU. Coach Hobson told Donald Erb of the offer one day on their walk home together.

"Well, now, you can't go to New York every year," the U of O president responded, pointing out the trip cost the players at least one week of school before the Christmas break began.

Told of Erb's objections, John MacGregor, the NYU law professor and U of O alumnus, called Erb and appealed, and Erb gave in.

The other game on the December 16, 1939, doubleheader was Henry Iba's Oklahoma A&M squad facing CCNY.

This time, the Oregon trip lasted nearly three weeks and nine games. Hobson realized making the train trip to New York in one long ride had left the Webfoots sluggish, so he scheduled a tune-up game in New Orleans against an AAU team on the way. If Ned Irish protested, he wasn't able to do anything about it because it was the dedication game for New Orleans's new arena.

Of course, some scribes attempted to build the December game into a retroactive national championship game, but that was ridiculous considering the graduation losses for *both* teams. John Dick was the only returning starter for the Webfoots, and he had been switched to center to step in for Slim Wintermute. One of the remaining Astoria Fishermen, Ted Sarpola, was starting as a senior and, as he had the season before, caught the attention of the New York scribes with his flashiness. Two other '39 championship team holdovers, Red McNeeley and Matt Pavalunas, were the other starters, along with Vic Townsend, a transfer from Compton Junior College.

Forward-center Si Lobello, a part-time starter as a sophomore the season before, was back for the Blackbirds and leading the way with a 17-point average, and Dolly King was a standout at center, but the Blackbirds had lost most of the stalwarts from the undefeated team of 1938–39.

Still, it turned out to be a terrific game, played in front of a crowd of 17,852.

At halftime, the Webfoots were up 32-20 and seemed in complete control. Frustrated, Bee mapped out a second-half strategy with his spools, but he also lost his temper and bashed his hand against a steel door. In considerable pain, he went out for the second half with his boys and watched as they fought back after the Oregon lead peaked at 14 points three minutes into the second half. The Blackbirds pulled into a 50-50 tie in the final minute with a bucket from King, described as a "220-pound Negro Hercules" in Arthur Daley's *Times* story and the "muscular negro veteran" in the AP account.

As the overtime was about to start, Hobson was flabbergasted to notice Bee approaching the Oregon bench. Before anything was said, though, Bee plopped down on the bench. Hobson remembered that his famous coaching opponent "was shaking like a leaf." It's unclear how long Bee stayed on the bench or where he went from there, but the Blackbirds managed to escape with a 56-55 win in overtime, with King getting the final points with 40 seconds remaining.[1] Lobello had 16 points for the winners and Sarpola had 13 and Dick 11 for the Webfoots. Sarpola drew his fourth personal and fouled out late in the first half, which was possible only because coaches couldn't call the time-outs, so Hobson wasn't able to get him out of the game in time on his own. Later, McNeeley also fouled out, so the Webfoots had a patchwork lineup on the floor in the overtime. Everett B. Morris of the *Herald Tribune* called it "the greatest game ever played in New York or perhaps anywhere."

Hobson said that when he went to the Blackbirds locker room to congratulate and check on Bee, he was unconscious on the training table. When Bee awakened, Hobson said, the LIU coach offered his left hand for the handshake. His right one, he told Hobson, was fractured.

At the time, despite the declarations of war, the absence of fighting in Europe for six months after the German conquest of Poland

---

1. The time remaining is according to the Associated Press story. Over the years, other retrospective accounts have had King's bucket coming at the buzzer. The *Times* story didn't mention a time for it at all. The AP version seems the most reliable.

would lead to the period being labeled "The Phony War." Few believed the quiet would last—and it didn't.

In that 1939–40 season, the Webfoots finished second to rival Oregon State in the PCC Northern Division, with Dick named a consensus All-American. They slipped to a tie for third in 1940–41, with only McNeeley, by then 24 years old, remaining from the NCAA championship team. The war years pushed all sports into the background, of course, scaling back schedules and especially travel even for the programs that could put together reasonable rosters. Hobson was on military leave in 1944–45, when Oregon defeated Washington State in a best-of-three series to claim the division title. The Webfoots advanced directly to the NCAA Western championships at Kansas City, where they lost to Arkansas in the first round and then beat Utah in a consolation game. While serving in the Navy, Hobson's primary duty was putting on basketball clinics for forces in the Mediterranean area. In the summers of 1945 and '46, he attended Columbia and obtained his doctorate. He was back at Oregon for the 1945–46 season, but resigned two years later to accept the head-coaching job at Yale. In 11 seasons under Hobson, the Webfoots were 212-124.

In his final seasons at Oregon, games between the Webfoots and Bee's Blackbirds were frequent. Hobson believed being able to say his team made annual trips to New York helped recruiting. So the Blackbirds and Webfoots met in mid-December in the Garden again in 1940 and, a week after Pearl Harbor, in 1941. LIU again won both of those games, 43-31 and 33-31. The series resumed in 1945, after the war, and Hobson's Webfoots won that game 60-50. After Hobson departed the program, assistant John Warren, the former Astoria High coach, inherited the Oregon job and brought the Webfoots back to the Garden for one more meeting with LIU in December 1947, with the Blackbirds winning again 49-47.

Hobson was ambivalent about leaving Oregon for Yale, but he said the opportunity to also supervise a master's degree program in physical education and athletics at the prestigious school was the deal-closer. Yale didn't offer a PE major for undergraduates, and the thinking was that adding the master's program would at least enable Yale grads to add a master's that would qualify them for coaching positions. A new president scuttled that program and many other graduate degrees in the early 1950s, which greatly disappointed Hobson. But he discovered that speaking engagements and other outside opportunities enabled him to more than double his income at Oregon. The Bulldogs won an Eastern Intercollegiate Basketball League title in 1949 and lost in the first round of the NCAA Eastern regional.

Hobson's 1949 book, *Scientific Basketball*, was stunningly detailed, presenting his arguments for ideas he had been pushing for many years. As familiar as much of it sounded to his former players, or anyone who had been around him, the book still was remarkably ahead of its time and innovative. He campaigned for going far beyond scoring numbers in evaluating the effectiveness of players. With an incredible amount of data to back it up, it read like a manifesto advancing what would become the modern box-score and more ambitious statistics, involving such things as "loss of ball" (i.e., turnovers) and "interceptions" (steals), plus far more attention paid to keeping track of rebounding. In a chapter titled, "A Proposed Area-Method of Scoring," he outlined his long-held ideas for a three-point field goal and a widened foul lane, or key. He was involved in an experimental game between Columbia and Fordham on February 7, 1945, in which a shot taken from outside a 21-foot line was worth three points. His proposal was to have the line at 24 feet. By then, he had abandoned as impractical and excessively complicated the idea of making lay-ups worth only one point. He stuck with the three-pointer, though, calling it "the home run of basketball" and arguing that it would:

- discourage zone defenses, which he used, but didn't particularly like;
- force tall players to become more well-rounded because of what Hobson envisioned to be more emphasis on three-point shots;
- cause the two-hand set shot to regain popularity because of its accuracy from long distance;
- enable teams to come from behind more often; and
- open up the game because tighter guarding outside would enable quicker players more opportunity to drive to the basket.

He was hit-and-miss on those points, but there can't be any disputing that he was a visionary and generally on track. When the lane finally was widened to 12 feet in 1955, he was given considerable credit for being the major proponent of the change for many years.

As chairman of the U.S. Olympic team for 1952, Hobson was part of the tryout process that selected six members of the University of Kansas varsity, including Clyde Lovellette, and AAU veterans as the core of the team. He went to Helsinki to see the American squad beat the Soviet Union for the gold medal. His son, David, served as the Bulldogs' captain in 1954–55, which turned out to be Hobson's next-to-last season as Yale's coach. Hobson stepped away from coaching at age 52, after the 1955–56 season, to go into publishing. He supervised sports books, mostly strategic and instructional texts sold to schools and coaches, for the Ronald Press Company of New York. That company had bought the Barnes Sports Library, which previously published a four-book series of instructional coaching texts by Clair Bee and Hobson's own *Basketball Illustrated*. With Hobson at the helm, Ronald Press's books were a financial success, and after four years, management allowed him to move back to Portland and run the operation out of an office there.

Hobson was inducted into the Naismith Memorial Basketball Hall of Fame in 1965. Three years later, because of Ronald Press Company policy, he retired at age 65 and, as the universally recognized "Hobby," enjoyed his time as the informal elder statesman of the Oregon sports scene until he passed away in June 1991. At his funeral, Laddie Gale mused: "If there's a basketball court in heaven, I know who's keeping statistics."

* * *

Clair Bee remained astoundingly busy. In addition to coaching, he served as Long Island's assistant to the president, the athletic director, and director of the physical education department, and even coached the revived football team for two seasons before the program was dropped again. His basketball coaching texts were regarded as mandatory for budding coaches. He owned a farm in upstate New York and used it as a retreat. His Blackbirds won the national invitation tournament again in 1941, and he took a leave of absence for two seasons during World War II to serve as a Merchant Marine commander.

In 1945, Bee mourned the death of Si Lobello, the sophomore big man on the 1938–39 Blackbirds. An Army private first class in the 13th Infantry Regiment, 8th Infantry Division, Lobello was killed in action in Belgium on March 3, less than two months before the German surrender. He was buried in the Henri-Chapelle American Cemetery and awarded the Bronze Star.

Bee's post-war formula was familiar: the Blackbirds became even more the "resident" college team of Madison Square Garden and their genuine road games were rare until two later barnstorming tours. One in 1949 included a pair of two-point wins at Oregon, and another in 1951 included a loss at California. After that 1951 trip, the Blackbirds returned to New York just as all hell was breaking loose on the college basketball scene.

When Milton Gross's extensive portrait of Bee appeared in the March 1951 *Sport*, the piece included a picture of Bee with his star forward, Sherm White, who was averaging an astounding 27.7 points per game that season. In the piece, Bee was quoted as saying: "If a boy convinces me he's sincere, I'll do anything short of paying him money to come to LIU. I'll give him tuition, fees, books, a job for spending money, and room and board if he comes from out of town. He'll have sympathy from me and understanding. I'll be for him all the way. He can call me day or night if he's in trouble and need advice or help of any kind. That's a coach's responsibility. But if I catch a player riding the gravy train, or if I find that everything he has told me about himself isn't true, then I want nothing further to do with him."

Bee's comments almost certainly alluded to the fact that in mid-January, three bookmakers and two players from the previous season's Manhattan team were arrested and charged with bribery and conspiracy in connection with game-fixing and point-shaving schemes. Rumors circulated that the scandal would spread to other New York teams. Bee had confronted his team and was assured none of his players were involved.

Only ten days before the magazine's cover date, three stars (Ed Warner, Ed Roman, and Al Roth) on the 1950 CCNY team that was the first and only squad to win both the NCAA tournament and NIT were arrested and charged, also. On February 20, apparently too close to the publication date for anything to be done about or with the story, three LIU players (White, LeRoy Smith, and Adolph Bigos) were arrested in connection with the growing scandal. The Blackbirds were 20-4 at the time. Their February 22 game against Cincinnati was canceled, and the season was ruled to be over. Eventually, three additional former LIU players from previous seasons (Natie Miller, Lou Lipman, and Dick Feurtado) also were arrested in district attorney Frank Hogan's crusade. Former LIU player Eddie Gard was the middleman between the "wise guys" and the Blackbirds, and Gard generally was offering $1,000 a game to each player involved. The total arrested reached 32 players from seven schools, with the fixed New York games taking place from 1947 to 1950. The other six schools were CCNY, Bradley, NYU, Kentucky, Manhattan, and Toledo.

White served nine months in jail on Riker's Island. The other five LIU players received suspended sentences. Bigos had earned the Bronze Star in World War II, and Smith had served in the Marines. That didn't mean much to Hogan. It might have to a judge.

LIU dropped basketball for six years.

Devastated, Bee never again coached in the college game. Discussing the scandal in a speech to coaches in Virginia, he said: "We, you and I, have flunked. We have not done the job that was expected of us in training the young people. I am not bitter. I am hurt, hurt desperately. When I was told that three of my boys had sold themselves, it was a deep bereavement. I am not ashamed to say I wept. It was then that something died within me."

Bee had started writing the Chip Hilton books in the late 1940s, and as the series continued, they were consolation. He could make his boys there not flawless (well, expect for Chip), but all worked out for them in the end—with bullies converted, villains defeated, wrongs righted, and lessons always learned . . . both by the boys within the pages and those reading the books. Bee coached the NBA's Washington Bullets from 1952 to 1954 and served as the athletic director at the New York Military Academy from 1954 to 1967. He was elected to the Naismith Memorial Basketball Hall of Fame in 1968 and died in 1983.

28.

The Tall Firs

---

28 Laddie Gale

Forward	6-4	195	Senior	Oakridge, Oregon
GP: 34	FG: 145	FT: 117	Points: 407	Average: 12.0

After turning down overtures for most of the 1939–40 season, Gale relented and played eight regular-season and three playoff games for the Detroit Eagles of the National Basketball League. Although he joined the Eagles late, his scoring average (7.5) led the team, barely beating out teammates Slim Wintermute (7.2) and former LIU star Irv Torgoff (6.6).

Gale was set to become Oregon's freshman team basketball coach in 1942 when he entered the service instead and became an instructor in water survival and a basketball coach for the U.S. Army Air Forces, including in Santa Ana, California. Following his release from the service, he played for several AAU teams. Moving to Oregon's capital of Salem in 1950, he ran his own gas station, owned a bread distributorship, and sold cars. In the mid-1960s, he briefly lived in Eugene, selling cars for Dunham Motors, and then entered the real-estate field in, first, Florence, and then Gold Beach on the Oregon coast, with his Sportsman's Realty.

Thanks in part to the tireless advocacy of Howard Hobson, Gale was inducted into the Naismith Memorial Basketball Hall of Fame in 1977, and the first call of congratulations he got was from his former college coach. "Hobby actually spent half the time apologizing that Slim (Wintermute) didn't make it too," Gale said that day. "I agreed, and it was kind of funny because most of the time we were talking about how it was too bad that some of the other guys couldn't be honored, too. It was the type of team that made it awful hard to pick out one guy."

Gale retired in 1980, and in 1989, Gold Beach saluted him with the naming of a fir tree—yes, a Tall Fir—in his honor on the new Schrader Old Growth Trail. He died at age 79 in July 1996, and mourners were startled, but pleased, when his funeral service ended with a rousing playing of "Mighty Oregon." His ashes were scattered beneath the tree.

22 Slim Wintermute

Center	6-8	195	Senior	Longview, Washington
GP: 31	FG: 124	FT: 61	Points: 309	Average: 10.0

The Webfoots' renowned center averaged 7.2 points in his single season with the Detroit Eagles. He also played for several semi-pro and AAU teams, including the Portland Indians, ran his own leasing company, and worked as an analyst for Boeing in Seattle.

On October 21, 1977, when he was 60, he and a friend, Jerry Caldwell, took out his 37-foot boat from the Lake Union Yacht Club. Subsequent reports said that in the afternoon, Caldwell awoke from a nap and realized Wintermute was gone. The boat by then was on the Cozy Cove inlet in Lake Washington, meaning it had been taken through the strait connecting the two lakes. Wintermute's body never was found. His son, Scott, said there was no suspicion of foul play and that his father had suffered a heart attack earlier and undergone heart surgery. Scott theorized that he either had suffered another heart attack and had fallen overboard or had slipped over the rail. Scott dived under the lake surface, trying to find his father's body, but was unsuccessful in water that was as much as 200 feet deep.

18 John Dick

Forward	6-4	200	Junior	The Dalles, Oregon
GP: 34	FG: 90	FT: 49	Points: 229	Average: 6.8

In his 1939–40 senior season, when he also was Oregon's student-body president and served on the athletics board, Dick led the PCC in scoring and was a consensus first-team All-American. He didn't talk about any of that much because the team had a disappointing season. "He still felt years later that he let the team down, because he played well, but not well enough," says his son, John Michael Dick.

After his graduation, Dick played for an AAU team in Seattle and held down a nominal job as a parts manager for the team's sponsoring company. He looked at it as holding time until he decided what direction he would go in the workplace. On December 7, 1941, everything changed. The next day, Dick—and many, many others—lined up to enlist in Seattle. "I was still in great shape because I was still playing ball, and the Lieutenant Commander who was in charge at the place I enlisted called me aside," he recalled. "He told me he had seen the results of my physical and said they desperately needed men in good physical shape in Naval aviation, so he asked me to go in that direction. I was a little surprised, but told him I would go wherever they needed me."

Told he needed letters of recommendation, he got working on that, and one of the first came from Washington coach Hec Edmundson. Accepted in the program, Dick went to Corpus Christi, Texas, for flight school. He played intra-service baseball, too, and when major-league pitcher Johnny Sain offered up a fastball that Dick drove off the scoreboard, he saw nothing but curveballs from Sain again and was reminded why he wouldn't have made it as a pro baseball player. (That damn curveball . . .) Then when he suffered a leg injury when spiked in a game, he was held back in training and eventually was assigned to serve a stint as an instructor, a common occurrence that underscored the rushed nature of our training. Many pilots, both in the Navy and the Army Air Forces, were held back to teach what they had been taught to those in the next wave. Then he was dispatched to the Pacific, where he flew Grumman F8F Bearcat and F6F Hellcat fighters in support of ground missions or bombing of ground targets. Immediately after the Japanese surrender, he was among those assigned to fly around the Pacific Theater, scouting for Americans stranded and abandoned in prisoner-of-war camps. He later told his sons that he got help from "flexible" Navy authorities, since he likely was taller and heavier than the pilot maximums. He admitted he generally didn't wear his parachute, because that would have made the cockpit too cramped, and stowed it under his seat instead.

Dick decided to remain in the Navy. "He didn't say he did any soul-searching," John Michael says. "He just said he loved flying, and they had taught him to fly. He wanted to stay in and fly."

He married the girl next door (truly) from The Dalles, Fran, in 1946. Eventually their family would include three sons and a daughter.

In the Korean War era, after being trained in another Grumman naval fighter, the F9F Panther jet, he was set to go out on his first sortie in the afternoon when the word came that the war was over.

In the 1960s, he first was chief of staff for naval air operations, and he obtained a master's degree in international relations from George Washington University while stationed in Washington. He often played basketball in the Pentagon gym, sometimes enlisting his visiting son, John Michael, as his teammate in two-on-two "make it, take it" games against younger players that could leave the opponents astounded about what the "old man" officer still could do on the floor, especially with running hook shots with either hand.

He was the primary flight officer on the *USS Intrepid* and the nuclear-powered *USS Enterprise*, plotting the schedules and logistics in the launch and recovery of the planes. Transitioning to the captain's bridge, Dick was captain of the *USS Washburn*, an attack cargo ship, and the super-carrier *USS Saratoga* from September 1967 to April 1969 during the Vietnam War.

He retired as a rear admiral in 1973. As his teammates died, one by one, he became even more the spokesman for the 1939 champions as years passed. John Michael most vividly remembers one television interview when the questioner asked his father what it felt like to be the leading scorer in the first-ever NCAA championship game. The Admiral's response: "You shouldn't make so much of that. We were a smart team and all we were doing was taking advantage of what the defense offered."

Fran passed away in 1999.

Rear Admiral John Dick died in Eugene on September 22, 2011.

32 Wally Johansen

Guard	5-11	155	Senior	Astoria, Oregon
GP: 34	FG: 74	FT: 45	Points: 193	Average: 5.7

Johansen and his fellow Flying Finn, Bobby Anet, indeed played the 1939–40 season for a new Eugene AAU team, which turned out to be sponsored by Rubenstein's Furniture and called the Rubenstein's Oregonians. They won the state title and then, after picking up Oregon seniors John Dick, Ted Sarpola, and Matt Pavalunas after the

Webfoots' season ended, lost to the Colorado Springs Jewelers in the quarterfinals of the 1940 national AAU tournament in Denver.

Johansen was studying law as a post-graduate when his father's illness caused him to step away from school and return to Astoria, where he landed a job as a sportswriter for the local paper. "He was trying to help his family along," says his son, Kirk. When the U.S. entered World War II, Johansen joined the Navy in 1942 and was a gunnery officer on a transport vessel in the Pacific Theater. He and his girlfriend, Betty, were married in June 1945 in San Francisco, and they sent a wire to Bobby Anet telling him the news.

After the peace, Johansen re-entered graduate law school and he and Betty lived near the Oregon campus, on what they jokingly called "Poverty Alley," and their next-door neighbors were Oregon quarterback Norm Van Brocklin and his wife, Gloria. In 1948, Johansen joined the McKeown and Newhouse firm in Coos Bay, Oregon. Successful and respected, he became a partner in the firm and was president of the Oregon State Bar Association in 1967–68.

On September 10, 1971, he had just finished a fishing expedition on the Rogue River with Kirk and was headed back to the family vacation home near Bandon when he suffered his third heart attack. This one was fatal.

He was 54 years old.

Kirk scattered his father's ashes in the Rogue.

20 Bobby Anet

Guard	5-8	175	Senior	Astoria, Oregon
GP: 33	FG: 56	FT: 67	Points: 179	Average: 5.3

After briefly working as a graduate assistant coach under Hobson, Anet—who had turned down a chance to join Gale and Wintermute with the Detroit Eagles—went to the Los Angeles area in 1940 to work for Lockheed and play basketball on the side.

Knowing his father, a member of the Astoria draft board, had promised that his sons would be among the first young men called up, Bobby enlisted in the Navy and was officially inducted in January 1942. He started out as a chief specialist in physical training at the Naval Training Station in Dearborn, Michigan. He managed to play semi-pro ball on the side with the Detroiters. In one doubleheader, he and the Detroiters faced the Eber-Seagrams and the Harlem Globe Trotters faced the New York Rens. Eventually, Anet went to the Pacific Theater where, beginning in late 1943, he served on ships as a lieutenant commander.

In San Francisco two months after the war ended, Wally and Betty Johansen announced to a visiting Anet that they had a friend named Paula they wanted him to meet. Raised in Walnut, Kansas, the future Paula Anet taught school briefly before deciding to join two of her aunts in San Francisco after the outbreak of the war, and she found work as a secretary in an architect's office.

Paula and Bobby were married in the spring of 1946. Wally and Betty Johansen stood up for them at the ceremony.

Anet had been accepted to attend graduate school at Harvard, but instead moved back to Oregon with his new wife. He spent most of his professional life as a lumber broker in the Portland area. He died in July 1981, and he was the third starter from Howard Hobson's most famous team that the retired coach had to memorialize. "Bobby was a great floor leader and always led the fast break," Hobson said. "I think people known as fast-break artists today would be slow walkers compared to Anet. He's the best I've ever seen, before or since. Other players did our scoring, but Bobby was clearly the director of the team."

40 Bob Hardy

Forward	6-3	180	Senior	Ashland, Oregon
GP: 30	FG: 46	FT: 22	Points: 114	Average: 3.8

As the Webfoots' ace pitcher, Hardy was 7-0 as a senior in 1939, and he and basketball teammate Ford Mullen led Oregon to the 1939 PCC Northern Division baseball championship. Hardy signed with the Detroit Tigers, receiving a bonus of about $1,500, and was sent to Beaumont of the Texas League. But as happens to so many hard-throwing left-handed pitchers, he was derailed by shoulder and arm trouble in his short minor-league career. He also served in the U.S. Navy in the Pacific during World War II, then returned to his native Ashland and purchased the family grocery store from his father. Next, he founded a lumber company in Happy Camp, California, and it did well. After his retirement, he lived on the Oregon coast at Brookings, and he died in 2006.

25 Ted Sarpola

Forward	6-2	160	Junior	Astoria, Oregon
GP: 27	FG: 37	FT: 17	Points: 91	Average: 3.4

Sarpola stepped up to become a starter the next season, too, and he and John Dick were the Webfoots' leading scorers. After his graduation, Sarpola served in the Coast Guard, and then had a long teaching and coaching career in Oregon high schools, including in The Dalles and Astoria, and was renowned for playing serious AAU ball well into his 50s. He retired in 1981, but continued coaching on a volunteer basis in his hometown and Knappa, Oregon. He died in his Knappa home in 1986.

11 Matt Pavalunas

Guard	6-0	170	Junior	Raymond, Washington
GP: 33	FG: 38	FT: 12	Points: 88	Average: 2.7

The reserve guard who made the championship game box score entered the service before Pearl Harbor and eventually coached the 363rd Engineers basketball team to many service championships, including of the entire Middle East command. A picture of him shaking hands with the Shah of Iran, Mohammad Reza Shah Pahlavi, was among the family archives. After leaving the Army, he became a well-known high school coach in Washington, starting out in 1949 at Sequim, on the Olympic Peninsula, where he was head coach in basketball and baseball and an assistant in football. In the late '50s, he became friends with Jack Elway, a young coach at nearby Port Angeles High School. Pavalunas specialized in basketball after he moved on to Centralia and Auburn high schools, and he was inducted into the Washington Interscholastic Basketball Coaches Association Hall of Fame in 1977. He died of a heart attack in Ocean Park, Washington, in 1991.

13 Ford Mullen

Guard	5-8	165	Junior	Olympia, Washington
GP: 20	FG: 18	FT: 9	Points: 45	Average: 2.3

Bobby Anet's backup decided to forgo his final season of basketball eligibility and, like Bob Hardy, signed with the Detroit Tigers after the Webfoots' 1939 baseball season. Mullen played several seasons of minor-league baseball from the Class D to the Class AAA level. After a brief run with the Pacific Coast League's Seattle Rainiers in 1942, he retired from baseball and taught and coached at Eugene High for a year. But with the ranks of players thinned out by the war, he rejoined the Rainiers at the end of the 1942–43 school year. He spent the 1944 season playing second base with the Philadelphia Phillies, hitting .267 in 118 games and becoming a cult figure as "Moon" Mullen. He was drafted into the Army, too, but was kept back at Fort Lewis in Washington and both played on and eventually managed the base's powerful baseball team. Leaving the service in 1946, he went to spring training with the Phillies in 1947, but didn't stick with the big club and spent four more seasons in the minors, finishing up as the Boise Pilots' player-manager in the Pioneer League. He returned to his hometown and for 27 years was a fixture as a biology and zoology teacher and coach at his alma mater, Olympia High School. He was the final surviving member of the 1939 Webfoots and the oldest living former Phillies player when he died in February 2013.

15 Red McNeeley

Guard	6-2	180	Sophomore	Portland
GP: 18	FG: 9	FT: 5	Points: 23	Average: 1.4

After playing two more seasons for the Webfoots, McNeeley drew what he later laughingly labeled "a nice low number" in the draft lottery. In a discussion taped for family posterity, McNeeley said: "I decided that I didn't want to pack a rifle in the mud." He enlisted in the Navy in late 1941, before Pearl Harbor, and took his first training flight on December 31, 1941. On a leave in Portland, he married his college sweetheart, U of O sorority girl Jean Pauling, who was from—small world—Astoria. As a pilot of floatplanes and seaplanes, McNeeley was stationed at Attu Island in the Aleutians for 14 months before returning to the mainland for more training. By then, he was considered one of the Navy's most experienced "new" pilots and was given his pick of carrier-based aircraft. He ended up in a new squadron, piloting a Grumman TBF Avenger torpedo bomber with a radioman and a gunner. Eventually, the squadron went to the Pacific, assigned to escort the fuel tanker fleet. After six months of that, the squadron was deployed to the

Battle of Iwo Jima. The squadron flew Marine observers over the island to gather information about the status of the battle and try to spot Japanese troops, and the observers tended to ask the pilots to get lower . . . and lower. McNeeley became squadron commander when his predecessor's plane was shot down. His planes were hit twice by enemy fire, but he made it back to the carrier. In the second week of the battle, again carrying an observer, his plane was nailed again, more seriously, and he managed to land on the steel-matted runway the Marines had just finished. He became more directly involved in the battle, dropping torpedo bombs into caves on the northern side of the island and also destroying a Japanese blockhouse. For his work in the Battle of Iwo Jima, he was awarded the Distinguished Flying Cross.

After he left the service, he and Jean settled in Astoria, where Red served a stint as mayor and sold insurance for over 50 years. He died in 1994.

36 Earl Sandness

Center	6-4	190	Sophomore	Astoria, Oregon
GP: 12	FG: 4	FT: 0	Points: 8	Average: 0.7

The backup center played two more seasons for the Webfoots, and then also entered the Navy. Serving through the Korean War, he rose to the rank of lieutenant commander. He coached and taught in Alaska and then in Portland, and late in life went into the charter boat business in Ilwaco, Wash. He died in 1984.

Also Saw Action

According to the final statistics published in the *Register-Guard* on March 29, 1939, two of the other nine players considered part of the full 20-man team that season appeared in varsity games. Sophomore **Don Mabee**, who made the eastern barnstorming trip as an extra body, played in five games. Junior **Wellington "Wimpy" Quinn** appeared in one. Both also were better known for their prowess in other sports. Mabee played only that single season with the Webfoots in basketball, but was a three-year letterman as an end and halfback in football. He served in the army in

World War II and became one of Oregon's top high school football coaches at LaGrande (five years) and McMinnville (25 years). He died in 1996. Quinn, nicknamed after the character in the "Popeye" cartoons, was a standout third baseman for the Webfoots in baseball and played professionally for Vancouver of the Western International League and the Los Angeles Angels of the Pacific Coast League. The Chicago Cubs liked his arm enough to bring him to camp as a pitcher in 1941, and pitching coach Dizzy Dean said: "With my brain and his arm, they'll never get him out of the major leagues." Ol' Diz was wrong about that. Quinn also was in the service during the war and then was a player-manager in the minor leagues as late as 1951, but died at age 36 in 1954.

Honorable Mention

Sophomore **Toivo Piippo,** the fifth player on the full 20-man team from Astoria that season, went into the Army Air Corps in July 1941. Piloting B-26 bombers during the war, Piippo flew out of Braintree, England, and among his many decorations was the Distinguished Flying Cross. After leaving the service, he taught and coached at Marysville High School in Washington, and then spent over 30 years as a beloved middle school teacher and coach at Chief Joseph Middle School in Richland, Washington. He died in 2003.

Paul Simon, the son of the Eugene Lutheran minister and briefly a *Register-Guard* sports writer, became an Illinois newspaper publisher, a congressman, and a U.S. senator, and unsuccessfully sought the 1988 Democratic presidential nomination. He was renowned for his bow ties.

Simon's former boss, **Dick Strite,** remained sports editor of the *Register-Guard* until he died of a heart attack in 1965, at age 61. Also known as an expert fisherman, his fishing companions over the years in Oregon included longtime state resident Bobby Doerr and his Boston Red Sox teammate, Ted Williams; and Yankees and Indians second baseman Joe Gordon, the former Webfoot.

Strite's friend and Portland rival, **L. H. Gregory** of the *Oregonian,* retired in 1973 and died two years later in a Portland nursing home.

Wayne Morse, the U of O law school dean, was elected to the Senate in 1944 as a Republican. He served four terms, leaving the GOP to become unaffiliated and then a Democrat, before being unseated in 1968 by Republican Robert Packwood. He ran for the Democratic presidential nomination in 1960 and was one of two senators to vote against the 1964 Gulf of Tonkin Resolution, which led to the widening of U.S. involvement in the Vietnam War.

Oregon Daily Emerald co-sports editor **George Pasero** became a longtime Portland sports editor and columnist with the *Oregon Journal,* and then sports columnist for the *Oregonian* after the *Journal* folded. He wrote the feature on the first championship team that appeared in the official program at the Final Four in Portland in 1965, but didn't mention that he had been on the U of O campus at the time.

Wendell Wyatt, Beta Theta Pi fraternity brother of Matt Pavalunas and Red McNeeley, was a prominent Portland attorney and a five-term Republican congressman from Oregon's 1st District. The federal building in downtown Portland is named after him and fellow U.S. representative Edith Green.

Miami of Ohio coach **Weeb Ewbank** went on to greater fame in football, coaching the Baltimore Colts of the NFL and the New York Jets of the AFL to world championships.

Associated Press Writer **Drew Middleton,** who so badly imitated New Mexico A&M star Kiko Martinez's accent, joined the *New York Times* and became a celebrated war correspondent during World War II, and in later years was the newspaper's chief military correspondent.

New York Times sportswriter **Arthur Daley** took over the "Sports of the Times" column from John Kieran in 1942, won the Pulitzer Prize in 1956, and stayed in the position until his 1974 death.

Metropolitan Basketball Writers Association president **Everett B. Morris,** of the *Herald Tribune,* was a beachmaster in the D-Day landings and then, as a naval reserve officer, was recalled to active duty during the Korean War era.

Ohio State captain **Jimmy Hull** was a longtime orthodontist in Columbus. He practiced until suffering a stroke in 1990 and died the next year, at age 74.

Long Island star **Irv Torgoff** played in the National Basketball League, American Basketball League, and Basketball Association of America through 1949. He then was a fabric and yarn salesman and died in Florida in 1993.

Bradley Tech standout **Charles Orsborn** went on to serve as, first, Bradley's coach and then the school's athletic director.

St. John's coach **Joe Lapchick** was the New York Knicks' head coach from 1947 to 1956, working for Ned Irish. He went back to St. John's and finished up his career with a nine-season stint with the Redmen.

Texas Longhorns reserve **Denton Cooley** became a surgeon and performed the first artificial heart implantation in the world and the first successful human heart transplant in the U.S.

After playing for Colorado in the invitation tournament and then for the Steelers in 1938, **Whizzer White** headed off to a year of Rhodes Scholar study at Oxford. He returned to the NFL with the Detroit Lions in 1940. President **John Kennedy**, the son of U.S. ambassador Joseph Kennedy, appointed White to the U.S. Supreme Court in 1962 and he served until his 1993 retirement.

Charles Buxton, the young *Oregonian* reporter who traveled with the team to Evanston and back, and covered the trip and the national championship game, served in the military in World War II. Later, Buxton joined the *Denver Post* as a reporter and ultimately was the newspaper's editor and publisher from 1970 to 1977.

U of O president **Donald Erb** died of pneumonia in 1943, at age 43. The Erb Memorial Union, honoring him and Oregon students killed in World War II, opened in 1950 at 13th and University streets and remains the school's student union.

Star Idaho forward **Steve Belko** became one of Howard Hobson's successors, serving as Oregon's head coach from 1956 to 1971. He later was commissioner of the Big Sky Conference.

Shortly after making the rounds of the New York and NCAA tournaments, **Dr. James Naismith** died on November 28, 1939, in Lawrence, Kansas. He was 78. His game lived on.

Acknowledgments

In 2011, I wrote to Admiral John Dick in Eugene, saying I was exploring the possibility of writing a book about the 1938–39 national champion Webfoots. By then, he was the final surviving starter. In the letter, I explained that if I decided to move forward, and if he were agreeable, I would hope to travel to Eugene with an old-fashioned tape recorder and cassettes in my computer bag to meet with him for more extensive sit-down sessions. (I still smile when I think of noted sports writer Blackie Sherrod's reaction to *Horns, Hogs, and Nixon Coming*. He wrote that I "must have worn out a dozen tape recorders.")

At the time, I was also researching 1936 Olympic decathlon champion Glenn Morris's toxic affair with German actress/filmmaker Leni Riefenstahl for a possible nonfiction book.

Soon after, Admiral Dick and I connected on the phone. Thinking we might talk a bit about the Tall Firs that day, I taped the conversation. I just listened to it again.

"I was awakened with fond memories of the Frei family," he said. "I remember your days here and your dad's days before you. I'm very favorably inclined to do whatever I can to help you."

I was both honored and flattered, and also struck that, at age 92, he still sounded like an admiral.

He explained that he had recently fallen in his home and wasn't yet up to speaking more than a few minutes on the phone, and certainly not going through long interviews. "I just had a little mishap not long ago and I wound up being briefly hospitalized and having to go through rehab," he said. "I'm still in the rehab end of things there. I'm more than willing to talk to you, but it's just that I have to complete this other requirement."

Of course, I had waited too long. We weren't able to get together. But his endorsement and encouragement eventually became one of the many driving forces for me in deciding to turn to this after writing the Morris/Riefenstahl story as *Olympic Affair: A Novel of Hitler's Siren and America's Hero*. When I got word of Admiral Dick's death, I not only figuratively saluted a great man, I again regretted not moving sooner on a book about that team and those times. And I mean *years*, perhaps even many years, earlier. That was selfish, but I would have loved to have had the opportunity to speak directly and at length with Hobby and the Admiral and Bobby and Wally and Laddie and their teammates, whether the discussions ended up as part of a book project or otherwise. As with *Third Down and a War to Go*, another book I waited too long to do, when I came back to this project, I was determined to do justice to the men and the story, and I treated the research process as a means of answering my own questions and satisfying my own curiosity. All along, I was determined to place the Webfoots' accomplishments in the context of the college basketball scene, the country, and the world of 1939. That, of course, included the rivalry between the two major basketball tournaments. My virtually lifelong reverence of Clair Bee was a backdrop. During breaks from the writing, I went back and re-read several of the Chip Hilton basketball stories. As always, Chip's Valley Falls Big Reds or the State U. Statesmen either won gloriously . . . or lost gallantly.

At the end of our conversation in 2011, John Dick thanked me for understanding.

So now to the Admiral and all his teammates, I again say: *No . . . Thank you.*

My gratitude also goes to offspring and survivors, including (but not limited to) Peggy Anet, John Michael Dick, David Hobson, Hank Gale, Kirk Johansen, Jim and Scott McNeeley, Jessie Mullen, Bob Pavalunas, Dan Strite, and Robin (Gale) Terrett.

Fellow scribe and longtime buddy Jim Beseda is an Oregon grad who as a Sigma Nu fraternity member was required to learn the names of the 1939 Webfoots who walked the same halls. He again provided help on several fronts.

Matt Walks, a *Denver Post* sports department intern in 2012 and the *Oregon Daily Emerald*'s sports editor in 2012–13, pitched in, too, with looks back into the student paper's archives. He's now a sports web producer for Digital First Media.

I appreciate the acknowledgment and support of the University of Oregon athletic department, including Rob Mullens, Jim Bartko,

Craig Pintens, and Jeff Eberhart; and the help from the University of Oregon Library's Jennifer O'Neal, Karen Estlund, and Lesli Larson, and the Oregon Historical Society's Scott Daniels.

Finally, I again offer my gratitude to all the folks at Taylor Trade, especially Rick Rinehart, who have shown faith in me, taken chances with me, and stuck with me.

Terry Frei
Denver, Colorado

IV

APPENDICES

1939 NCAA Tournament Bracket

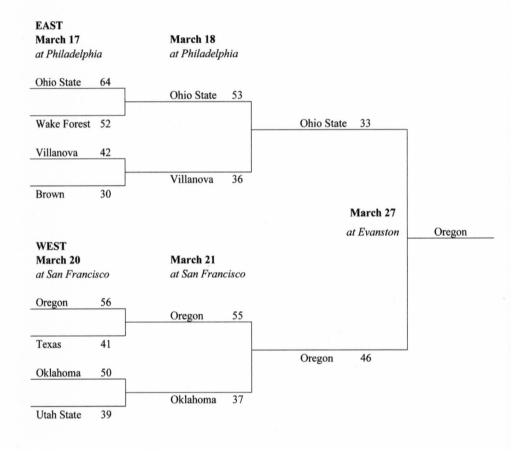

EAST
March 17
at Philadelphia

March 18
at Philadelphia

Ohio State   64

Ohio State   53

Wake Forest   52

Ohio State   33

Villanova   42

Brown   30

Villanova   36

March 27
at Evanston   Oregon

WEST
March 20
at San Francisco

March 21
at San Francisco

Oregon   56

Oregon   55

Texas   41

Oregon   46

Oklahoma   50

Utah State   39

Oklahoma   37

Appendix A: 1939 NCAA Tournament

Legend

Free throws taken and missed figures not available for all games. Figures such as x-x-x denote field goals made, free throws made, and total points. Figures such as x x-x x denote field goals made, free throws made and attempted, and total points.

Eastern Championships at Philadelphia
March 17 Semifinals
VILLANOVA 42, BROWN 30

VILLANOVA: Michael Lazorchak 3 0-1 6; James Montgomery 5 2-3 12; Louis Dubino 2 0-0 4; John Krutilis 6 2-3 14; Paul Nugent 1 0-0 2; Ernest Robinson 0 0-1 0; William Sinnott 1 0-0 2; Lloyd Rice 0 0-0 0; Arthur Vigilante 1 0-0 2; Charles Yung 0 0-0 0. TOTALS 19 4-8 42.

BROWN: John Padden 2 2-2 6; Harry Platt 3 1-2 7; Robert Person 3 2-3 8; Francis Wilson 2 1-4 5; G. W. Fisher 1 0-0 2; Leonard Campbell 0 0-0 0; W. B. Mullen 0 1-1 1; George Truman 0 1-1 1. TOTALS 11 8-13 30.

Halftime: Villanova 17, Brown 7.
Fouls: Villanova 10, Brown 7.

OHIO STATE 64, WAKE FOREST 52

OHIO STATE: Jimmy Hull 7 4-5 18; Dick Baker 10 5-7 25; John Schick 1 0-1 2; Dick Boughner 0 0-0 0; Bob Lynch 2 3-3 7; Gilbert Mickelson 1 2-2 4; William Sattler 2 0-4 4; Jack Dawson 2 0-1 4. TOTALS 25 14-23 64.

WAKE FOREST: Jim Waller 5 4-5 14; Vince Convery 3 1-1 7; Boyd Owen 7 5-9 19; Bill Sweel 0 1-3 1; Stanley Apple 4 2-2 10; Smith Young 0 1-1 1; Dave Fuller 0 0-1 0. TOTALS 19 14-22 52.

Halftime: Wake Forest 29, Ohio State 23.

Fouls: Ohio State 19, Wake Forest 16.

March 18 Final
OHIO STATE 53, VILLANOVA 36

OHIO STATE: Hull 10 8-8 28; Baker 2 0-0 4; Schick 3 1-1 7; Lynch 0 0-1 0; Boughner 0 0-0 0; Dawson 1 0-2 2; Stafford 1 0-0 2; Mickelson 1 0-0 2; Sattler 3 2-3 8; Charles Maag 0 0-0 0; Jed Mees 0 0-0 0; Don Scott 0 0-0 0. TOTALS 21 11-15 53.

VILLANOVA: Lazorchak 2 0-0 4; Montgomery 1 1-3 3; Duzminski 2 2-3 6; Krutilis 2 1-1 5; Nugent 7 2-3 16; Dubino 1 0-3 2; Sinnott 0 0-0 0; Rice 0 0-0 0; Robinson 0 0-0 0; Yung 0 0-0 0. TOTALS 15 6-13 36.

Halftime: Ohio State 25, Villanova 10.

Fouls: Ohio State 15, Villanova 11.

Western Championships at San Francisco
March 20 Semifinals
OKLAHOMA 50, UTAH STATE 39

UTAH STATE: Del Bingham 1 4-5 6; Floyd Morris 6 3-5 15; Roland Reading 4 1-2 9; Leonard James 1 1-1 3; Calvin Agricola 0 2-3 2; Ray Lindquist 1 0-0 2; Clyde Morris 1 0-1 2; Lloyd Jacobsen 0 0-0 0. TOTALS 14 11-17 39.

OKLAHOMA: Jimmy McNatt 5 2-3 12; Garnett Corbin 5 2-3 12; Herb Scheffler 1 3-4 5; Marvin Mesch 3 1-1 7; Marvin Snodgrass 3 0-0 6; Gene Roop 1 3-4 5; Matthew Zoller 1 0-1 2; Ben Kerr 0 1-1 1; Vernon Mullen 0 0-0 0; Roscoe Walker 0 0-0 0. TOTALS 19 12-17 50.

Halftime: Oklahoma 25, Utah State 14.

Fouls: Oklahoma 15, Utah State 12.

OREGON 56, TEXAS 41

OREGON: Laddie Gale 3-3-9; John Dick 6-1-13; Slim Wintermute 7-0-14; Wally Johansen 3-1-7; Bobby Anet 1-2-4; Ted Sarpola 0-1-1; Matt Pavalunas 1-1-3; Ford Mullen 0-1-1; Bob Hardy 1-0-2; Earl Sandness 1-0-2. TOTALS 23-10-56.

TEXAS: Willie Tate 3-1-7; Elmer Finley 2-2-6; Thurmon Hull 1-4-6; Bobby Moers 3-0-6; Oran Spears 2-1-5; Warren Wiggins 1-2-4; Denton Cooley 1-1-3; Chester Granville 0-2-2; Tommie Nelms 1-0-2. TOTALS 14-13-41.

Halftime: Oregon 19, Texas 16.

Fouls: Texas 17, Oregon 11.

March 21 Final
OREGON 55, OKLAHOMA 37

OREGON: Dick 6 2-2 14; Gale 3 5-7 11, Wintermute 4 2-2 10; Johansen 4 0-1 8; Anet 1 4-5 6; Hardy 0 3-3 3; Pavalunas 1 0-0 2; Mullen 0 1-2 1; Sarpola 0-0-0 0. TOTALS 19 17-22 55.

OKLAHOMA: McNatt 5 2-3 12; Corbin 2 0-0 4; Scheffler 1 2-2 4; Mesch 1 0-1 2; Snodgrass 0 1-1 1; Walker 1 0-1 2; Kerr 3 3-3 9; Mullen 0 0-0 0; Zoller 0 0-0 0; Roop 1 1-2 3. TOTALS 14 9-13 37.

Halftime: Oregon 21, Oklahoma 14.

Fouls: Oklahoma 18, Oregon 13.

Third-Place Game: Utah State 51, Texas 49

National Championship Game
May 27 at Evanston, Illinois
OREGON 46, OHIO STATE 33

OREGON: Dick 4 5-5 13; Gale 3 4-5 10; Wintermute 2 0-1 4; Johansen 4 1-2 9; Anet 4 2-3 10; Mullen 0 0-0 0; Pavalunas 0 0-0 0. TOTALS 17 12-16 46.

OHIO STATE: Hull 5 2-4 12; Baker 0 0-0 0; Schick 1 0-0 2; Lynch 3 1-3 7; Boughner 1 0-0 2; Stafford 0 0-0 0; Sattler 3 1-2 7; Dawson 1 0-0 2; Mickelson 0 0-0 0; Maag 0 0-0 0; Scott 0 1-1 1. TOTALS 14 5-10 33.

Halftime: Oregon 21, Ohio State 16.

Fouls: Ohio State 13, Oregon 8.

Appendix B: Oregon's 1938–39 Results

Nov. 29 at Eugene: Oregon 51, Portland 24
Dec. 2 at Eugene: Oregon 83, Multnomah Athletic Club 25
Dec. 3 at Eugene: Oregon 46, Signal Oil 34
Dec. 10 at Portland: Oregon 54, Pacific Packards 39
Dec. 17 at New York: CCNY 38, Oregon 36
Dec. 19 at Philadelphia: Oregon 54, St. Joseph's 44
Dec. 20 at Cleveland: Oregon 74, Miami (Ohio) 38
Dec. 22 at Buffalo: Oregon 53, Canisius 41
Dec. 23 at Detroit: Oregon 52, Wayne 31
Dec. 26 at Peoria: Bradley Tech 52, Oregon 39
Dec. 27 at Chicago: Oregon 60, Macomb Teachers 45
Dec. 29 at Des Moines: Oregon 42, Drake 31
Dec. 31 at San Francisco: Stanford 50, Oregon 46
Jan. 6 at Eugene: Oregon 46, Washington State 35
Jan. 7 at Eugene: Washington State 39, Oregon 34
Jan. 13: at Corvallis: Oregon 31, Oregon State 26
Jan. 17 at Pullman: Oregon 56, Washington State 44
Jan. 18 at Pullman: Oregon 57, at Washington State 31
Jan. 20 at Moscow: Oregon 38, Idaho 30
Jan. 21 at Moscow: Oregon 35, Idaho 31
Jan. 27 at Eugene: Oregon 46, Oregon State 39
Jan. 31 at Eugene: Oregon 57, Washington 49
Feb. 1 at Eugene: Oregon 58, Washington 42
Feb. 10 at Eugene: Oregon 45, Idaho 28
Feb. 11 at Eugene: Oregon 53, Idaho 36
Feb. 17 at Corvallis: Oregon State 50, Oregon 31
Feb. 24 at Eugene: Oregon 48, Oregon State 37
March 3 at Seattle: Oregon 39, Washington 26
March 4 at Seattle: Oregon 54, Washington 52

Pacific Coast Conference Championship

March 16 at Eugene: Oregon 54, California 49
March 17 at Eugene: Oregon 53, California 47

Western Championships

March 20 at San Francisco: Oregon 56, Texas 41
March 21 at San Francisco: Oregon 55, Oklahoma 37

National Championship

March 27 at Evanston: Oregon 46, Ohio State 33
Record: 29-5

1939 National Invitation Tournament Bracket

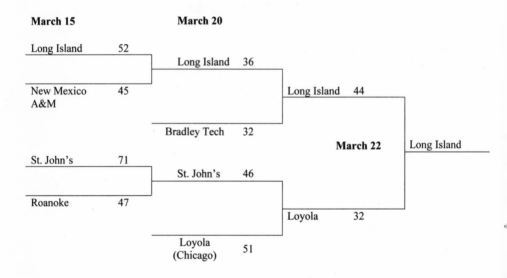

March 15

March 20

Long Island   52

Long Island   36

New Mexico   45
A&M

Long Island   44

Bradley Tech   32

March 22   Long Island

St. John's   71

St. John's   46

Roanoke   47

Loyola   32

Loyola   51
(Chicago)

Appendix C: 1939 National Invitation Tournament

March 15 Quarterfinals
LONG ISLAND U. 52, NEW MEXICO A&M 45

LIU: Irv Torgoff 5-4-14; Dan Kaplowitz 2-0-4; Si Lobello 3-0-6; John Bromberg 6-1-13; George Newman 0-0-0; Ken Ehlers 0-0-0; Ossie Schechtman 2-0-4; William King 4-1-9; Max Sharf 0-0-0; Butch Schwartz 0-2-2. TOTALS 22-8-52.

NEW MEXICO A&M: Martinez 4-0-8; Finley 5-1-11; Jackson 5-2-12; Wood 0-2-2; Ritchey 5-2-12; McAdam 0-0-0; Showa 0-0-0; Cunico 0-0-0. TOTALS 19-7-45.

ST. JOHN'S 71, ROANOKE 47

ST. JOHN'S: Dolgoff 1-0-2; Lloyd 12-7-31; Palmer 0-0-0; Vocke 4-0-8; Garfinkel 2-1-5; Wosnitzer 1-0-2; Gill 1-0-2; McKeever 2-0-4; Gorman 1-2-4; DeStefano 2-0-4, Krajcovic 1-1-3; Amoross 0-0-0; Haggerty 3-0-6; Ferrara 0-0-0; Joos 0-0-0. TOTALS 30-11-71.

ROANOKE: Rice 4-0-8; Studebaker 10-6-26; Sheffield 1-2-4; Wagner 1-2-4; Lieb 1-0-2; Moore 0-1-1; Southat 1-0-2. TOTALS 18-11-47.

March 20 Semifinals
LONG ISLAND 36, BRADLEY TECH 32

LONG ISLAND: Torgoff 2-0-4; Kaplowitz 2-0-4; Lobello 3-1-7; Bromberg 4-4-12; Newman 1-0-2; Schwartz 0-0-0; Schechtman 0-1-1; Sharf 0-0-0; King 1-1-3; Zeitlin 0-1-1; Shelly 1-0-2. TOTALS 14-8-36.

BRADLEY TECH: Schunk 4-0-8; Orsborn 4-1-9; Hutchins 1-0-2; Panish 3-1-7; Olson 1-1-3; Bortel 1-1-3. TOTALS 14-4-32.

LOYOLA 51, ST. JOHN'S 46 (OT)

LOYOLA: O'Brien 1-2-4; Hogan 3-1-7; Novak 8-4-20; Kautz 7-2-16; Wenskus 1-2-4; Graham 0-0-0; Driscoll 0-0-0. TOTALS 20-11-51.

ST. JOHN'S: Dolgoff 3-2-8; Lloyd 5-7-17; Palmer 0-1-1; Garfinkel 5-0-10; Vocke 4-1-9; Haggerty 0-0-0; Ferrara 0-0-0; Gorman 0-0-0; McKeever 0-0-0; DeStefano 0-1-1. TOTALS 17-12-46.

March 22 Championship
LONG ISLAND 44, LOYOLA 32

LONG ISLAND: Torgoff 5-2-12; Kaplowitz 4-1-9; Myron Sewitch 0-1-1; Newman 1-1-3; Bromberg 2-1-5; King 0-0-0; Schwartz 0-2-2; Scharf 0-0-0; Lobello 0-0-0; Shelly 1-0-2; Schechtman 4-1-9; Zeitlin 0-1-1. TOTALS 17-10-44.

LOYOLA: Hogan 2-0-4; O'Brien 4-1-9; Novak 0-1-1; Kautz 3-0-6; Wenskus 4-0-8; Schell 1-0-2; Graham 1-0-2; Driscoll 0-0-0. TOTALS 15-2-32.

Third-Place Game: Bradley Tech 40, St. John's 35

Appendix D: Long Island's
1938–39 Results

Dec. 1 at Brooklyn: Long Island 63, Alumni 36

Dec. 7 at Brooklyn: Long Island 64, Newark 14

Dec. 13 at Brooklyn: Long Island 41, Panzer College 35

Dec. 15 at Brooklyn: Long Island 82, Princeton Seminary 37

Dec. 19 at Brooklyn: Long Island 63, Stroudsburg Teachers 33

Dec. 21 at Brooklyn: Long Island 77, McGill 39

Dec. 23 at Brooklyn: Long Island 63, Montclair State 40

Dec. 30 at New York: Long Island 33, Southern California 18

Jan. 4 at New York: Long Island 52, Kentucky 34

Jan. 11 at New York: Long Island 41, Marquette 36

Jan. 18 at Brooklyn: Long Island 64, New York Athletic Club 43

Jan. 25 at New York: Long Island 46, Toledo 39

Jan. 28 at Brooklyn: Long Island 48, Geneva 39

Feb. 8 at New York: Long Island 48, Duquesne 41

Feb. 10 at Brooklyn: Long Island 65, Scranton 53

Feb. 14 at Brooklyn: Long Island 62, Canisius 50

Feb. 18 at Brooklyn: Long Island 61, St. Francis 20

Feb. 21 at Brooklyn: Long Island 70, St. Bonaventure 31

Feb. 23 at Brooklyn: Long Island 52, Baltimore 34

Feb. 28 at Brooklyn: Long Island 65, John Marshall College of Law 25

March 3 at Philadelphia: Long Island 28, La Salle 21

National Invitation Tournament at New York

March 15: Long Island 52, New Mexico A&M 45

March 20: Long Island 36, Bradley Tech 32

March 22: Long Island 44, Loyola (Chi.) 32

Record: 24-0

Notes

Dates listed for wire-service dispatches cited are when they were transmitted on the newswires. Many of the stories ran in afternoon papers on the date listed. Others appeared in newspapers the next day.

For newspaper stories, if no writer is named, story was published without a byline.

Introduction

4 "The first college championship . . . ": *Oregonian* (Portland), Nick Bertram, April 1, 1988.

1. Hobby

11 "I grew up with a basketball . . . ": Howard Hobson, *Shooting Ducks: A History of University of Oregon Basketball* (Portland: Western Imprints, 1984). Hereafter: *Shooting Ducks*.

12 "Don't bother him, he has a game . . . " and "You better watch out for that boy . . . ": Author interview with David Hobson.

13 "We spent many, many hours . . . ": *Eugene Register-Guard*, Blaine Newnham, October 28, 1977. Hereafter: *RG*.

13 "We sold candy and cigarettes . . . "; "McArthur Court was built by . . . "; "At that time it was probably the greatest basketball pavilion . . . "; "I thought with a master's degree . . . "; "What do you teach? . . . "; "the best press I ever had"; and "a wonderful three years": Interview with Howard Hobson for Oregon Historical Society's oral histories, conducted in June 1982 by Linda Brody. Hereafter: OHS.

16 "We feel that in Hobson . . . ": *Oregon Daily Emerald* (University of Oregon), Clair Johnson, April 18, 1935. Hereafter: *Emerald*.

2. Fishermen

23 "Dick Strite wrote . . . ": Paul Simon, *P.S.: The Autobiography of Paul Simon* (Chicago: Bonus Books, 1998). Hereafter: *P.S.*

3. Laddie and Slim

25 "Shut up, kid . . . ": Author interview with Hank Gale.

4. From the Gorge

30 "Sports and the local trials . . . "; "I wanted to be a student . . . "; and "Managing my time became an issue . . . ": From Oregon athletic department official Jeff Eberhart's interview of John Dick. Hereafter: Eberhart.
31 "You can't have too few enemies . . . ": Author interview with John Michael Dick.

5. Basketeers

36 "At the end of each season . . . ": Associated Press dispatch, January 5, 1935. Hereafter: AP.
37 "I liked Wintermute from the start . . . ": *Oregon Journal* (Portland), Richard H. Syring, December 3, 1939. Hereafter: *Journal.*
38 "He was in his day the best center . . . ": *RG*, October 24, 1977.
38 " . . . and there the tall-fir Webfoots . . . ": *Oregonian*, L. H. Gregory, March 3, 1938.
38 "The only way Oregon's tall-fir basketeers . . . ": *Oregonian*, Gregory, March 5, 1938.
39 "Anet was an indifferent shot . . . ": *Journal*, Syring, December 3, 1939.
39 "the greatest dribbler I have ever seen . . . ": *RG*, Ron Bellamy, February 19, 2009.
40 "Next year, we're going . . . " and "After getting past us . . . ": Eberhart.
42 "There are about 500 people . . . ": AP, March 17, 1938.
43 "In the last game, I got to check . . . ": *Willapa Harbor Herald* (Washington), March 1938.

6. Floating Ideas

44   "Interest was not great.": *Shooting Ducks.*
46   "From that moment on . . . ": Eberhart.
47   "It was not a helter-skelter fast-break . . . ": *RG*, Newnham, October 28, 1977.
47   "I used to kid Anet all the time . . . ": *RG*, February 13, 1977.
48   "He was relatively soft-spoken . . . ": *Oregonian*, Ken Wheeler, June 10, 1991.
49   "wasn't sure that Oregon existed": OHS.
50   "He felt that the benefits of the trip . . . ": Eberhart.

7. Bee and the Blackbirds

51   "After a while, the priests caught on . . . ": *New York Times*, Sam Goldaper, May 21, 1983. Hereafter: *NYT.*
53   "He is salty, profane, a two-fisted fighter . . . ": *Sport* magazine, Milton Gross, March 1951. Hereafter: *Sport.*

8. Taking the Show on the Road

59   "The National Collegiate Athletic Association's plan . . . ": AP, December 14, 1938.
62   "basketball rivals salmon fishing . . . "; "could do more tricks with a basketball . . . "; and "terrifically fast break": *New York Herald Tribune*, Everett B. Morris, December 16, 1938. Hereafter: *NYHT.*
64   "small hall that bulged at the seams . . . ": *NYHT*, Richards Vidmer, December 17, 1938.

9. Garden and Beyond

65   "Now we aren't going to call every little . . . ": *Shooting Ducks.*
65   "hampered in the beginning . . . "; "slowed down to a walk . . . "; and "a drab sort of battle in its early stages . . . ": *NYT*, Arthur Daley, December 18, 1938.
66   "small, but mighty classy City College of New York . . . "; "thrill-a-minute first game"; and "couldn't quite solve . . . ": *New York Daily News*, Jack Mahon, December 18, 1938.
70   "look like P.S. 9 on a bad night": *NYT*, Daley, January 6, 1939.

71   "obviously weary from a . . . ": AP, Dec. 31, 1938.
71   "We learned to adapt . . . ": Eberhart.

10. White Smoke

77   "The German air force is the terror . . . ": AP, March 1, 1939.
78   "That's as good a team . . . ": Eberhart.
79   "Yeah—the second-best team . . . ": *RG*, Dick Strite, March 1, 1939.
80   "Washington's formula is to build up . . . ": *Emerald*, March 2, 1939.
81   "If she clicks . . . ": *International News Service* dispatch, March 1, 1939. Hereafter: *INS*.
82   "The kids have shown improvement . . . ": *Emerald*, George Pasero, March 2, 1939.
83   "The boot blacks . . . ": *RG*, Strite, March 3, 1939.
83   "For the third year . . . ": Eberhart.
83   "It's a peculiar floor . . . ": *Oregonian*, Gregory, March 2, 1939.
84   "We'll win . . . " and "The boys are as high . . . ": *RG*, Strite, March 3, 1939.

11. Cayuse with a Saddle

86   "wading like a waterfront brawler . . . ": *Sport*, Gross, March 1951.
86   "Oregon virtually ran . . . " and "one of the greatest exhibitions . . .": *RG*, Strite, March 4, 1939.
87   "It was the best officiated game . . . ": *Oregonian*, Gregory, March 4, 1939.
87   "How'd you like that?": *Shooting Ducks*.
88   "With many other democracies . . . ": AP, March 4, 1939.
89   "rode the ball as if it had been a Cayuse": *Oregonian*, Gregory, March 4, 1939.
89   "It still goes . . . ": Eberhart.
91   "After misrepresentations and curious opinions . . . ": *INS*, March 5, 1939.

12. Maneuvers

95   "It looks to me . . . ": *RG*, March 7, 1939.

13. RSVP

99   "What in the world is the NCAA . . . ": *Columbus Dispatch*, Dick Fenlon, April 1, 1988. Hereafter: *CD*.

99   "We didn't even know what it was . . . ": *CD*, Bob Hunter, March 24, 1999.

101   "based on recommendations by coaches and sports writers . . . ": National Enterprise Association dispatch, Jerry Brundfield, March 9, 1939.

103   "If we should win the conference . . . ": *RG*, March 10, 1939.

103   "if his father starts another war.": AP, March 11, 1939.

104   "the national invitation tournament that . . . "; "Six teams have been invited to the tournament by the scribes . . . "; and "a tremendous success . . . ": *NYT*, Daley, March 12, 1939.

104   "The boys have been coming up fine . . . ": AP, March 11, 1939.

14. Jumping Either Way

105   "overwhelming in its solemnity . . . ": AP, March 12, 1939.

106   "No force stands between . . . ": AP, March 10, 1939.

108   "I've only seen California play . . . ": *RG*, March 15, 1939.

109   "We didn't see how they could pass us up . . . ": *Philadelphia Daily News*, Ray Didinger, March 23, 1988. Hereafter: *PDN*.

109   "Ten-gallon hats, cowboy boots . . . " and "I can jump either way . . . ": *NYT*, John Kieran, March 15, 1939.

109   "No grass . . . ": AP, March 14, 1939.

110   "four teams who thought . . . ": AP, March 15, 1939.

111   "Hitherto Germany has only . . . ": AP, March 15, 1939.

111   "We are now living . . . ": *NYT*, March 16, 1939.

111   "had the crowd in ecstasies of delight . . . ": *NYT*, Daley, March 16, 1939.

112   "It will be the same . . . ": *RG*, March 16, 1939.

15. Spotlights

113   "the law of self-survival . . . ": AP, March 16, 1939.

113   "We were the two of the tallest teams . . . ": Eberhart.

114 "With a lull here over the weekend . . . ": *NYT*, Joseph M. Sheehan, March 17, 1939.

115 "We got our fast break rolling . . . " and "We got the ball to Laddie . . . ": Eberhart.

115 "did a beautiful job . . . ": *Oregonian*, Gregory, March 17, 1939.

116 "As long as they don't boo . . . ": *Emerald*, Buck Buckwach, February 3, 1939.

116 "We played our best ball . . .": *RG*, Strite, March 17, 1939.

116 "Listen, we'll stop those big horses . . . ": *Shooting Ducks*.

116 "to the utmost of its power . . . " and "I have never denied that the terms . . . ": *AP*, March 17, 1939.

118 "I think he covered his eyes on every one . . . " and other Krutulis comments: *PDN*, Didinger, March 23, 1988.

16. Moving On

119 "wanton lawlessness and arbitrary force . . . ": *INS*, March 21, 1939.

120 "guarded like a prisoner . . . ": *Oregonian*, Gregory, March 18, 1939.

120 "In the second game . . . ": Eberhart.

120 "I told you, we stopped 'em . . . ": *Shooting Ducks*.

121 "Greatest basketball team we ever played . . . ": *Oregonian*, Gregory, March 18, 1939.

121 "Coming from a coach . . . ": Eberhart.

121 "I've said all season that . . . ": *Oregonian*, Gregory, March 18, 1939.

121 "Well, we got what . . . "; "looking for bigger game . . . "; and "most brilliant game of his career": *RG*, Strite, March 18, 1939.

17. Suitcase Test

123 "Just think, I'm going to see . . . ": AP, March 18, 1939.

123 "Experts predicted that the Webfoots . . . ": *INS*, March 18, 1939.

124 "Gentlemen, this is a little embarrassing . . . " and subsequent exchange: *CD*, Bob Hunter, March 24, 1999.

125 "That won't be enough . . . ": *RG*, March 23, 1939.

126 "I figure the boys . . . ": *Oregonian*, Gregory, March 20, 1939.

128 "They were just too fast . . . ": AP, March 20, 1939.

128   "We were asked . . . ": Eberhart.
128   "Picked by the Southern casaba favorites . . . ": *Emerald*, Pasero, March 20, 1939.
128   "Imagine 350,000 pairs of eyes watching every move you make . . . ": *Emerald*, March 20, 1939.

18. Eighth Avenue

131   "Kautz was not just a stooge . . . ": *NYT*, Daley, March 21, 1939.

19. Treasure Island

132   "embroil the United States . . . ": AP, March 20, 1939.
134   "The tall-fir Oregon boys": *Oregonian*, Gregory, March 21, 1939.

20. How the West Was Won

136   "followed athletic scores and the sports pages faithfully . . . ": *P.S.*
138   "We will win it for the west": *RG*, Strite, March 23, 1939.
138   "We were head and shoulders . . . ": OHS.

21. 49th Street

140   "Although the Metropolitan Basketball . . . ": *NYHT*, Morris, March 21, 1939.
140   "the Wonder Team . . . " and "the unbeaten . . . ": *NYT*, Daley, March 22, 1939.
142   "What can you do . . . ": *NYHT*, Irving T. Marsh, March 23. 1939.

22. Destinies

143   "I believe that now . . . ": AP, March 23, 1939.
144   "He was always a tall boy . . . " and other Ivie Wintermute comments: *RG*, March 23, 1939.

144 "rolled up an amazing total of 835 points . . . ": *Chicago Tribune*, March 23, 1939.

145 "In the last year, two republics . . . ": *New York Daily Mirror*, Walter Winchell, March 24, 1939.

146 "The train ride apparently . . . " and other comments on the train ride: *Oregonian*, Charles Buxton, March 25, 1939.

147 "The Berlin-Rome axis is unbreakable . . . ": AP, March 25, 1939.

147 "if he has a brain . . . ": AP, March 25, 1939.

149 "It degenerated into an interview . . . ": Eberhart.

151 "This was the only recommended change . . . ": AP, March 27, 1939.

23. Broken Trophy and All

153 "Bob, run 'em to death . . . "; "We'll run them . . . "; "I wish they'd run . . . ": *Shooting Ducks*.

154 "He clipped off the figure . . . ": Eberhart.

154 "He said, 'Well . . . ": Author interview with Peggy Anet.

155 "You told me not to call one until we were tired . . . ": *Journal*, Syring, December 3, 1939.

155 "Both teams shot . . . ": Eberhart.

155 "My leg just felt terrible . . . ": *CD*, Fenlon, April 1, 1988.

156 "In the final 12 days . . . ": Eberhart.

156 "Ohio State was really . . . ": AP, March 30, 1939.

156 "The University of Oregon . . . ": AP, March 27, 1939.

156 "Oregon's rangy sharpshooters . . . ": United Press dispatch, March 27, 1939.

159 "I think some of us had a couple of Heinekens . . . ": *RG*, Neil Cawood, March 26, 1979.

24. Ride Home

160 "a fancy ball-handling . . . ": AP, March 28, 1939.

161 "Years from now . . . ": *RG*, March 28, 1939.

163 "a foot of our land nor . . . ": AP, March 30, 1939.

25. Dance of Champs

167 "send it gracefully through the air like the Yankee Clipper": *Emerald*, March 28, 1939.

167 "We never imagined . . . ": *RG*, April 1, 1939.
167 "The sad part about this occasion . . . ": *Oregonian*, April 1, 1939.
168 "The athletic committee realizes . . . ": AP, March 31, 1939.
168 Bobby Anet, Howard Hobson, and Donald Erb comments at the Monday Morning Quarterbacks' dinner: *Emerald*, J. Robert Penland, April 1, 1939.
169 "There was no hollow victory . . . ": *RG*, Strite, April 2, 1939.
170 "When today an English statesman . . . ": AP, April 1, 1939.

27. Coaches

178 "Well, now, you can't go . . . ": OHS.
179 "220-pound Negro Hercules": *NYT*, Daley, December 17, 1939.
179 "muscular negro veteran": AP, December 16, 1939.
179 "was shaking like a leaf": *Shooting Ducks*.
179 "the greatest game ever played . . . ": *NYHT*, Morris, December 17, 1939.
182 "If there's a basketball court in heaven . . . ": *Oregonian*, John Nolen, June 15, 1991.
183 "If a boy convinces me he's sincere . . . ": *Sport*, Gross, March 1951.
184 "We, you and I, have flunked . . . ": *NYT*, Goldaper, May 21, 1983.

28. The Tall Firs

185 "Hobby actually spent . . . ": *RG*, February 13, 1977.
186 "He still felt years later that he let the team down . . . " and other remarks in this passage: Author interview with John Michael Dick.
187 "I was still in great shape . . . ": Eberhart.
190 "Bobby was a great floor . . . ": *RG*, July 27, 1981.
192 "I decided that I didn't want . . . ": McNeeley family taped interview.
194 "With my brain and his arm . . . ": *RG*, Strite, June 1, 1941.

Acknowledgments

197 "I was awakened with fond memories . . . ": Author phone conversation with Rear Admiral John Henry Dick.

Selected Bibliography/Sources

Newspapers

Daily Astorian, Astoria, Oregon
Berkeley Daily Gazette
Boston Globe
Columbus Dispatch
Curry Coastal Pilot, Brookings, Oregon
Dalles Chronicle, The Dalles, Oregon
Denver Post
Deseret News, Salt Lake City
Eugene Register-Guard
Kentucky New Era, Hopkinsville
Newsday, New York
New York Daily News
New York Herald Tribune
New York Times
Oregon Daily Emerald, University of Oregon, Eugene
Oregonian, Portland
Oregon Journal, Portland
Philadelphia Daily News
Rocky Mountain News, Denver
Seattle Post-Intelligencer
Seattle Times
Spokane Spokesman-Review
Tacoma News Tribune
Toledo Blade
Tri-City Herald, Washington
USA Today

Other Publications

Duck Dope
Sport magazine
Sports Illustrated

Books

Bee, Clair. *Drills and Fundamentals*. New York: A.S. Barnes and Company, 1942.

————. *Man-to-Man Defense and Attack*. New York: A.S. Barnes and Company, 1942.

————. *Zone Defense and Attack*. New York: A.S. Barnes and Company, 1942.

————. Original Chip Hilton series. New York: Grosset and Dunlap. 1: *Touchdown Pass*, 1948; 2: *Championship Ball*, 1948; 3: *Strike Three*, 1949; 4: *Clutch Hitter*, 1949; 5: *Hoop Crazy*, 1950; 6: *Pitchers' Duel*, 1950; 7: *A Pass and a Prayer*, 1951; 8: *Dugout Jinx*, 1952; 9: *Freshman Quarterback*, 1952; 10: *Backboard Fever*, 1953; 11: *Fence Busters*, 1953; 12: *Ten Seconds to Play*, 1955; 13: *Fourth Down Showdown*, 1956; 14: *Tournament Crisis*, 1957; 15: *Hardcourt Upset*, 1957; 16: *Pay-Off Pitch*, 1958; 17: *No-Hitter*, 1959; 18: *Triple-Threat Trouble*, 1960; 19: *Backcourt Ace*, 1961; 20: *Buzzer Basket*, 1962; 21: *Comeback Cagers*, 1963; 22: *Home Run Feud*, 1964; 23: *Hungry Hurler*, 1966.

Hobson, Howard. *Basketball Illustrated*. New York: A.S. Barnes and Company, 1948.

————. *Scientific Basketball*. New York: Prentice-Hall, 1955.

————. *Shooting Ducks: A History of University of Oregon Basketball*. Portland: Western Imprints, 1984.

Isaacs, Neil D. *All the Moves: A History of College Basketball*. New York: Harper and Row, 1975.

Leedom, Karen L. *Astoria: An Oregon History*. Pittsburgh: The Local History Company, 2008.

Olson, Lynne. *Those Angry Days: Roosevelt, Lindbergh, and America's Fight over World War II*. New York: Random House, 2013.

Palmberg, Wally. *Toward One Flag: A History of Lower Columbia Athletics*. Astoria, Oregon: Astorian Printing Company, 1993.

Rosen, Charles. *The Scandals of 1951: How the Gamblers Almost Killed College Basketball*. New York: Holt, Rinehart and Winston, 1978.

Simon, Paul. *P.S.: The Autobiography of Paul Simon*. Chicago: Bonus Books, 1998.

Author Interviews

Peggy Anet, Portland, Oregon.
Rear Admiral John Henry Dick, Eugene, Oregon.
John Michael Dick, Renton, Washington.
Hank Gale, Westlake, Oregon.
David Hobson, Portland.
Kirk Johansen, Lake Oswego, Oregon.
Jim McNeeley, Portland.
Scott McNeeley, Springfield, Oregon.
Jessie Mullen, Stanwood, Washington.
Bob Pavalunas, Auburn, Washington.
Dan Strite, Warrenton, Oregon.
Robin (Gale) Terrett, Gold Beach, Oregon.

Other Recorded/Transcribed Interviews

John Dick, 2003. Conducted by Jeff Eberhart for the Oregon athletic department's *Order of the O* newsletter, only portions of which were published.
Howard Hobson, June 28, 1982. Conducted by Linda Brody for the Oregon Historical Society's Oral Histories.
Evert "Red" McNeeley, circa 1985. Courtesy Steve McNeeley.

Websites

Goducks.com, University of Oregon Athletics website
KVAL.com (Eugene)
Saratogamuseum.org
Sports-reference.com

Index

Italicized page numbers refer to illustrations between pages 112 and 113. They are numbered *112(a)* through *112(h)*

227